EXILE'S RETURN

EXILE'S RETURN

The Making of a Palestinian American

FAWAZ TURKI

THE FREE PRESS
A Division of Macmillan, Inc.
NEW YORK

Maxwell Macmillan Canada
TORONTO

Maxwell Macmillan International
NEW YORK   OXFORD   SINGAPORE   SYDNEY

The Free Press
A Division of Macmillan, Inc.
866 Third Avenue, New York, N.Y. 10022

Maxwell Macmillan Canada, Inc.
1200 Eglinton Avenue East
Suite 200
Don Mills, Ontario M3C 3N1

Macmillan, Inc. is part of the Maxwell Communication Group of Companies.

Printed in the United States of America

printing number

1 2 3 4 5 6 7 8 9 10

Library of Congress Cataloging-in-Publication Data
Turki, Fawaz
    Exile's return: the making of a Palestinian American / Fawaz Turki.
        p.   cm.
    ISBN 0-02-932725-3
        1. Turki, Fawaz. 2. Palestine—Exiles—Biography.
    3. Palestinian Arabs—Biography. 4. Jewish-Arab relations—1949-
    I. Title.
    DS119.7.T833 1994
    956.9405'092—dc20   93-36435
        [B]   CIP

Contents

Preface

O n September 13, 1993, representatives of the Palestine Liberation Organization and the Israeli government signed a bold and
complex peace agreement putting an end to their long conflict.

The ceremony on the White House lawn that day carried all the
weight of a historic moment. Israelis were prepared, after a quarter
century of military occupation, to relinquish control over the West
Bank and Gaza, and the Palestinians there were being given the
opportunity to rule themselves, and potentially become a state, for
the first time in their modern history.

The majority of Palestinians in the occupied territories rejoiced,
but there were many others, not all of them fundamentalists or rad-
icals, who felt great anxiety over the agreement. These are the
refugees, or descendants of refugees, who left Palestine in the exodus of 1948 and, living in exile since that time, have struggled for
the realization of their own dream, what they call the *awda*, the
return to home and homeland.

For many years, world attention was focused on the plight of
Palestinians in the occupied territories—and well it might have
been, for the pain they endured was at times beyond all understanding. But the Palestinians who lived in exile—and there are four million of them scattered around the Arab countries and beyond—have

a story to tell about their own unspoken pain and about their striving, all these years, for a sense of at-homeness.

My book is the story of one Palestinian exile who tries to come to grips and, finally, to terms with his condition.

Exile is a demanding habitat. The spirit bends under its weight, and the mind bruises under the agony of otherness it inflicts. My father (not unlike others of his generation who left the homeland in 1948 and refused to accept life in exile) died mumbling incoherences about the *awda* and curses at the gods for having made such a mess of his life.

My generation of Palestinians were born in exile or came to it as children. Left to our own devices, in our own parcel of hell, we had to learn to survive by ourselves. We finally came, with the unperturbed naiveté of children, to look upon exile itself as our homeland, and we grew, by force of time, to acquire a sensibility only remotely connected to the notion of statehood. Though the *awda* continues to find an echo in our sensibility, it will never have a mastering grip on our dreams as it had for my father's generation. Long stretches of time in exile can, like some kind of detergent, scrub off your feelings of rage. Still, for the many Palestinian refugees who live in crowded camps, the thought that they may never, ever go home again will surely wreak havoc on their souls.

This book is both a backward glance at my life as a Palestinian writer, activist, and unhoused wanderer, and an account of my visit to Palestine on the eve of the Persian Gulf War, in which I reflect on the tensions that exist between Palestinians who have always lived in their homeland and those who, like myself, have lived in exile.

English-speaking readers may find my narrative informative. My former colleagues in the PLO will surely find it scandalous. And my fellow Palestinians will likely be shocked at my harsh critique of Palestinian popular culture and its antiquated mores.

I have drawn on my own experiences to tell this story. For it is from the echo of our lives, and what we let that echo yield, that we arrive at our own truths.

EXILE'S RETURN

1

Journey to the Homeground

Once, to celebrate the end of Ramadan, the Moslem month of fasting, my parents packed a picnic lunch and took us by bus to the park at Mount Karmel in Haifa.

It was one of those days that fall between seasons, with no clearly defined identity, when spring was about to surrender itself to summer. I was a few months shy of my eighth birthday. In less than two weeks my sister, Jasmine, who was turning into a precocious child, would be six. My older brother, Mousa, somewhat aloof and conscious of his privileged status as the oldest son, was twice my age. And Mom was pregnant with Samir, who was to wait for another six months, until we all got to the refugee camp in Beirut, before he decided to come into the world.

After we ate our lunch, Jasmine and I ran around the park rattling a stick on fence palings and playing hide and seek. Mousa lay on the grass with his arms holding the back of his head. At his age, he would have surely looked foolish playing with us. Instead, he joined my parents in discussing the political situation in what was then called Palestine. At that time in 1948 it was slowly being devoured by a madness in its history, the kind of madness that robs men and women of their human compassion and children of their innocence.

I remember the day I asked a Jewish boy I knew from the neigh-

1

borhood if he wanted to play. Uri and I had been friends for well over a year—and that is a long friendship in the life of a child. He just looked at me level-eyed, face set, with his chin up, in the typical manner of a boy snubbing another, and said, "My mother told me I can't play with Arabs."

The next time I saw Uri, I asked him aggressively why he had his shirtsleeves rolled all the way up. "You some kinda tough guy?" I demanded.

"You wanna fight?"

"What about you, you wanna fight?"

We looked at each other and nodded, frowning all the while. We did not, finally, fight. We just moved away from each other, troubled by the inexplicable absurdity of it all.

I never got to speak to Uri again. His family and mine lived on Miknass Street in a neighborhood that was predominantly Arab. The madness in our history was not only propelling Arabs and Jews—later to become known to the world as Palestinians and Israelis—to turn their backs on each other but to live in their own separate enclaves. So Uri's family moved out. The day they moved, I stood on the steps leading to our house, leaning against the railing, both hands in my pockets, watching Uri get into his parents' car just before it screeched off violently into the distance. I found myself involuntarily taking both hands out of my pockets and waving at him, but I don't think he saw me. The scene was sad in the extreme, but I couldn't tell any adult about it. I would have been harshly lectured about "the enemy," just as Uri had been. Adults cannot bring themselves to admit that children are special guardians of human truth. So Jews and Arabs first turned their backs on each other, then moved away from each other, and finally proceeded to murder each other. Who started it? Who cares. History had already poured fire into our blood and ritual reference into our meaning.

My uncle was killed as his car was ambushed while driving past a Jewish settlement on the coast road leading to Haifa. Mousa, my older brother, joined the *Mojahedeen*, the Arab guerrilla group of the day. When he came home it was with guns and hand grenades, but often he took off for days, even weeks, on end. Innocent Jews and Arabs caught on the fringes of their respective neighborhoods were stabbed and killed. And then the matchless cruelty of the massacres started—massacres whose perpetrators, along with their supporters on each side, would describe as heroic, as if their justification lay in some book of sacred law. Both sides soldiered on, a fierce madness at their heels.

One day a convoy of five Jewish trucks driving down Miknass Street was ambushed just outside our house. It was broad daylight, and the men—Mousa and a dozen or so of his fellow *Mojahedeen*—lay in wait behind cement blocks with their weapons. I watched through a window on the second floor of our house, thinking it was all a game. As the convoy arrived, with two drivers in each truck, suddenly they received fire and hand grenades. Three of the trucks sped away unharmed, but two caught fire. Three of the drivers were killed, their bodies lying motionless in their burning vehicles. The one survivor, a man in his late thirties dressed in overalls, jumped out of his truck on the passenger side, away from the gunfire, and sought shelter behind the walls of an unfinished building. He clutched a pistol in one hand and some kind of rifle in the crook of his arm as he ran across the road. Within minutes, dozens of British soldiers were swarming over the neighborhood, and they rescued him. It was the smell of this grim and intensely vivid event that stayed with me—the smell of gunpowder and smoke mixed with the smell of burning bodies, a dense, concentrated smell that seemed to have a meaning of its own, ugly and suffocating and vile. In later years, as I would find myself succumbing to the force of memory, I would recall that smell, and feel it rising in my chest like held-in vomit.

I took another memory with me from Palestine as madness devoured the land. As we finally trekked north on the coast road to seek refuge in Lebanon, with thousands of other refugees fleeing the carnage, we came upon a pregnant woman lying by the wayside, emitting the ghostly sounds of the pain of labor. Her husband was running up and down the road, flailing his arms and pleading, "Brothers and sisters, I beg of you, brothers and sisters, I beg of you. Is there a midwife in your midst? In the name of Allah, the Merciful, the Compassionate, is there a midwife in your midst?"

People crowded around the young woman, among them my mother, who knelt to comfort her and wiped her face with a wet cloth, waiting for a midwife to be found among the refugees on the road. As we waited, those haunting sounds emitted by the woman in labor seemed to splinter their surroundings into raw wounds.

A midwife was finally found, and we moved on.

The image of that woman lying by the wayside may have diminished in time or choked on some inexplicable subconscious impulse, but the remembered sounds keep rattling around in every corner of my being. When I hear them, I give the world the bitter smile of a thousand sleepless nights. Those sounds had their mad echoes in everything destructive I have done to myself and to others in my life.

Out of the havoc of my early childhood, it was the memory of a single day—the last of Palestine's halcyon days, that I spent on Mount Karmel picnicking with my family—that has acquired an irrevocable tenure in my soul. Time has not excised it. Nor has my encounter with despair in later years. No one knows, save other exiles, the unutterable solitude that is the private fate of those severed from home and homeland, how they are forever haunted by images of themselves as unhoused wanderers, carrying on their backs what little cargo they bring with them from their past: a name, a memory, an inner echo, a kind of dark meaning, and always the weight of a nearness out of reach.

That is why I am back here today, at Mount Karmel, standing in the same spot where I had that picnic on that cloudless day four decades ago, and I feel its energy enfold me like my skin enfolds my body.

I am home.

Yet as I say that to myself, I know how facile and illusory that outcry is. It is tawdry, I tell myself, for me to be saying that. I cannot return here, after forty years in exile, with my alternative order of meaning, my comfortable notions about homelessness being my only homeland, and say that I am home. The house is no longer as habitable as when I left it. The toys are no longer in the attic. An awry force in history has changed the place, and my own sense of otherness has changed me. This place could not be lived in by anyone other than its new inhabitants, and they have already stripped it clean of everything but themselves. From time to time I come across something here and there, inherited from nature— the view of the Mediterranean below, the cloudless sky above, the richly green trees around—that had always independently declared their own form of being, but apart from that, Haifa no longer speaks to me.

A few feet away, a man with a skullcap is holding a child on his shoulders. The child, a girl of five or six, is crying. As she cries, she leans so far out from his hold that I think she is going to fall. Her father sits her on his lap, claps her hands together, and begins to speak to her. In English. With a Brooklyn accent. Elsewhere, I would not have found this scene charged with any meaning beyond the touching sight of a father out for a walk with his child. Here it is a scene with the unlogic of dreams and reality turned on its hinges.

This land is so pervaded by symbols, so defined by them, that even the people who live here have themselves become symbolic. I could not even see a father and his daughter in a park but as a symbol of disruption in my life. He is from America, and this place is now his. I am from this place, and America is now mine. In between his trip and mine, as we changed places, something happened to me. People who live in exile guard their names the way they shield their eyes from the sun. In exile everything is excitable, like storms in wintertime, the only season you know there. Without your name, without those lips from childhood's mirror, you will be forgotten inside the American dream. I'm a first-generation American, still covered with the blood of ancient wounds.

I leave the park, wander down to the port (port areas remain the same, like the sea), and walk a few blocks north in search of the house where I was born. Something in me, in the central knot of my being, is still saying: You're back home. *Home*—a mystical, healing incantation that affirms that the link between the world in me and the world around me has not been irreparably ruptured.

There is the house, as nondescript as ever, standing at the corner of Miknass and Talal streets. The names, like everything else in this city, have been changed. Three steps lead up to the front door. I climb them and knock. The glow from the sun is so powerful that when I close my eyes they are instantly flooded by red. For a moment I swim in it. I feel the floor rock like the deck of a ship. A man in his late sixties opens the door and says something in Hebrew.

What can I say to this man? What am I doing here? Why am I driven to return to this country, this city, this street, this house, after forty years in exile?

Perhaps there lurks in each of us who have been severed from our homeground a craving to return. Whatever it is, I know I came here to remember. "I will remember," wrote Thomas Wolfe. "When I come to the place, I shall know." Here and there, I will meet Palestinians who, unlike me, had remained anchored to what they remember. They will help me to know.

"Do you speak English, sir?" I ask the old man.

He tells me, in a heavy East European accent, that he does. And I ask him if I could just look around the house a bit. He has wrinkled eyebrows and a pouting underlip that expresses his puzzlement at my odd request.

"I was born here," I offer, in the way of explanation.

He lets me into the hallway without saying another word.

"You want that I show you the house?" he asks.

"That'll be very kind of you."

"You do not speak Hebrew?"

"I'm afraid not."

"And you were born here?"

He obviously thinks I'm Jewish, but I don't want to deceive him, so I say: "I am not a Jew. I am an Arab."

He looks at me uncomprehendingly. I can see the man has arthritis and his hands are shaking.

"I mean I'm Palestinian. I'm not an Israeli," I add redundantly, but this only excites the language of his wrinkled eyebrows and pouting underlip, and he looks at me as if I had smacked him. His hands begin to shake more visibly.

"I mean, like, you know, I'm actually American," I blurt out defensively. But the man wants me out of his house. His house. My house. Our house.

I leave without either of us saying another word.

I should have told him I wasn't there to reclaim the place, just the passions it once housed. I think he would have understood. He too was once in exile, after all. I should have shared my memories from this place and the memories I acquired outside it—like the time I was a child in the refugee camp and overheard the peasant women talking to each other at the water pump about the good harvest beyond the barbed wire, south of the border. Above all, I should have told him about Abla.

In 1979, I decided to return to Borj el Berajni, the refugee camp I grew up in, and live with my people again. I stayed with my cousin Abla and her husband, Adnan. That was soon after the Palestinians had scrubbed off the grime of a name given to them by the outside world, *Arab refugees*, and wrested control of their own, *Palestinian*. I guess the Israelis did not like that. If we are *Palestinians*, we must have come from Palestine. And if we came from Palestine, then why are we not allowed to return? So they decided to bomb the name. Names are dangerous.

Abla was hanging the bed sheets and children's clothing on the line outside the house when the F-15s came. She was standing back like an artist contemplating her work, watching every piece of laundry pegged to the line flying in the sun.

Abla was carried to the hospital propped on a stretcher, bandaged in vivid red. And buried later in plain white. Abla, like all Palestinian exiles, had gathered her name moment by moment, encounter by encounter. And after it became a name, the history of all that came before was added to it. Names are subtle. You can watch them gather meaning, watch them glow with a kind of warmth and happy enormity. A name is like a home to which you bring a new object every day. A new book. A new color. A new breath. And as the bombs make it bleed, they also make it deepen, like a leaf with its own million tiny cells, each one growing with every new dawn.

When I attended Abla's funeral, I realized that her name would forever eddy around in my mind like some fragment of history. To me, Abla is a memory—another of those from my excitable wintertime. To me she is dazzling, graceful, and pure, like the moon.

I want to remember, so I will know. Sometimes when I remember, I see how we and history have become like old lovers. We lie beside each other every night, in silent darkness, and share touches that startle the heavens.

How could a little people like the Palestinians go on like that, expecting to be reborn from the shadows of a place that no longer waits for them? A place where they no longer live but that still lives in them?

I walked around Haifa all day. I had thought so often about doing it that I was convinced the experience was somehow going to enter my consciousness and catch fire.

It did not. I was a stranger in a strange city that under different circumstances I would have found boring, tacky, and uptight. I was angry at myself for having thought that the experience was somehow going to be existentially enriching, emotionally rewarding, and intellectually edifying, but I felt nothing. My sensibility had become so honed at the whetstone of exile that it revolted at the notion of rootedness to a place. And my intellect had long since developed an abhorrence for the obsessive preoccupations of nationalism. But I *had* to imagine what I wanted to imagine about Haifa. I was born here. There are people everywhere, walking around me, in front of me, behind me, bumping into me, some even exchanging glances with me, the whole place readily communicating the quick of the human spirit that inhabits it. But I feel nothing. If I were to tell these people who I am, they would call my heart my head and declare my roots to be my horoscope. I cannot speak to them. I cannot drag the ocean, holding it by the scruff of its neck, to the house of our past. I cannot tell these people how my very breath has bound me to this land, this sea, this morning.

Later today I will leave Haifa and go to East Jerusalem, where I will meet Palestinians from the homeground. I will tell them that. I wonder what they'll say.

...

I do not know how Palestinians here will receive me. Perhaps they will think that my way of being Palestinian is inadequate because it does not involve the same emotional investment and reserves of political perception with which they have imbued it. Palestinians on the homeground, consumed by the cruel fetish of constantly pondering their victimized condition, are weary of contemplating an alternative way of being Palestinian. I am not concerned. Time will show that those of us who left to inhabit the lands of others are the ones who became more themselves as Palestinians.

When I was growing up in a refugee camp in Beirut and beginning to acquire a past of my own, my soul forever gasped for breath. I lived in a society whose intolerance for innovation laid waste to our personal meaning. It daily tampered with our individuality and so subverted free utterance that people lost the faculty of communicating anything worthwhile even to themselves, let alone to others. The only freedom possible there was the freedom of madness and death.

Eventually I escaped that world and traveled to Australia, India, Europe, and finally the United States. It was there that I discovered that I wanted to be—needed to be—Palestinian again. America has a way of allowing people to experience the defining feature of their old culture, after they have given themselves to a new one.

I had lived outside Palestine since childhood and outside my own cultural skin since my late teens. And in all these lands I had lived in since I left, nothing really was what it appeared. The center was always hollow, unstable, and formless. My Palestinian identity always lurked in my subconscious, like an old toy stored in the attic.

I joined the Palestinian movement. The PLO was, and still is, an incompetent, at times cynical organization, engaged more in political posturing than in inspired leadership. It bore directly—and sadly—on the fortunes of Palestinian society and its struggle for cultural awareness, itself a precondition to a people's ability to achieve insight into their place in historical life.

When I came upon them, after my "return," Palestinians still stood orphaned at the gate of history. All the energies of spirit their community had generated remained without a mature response from their leaders. This was a pitiless realization, but I was not daunted by it. Palestinian functionaries may have ruled, and their rule may have been tainted with corruption, larceny, and cynical disregard for the interests of the governed, but it was the people and the cause I worked for.

The Palestinian community in the United States is brand new. To be sure, a trickle of immigrants had arrived after the two upheavals in Palestine in 1936 and 1948, and another trickle subsequent to that, numbering in the thousands, who came to live here as legal immigrants or, through the back door, as tourists. But the overwhelming majority made it to these shores after the June War of 1967. In addition, there are always 60,000 or so students to be found in North America every year who hail from both the homeground and the diaspora. And every year, no fewer than half of these students remain after graduation. Given the choice between returning to their host states in the Gulf, Jordan, Saudi Arabia, or Lebanon—and living in America, they understandably prefer the latter.

No one knows precisely how many Palestinian Americans there are. Many have changed their names and escaped into the heartland of the American dream, perhaps to avoid the ache of dealing with their background. But many, many more have not escaped; they remain true to their identity and have become active in the struggle of their compatriots in the old country.

Among these it was the new generation, especially the students, for whom I was now becoming the model activist and lecturer of choice, a kind of legend actually. We were in love with each other. I loved them because they represented the future of my past. They loved me because Palestinians love other Palestinians who are not like them.

So I soldiered on, unconcerned with the excesses of Palestinian officials, until that day in September 1982 when the frenzied packs came to the two refugee camps of Sabra and Shatila, inhabited exclusively by old men, women, and children, and perpetrated their massacre, piling stacks of bodies on top of each other and leaving them in the muddy lanes to rot in the sun.

Palestinian officials wanted to "gain publicity" from the event.

I, on the other hand, wanted to die.

The thought of Sabra and Shatila invaded my mind and caught fire, and the fire began to consume me bit by bit, moment by moment, image by image. It encroached on my mind like a nightmare.

I knew Sabra and Shatila as a teenager, when I lived in Beirut in a neighboring camp. They were home to thousands of Palestinian exiles like myself and, for close to a decade, home to the southerly wind from Palestine and some crazy shadows from our homeland. Home to a people living there in a kind of silent orgy of intricate sounds.

What stood between our camps and the outside world was an aggregate of Palestinian childhoods, silhouetted against the walls of the mudhouses and proclaiming their own unique formality. A separateness of tone. A kind of absurd purity.

In September 1982, the children died in silence. The ones who did not die in simple silence begged for mercy first. The few who survived learned the ritual terrors of a journey through hell, and they would lie every night unable to sleep, their hands reaching out for tough argument with their deity. One day they will learn how to smother their screams and their fury. I know. I am from their camps and of their pain. I am one with them. I've learned to smother the screams and the fury from my own past. All I left myself with was a flash of images, a pungency of nameless pain.

I wanted to talk about Sabra and Shatila because I like my voice and I like my pain. I like them in my aloneness, because only in that way can I define our Palestinian solitude in a fraternity of screams at sunrise. I never tire of talking about death. How could I? We have mass graves all over Lebanon, Syria, Jordan, and Palestine. I am tired of books that describe them. I am tired, too, of my own books, of fleeing into the confines of my poems where I am sure of shelter.

I know, I said to myself, one day soon I will meet one of the children who survived, and I will tear off my skin with grief and ram my head against his eternity. Above all, I will cut my fingers off, for what is the use of hitting them on the dumb keys of a typewriter, in my comfortable diaspora dream, in order to write a poem, and play with my child on a carpeted floor, and complain to myself that the whole world is taking its revenge on the defenseless children of our exiled nation. It is so helpless a project—so vain and absurd.

They all died, even those who survived, and I died too. For when the fascists came, they came also looking for *me*. When they came to Sabra and Shatila, they didn't come looking for radical Palestinians or conservative Palestinians, Moslem Palestinians or Christian Palestinians, rich Palestinians or poor Palestinians, young Palestinians or old Palestinians. They came looking for *Palestinians*. I am a Palestinian. I was not there only by a trick of fate.

Why was I not there? God, I tell you now, I would have wanted to be there. Hell, why am I addressing God? I should be addressing the devil. God has nothing to do with us. Our pact was signed with the devil, a long time ago. At least the devil knows his job. He delivers. God does not. God has shown us nothing but indifference.

I had no desire to be an activist after that. I did not wish to speak to anyone anymore, to re-create myself in words anymore. How can you speak the unspeakable, imagine the unimaginable?

A group of officials from the PLO, headed by a man with a belly that looked like a drum, arrived in Washington and told the Palestinian community that we should "work on this thing" and "gain publicity" for the cause by capitalizing on the sympathy of the American public. "Don't worry about it," he assured us, "only hundreds died, not thousands. We only say that for public consumption."

Go away from me, you bastards. And if you will not go away from me, I will go away from you.

I went away from them all. I wanted, literally, to die. Dying, no less than living, is an art. When you are prevented from choosing how to live, you seek the freedom of choosing how to die.

Then one day, I met a twenty-three-year-old Palestinian boy at a casual dinner party. Ibrahim was a survivor of Sabra whose entire family, with the exception of his younger brother, was wiped out. He and his brother had been brought here by an Arab-American organization and since the massacre had lived and gone to school in the Washington area.

During dinner, he and I exchanged glances. I was not going to ask him any indecent questions about his experiences. In no time, however, someone else asked both an indecent and a frivolous question. "What was it like, brother Ibrahim?"

"I don't know," he said quietly.

The questioner, along with the other five guests, looked blankly at the boy.

"I don't know what it was like," he persisted. "All I know is that we ran when we heard them coming. All of us ran, except for my brother, Jaafar, who was not at the camp that day. I was in the front, and my grandmother was some yards behind us because she couldn't catch up with us. She was shot first. Then more shots were fired, and my two sisters, my other brother, and my parents were hit. They all fell on top of me. I lay still. A few moments later the fascists approached and fired about half a dozen bullets into the bodies of my family members. I thought I was hit too, but I was not. I still lay quiet after they left. Before they left, I heard one of them boast that they managed to kill not just one but six Palestinians. They were referring to one of their fascist slogans about how it was the duty of every Lebanese to kill at least one Palestinian. That's all I know until I was rescued by the Red Cross."

There was silence around the dinner table. Then the boy added: "That's all I know, really. That's it."

There was a finality to the way he said that, and mercifully, the guests respected the boy's wishes and no more questions were asked.

Two weeks later I met Ibrahim again in a classroom at George Washington University where I was giving a lecture. When I finished, I asked him if he would care to have coffee with me in the cafeteria. He seemed flattered by my offer.

"Ibrahim, I want to ask you a question," I said, after we had exchanged a few pleasantries about his studies. "This is a question I have been thinking about for the last two weeks, since I last saw you. I don't know why I have been thinking about it, but I have.

Before I ask it, though, could you tell me how long you were under that pile of bodies before you were rescued?"

"I don't know, brother, I really don't know," he offered innocently. "I'm told it was hours, but I had no idea of time passing. I was just there, and I didn't feel time stretching or contracting. I mean I just wasn't conscious of minutes or hours and such."

"Okay, here's my question," I said. "What were you thinking about the whole time you were buried under those bodies?"

"I only remember one thought," he said, looking pensively at his hands.

"What was it?"

"It is ridiculous. You don't want to hear it."

"Would you care to share it with me?" I pressed.

"I thought about the potted plant on the roof of our house. My father always made it face south, to get the southerly wind from Palestine."

I thought about that for days. Then for weeks.

Suddenly all these ideas, thronging my confused mind, spilled out with frantic energy. *I want to get the southerly wind from Palestine.*

I want to go home. The only wind I have felt all these years came at me from a placeless place where things are best understood when you look at the mask, not the face.

I too want to get the southerly wind from Palestine. I want to be in the homeground where meaning has finality, where my core may find its voice.

...

So here I am in Haifa waiting in a bus terminal. Two hours later, I find myself in West Jerusalem. From there I take a cab to my hotel in East Jerusalem. The trip takes about ten minutes, and in that short time I was, in effect, taken from one world to another, from one social reality to another, from one people to another. The ferocity of discord in this land of symbols, between Israelis and Palestinians, is no more starkly symbolized than in the two life-styles of "united" Jerusalem. In the western part, as I looked out of my cab window with weary fascination at the street, I could see how people everywhere were moving about in natural control of life, in zestful self-confidence, in a city bristling with the tension of a modern metropolis. In East Jerusalem, cultural identity and historical presence are explicit, but there is a muteness about the place—the muteness of an occupied people crippled by constant assaults on its emotional resources. In contrast to their counterparts in the West, the East Jerusalemites move about their streets as if going nowhere. They look listless, helpless, purposeless. Tormented by an unendurably harsh occupation, they look inward for direction.

The Israeli taxi driver breaks every tradition in his profession by not exchanging a word with me. He seems nervous about taking me to East Jerusalem. The *Intifada*, a popular uprising that was started mostly by young, stone-throwing Palestinians in the West Bank and Gaza, has disunited a Jerusalem that the Israeli occupation had united by force of arms twenty-three years before.

The driver lets me off outside my hotel, a hotel that some buffoon had called—in a part of the world that had long railed against colonialism—the American Colony Hotel.

As soon as I check in I call a number. A woman comes on the line. "Yes, can I help you?" she says in a formal voice.

I identify myself and ask, in my best Arabic, if I can speak to Faisal Husseini. Husseini, scion of a prominent family from Palestine, is one of the local leaders in the West Bank/Gaza and is unofficially recognized as the top PLO man in the territories. Fatah, the large PLO faction that he belongs to, often refers to him as "our man in Palestine." I don't care whose man he is. I don't care for PLO boys. I care less for "family boys"—the fellows who come from the dozen or so landowning families who have anointed themselves the chosen leaders of the Palestinian people. Because they owned 80 percent of the land and an equal percentage of its wealth, they felt entitled to 100 percent of the power. What could I, a Palestinian from the camps who grew up with radical politics like he grew up with his skin, have in common with them? To them, we are mere nameless, faceless creatures, foot soldiers to be sent to the front lines to die. Unlike us, these people have never been hungry in their lives. I feel anger at them, and I know that it is a destructive kind of anger. When you're angry at a foreign enemy, your anger is clearly defined and siphoning it off through struggle is a liberating experience. When you're angry at a class enemy, you're angry at something in *you*. To address it, you address yourself.

"Who was that who made the call for you?" the lady asks suspiciously.

I tell her it was the desk.

"That's wrong," she says cryptically and hangs up.

Her reaction seemed peculiar, but I am in the occupied West Bank, after all, and Husseini is a leading figure, so security concerns are uppermost in the mind of those who answer his phone. Now I call Salem's number. Salem is my other contact in the West Bank. He too is a family boy and works for Husseini as a runner. He runs from village to village to settle feuds between families, from town to town to resolve disputes between factions, and from hospital to hospital, or prison to prison, to address the needs of those injured and incarcerated by the occupation soldiers.

"I'm here," I tell Salem when he answers the phone.

"Thank the Lord for your safe arrival. Palestine shines by your light. The land is richer for your presence. Welcome, brother, welcome," he hollers his flowery Arabic into the phone. "Thank God, I say, for your safe arrival. Or should I say your safe return?"

I sit and wait in the hotel lobby. The place is almost empty, except for the odd resident journalist, the odd visiting UN official, and the odd tourist. The last type of visitor would have to be odd indeed to be visiting this part of the world at this time. It is December 21, 1990. Kuwait has been occupied by Iraqi forces for almost five months and close to a million allied forces, half of them American, are gathered in the Gulf to enforce a UN Security Council resolution calling on Iraq to pull out by January 15—or else. Talk of imminent war—inevitable war that would engulf the entire region, including Israel—is prevalent. One would have to be a truly unusual tourist to choose this part of the world for a vacation, like the black American lady in her mid-forties, sitting at a table next to me in the lobby, earnestly reading *The Golden Book of Prayer*. From time to time as she reads, she lifts her head and nods contentedly, as if she has just made a spiritual discovery. In the old days before the *Intifada*, thousands of such people came at this time of year to make the pilgrimage to Bethlehem and tour the Christian holy places in Jerusalem. Even during the *Intifada*, over the last two Christmases, many still came. But this year, with war seeming the inevitable conclusion of the Gulf crisis, few have decided to brave it.

Salem finally turns up, accompanied by Leila. Salem and I hug and kiss on both cheeks. That's customary. Leila and I . . . well, we just shake hands. Leila is now a professor of psychology at Beir Zeit

University, outside Ramallah. Seven years before, when she was doing her Ph.D. at the State University of New York in Buffalo and I was a writer in residence at the Communications Department, we were lovers. But here you do not hug and kiss a woman, even an old lover. That is not customary. It is even less customary to let on that, God forbid, a woman has had a lover at any time in her life. A woman who does that sort of thing is a tart. And a tart is shot and killed by a male member of her family or, at best, is ostracized. So Leila and I shake hands, and she sits between me and Salem in the lounge, a demure, blushful woman comporting herself with the linguistic propriety and sexual reticence expected of any female Palestinian in social life. Never mind that she is a thirty-six-year-old career woman, a brilliant intellectual, and an economically self-sufficient person. Here she lives with her parents, and if she is late returning home, she may be challenged by them or by any male member of the family, including a *younger* brother, to explain where she has been and with whom. The daring, impetuous, erotic Leila I had known in the United States, the girl of twenty-nine who had flaunted the glory of her youthful sensuality, and her readiness to share it, now sits across from me at the American Colony Hotel trying to communicate her feelings about seeing me again in ways other than words.

Over coffee, Salem, whom I had met a few years back when he was a student at George Washington University, gushes his ornate assurances that my stay in the homeland will be productive and enriching. He will see to that.

After our coffee, we leave the Colony and walk down the appropriately named Saladin Street, which hugs the walls of the Old City. It was here the Crusaders came in July 1099, laid siege to Jerusalem, and captured it from the Arabs, and where Saladin, returning with Arab forces eighty-eight years later, crushed the Frankish armies in the battle of Hittin near Lake Tiberias and reconquered the city, along with the greater part of the territories comprising the kingdom the Franks had established in Palestine.

It is early evening and all the shops, with the exception of the pharmacies, have long been closed. All over the West Bank, including East Jerusalem, business comes to a standstill at 1:00 P.M. That's the way the underground leaders of the *Intifada* want it. This confirms the popularity of their movement and that they, not the Israeli occupiers, are in charge. The people here willingly, even happily, go along with the communiqués issued by the Unified Command. To be sure, they also go along with the occupation authorities, but they do that under duress.

There are a lot of people around, but it is still early evening. Within two or three hours, by 8:00 P.M., the streets will be empty and the city will look like a ghost town. The same pattern of life is followed all over the West Bank and Gaza. You finish your work by early afternoon, dinner by early evening, and your entire day by 9:00 P.M. You are indoors, in bed, by that time. You don't go wandering around the streets after that hour, unless you want to get picked up by occupation soldiers or by the brutal border police. These people don't ask questions, and when they do, they don't bother with answers.

I can't believe all these people are *Palestinians*. Save for the few years that I had spent in Haifa, before Palestine became Israel, I had never before been in a city, town, or village where everybody was Palestinian and where, in the overlapping of energies, every Palestinian had somehow contributed to the ethos of the place. As I walk with Salem and Leila, taking shortcuts through side streets, I feel a sharpening of my senses, a strange excitement of the kind we ordinarily keep in check because it resembles the boundless, hysterical excitement of a child. I want to walk up to people and say, Hey brother, I'm Palestinian too. I too grew up crying on the shoulders of a dispassionate world, screaming helpless jokes about our condition, building my naked fear into a sigh of self-destruction. But these Palestinians would only look askance at me—as they did when we finally arrived at our destination, the home of Hatem Sharif.

Hatem, who at one time had been director of a Palestinian charity organization in Washington, D.C., was a friend of fifteen years. He was in town for a short while to attend the funeral of his father, a noted scholar who had died three days before. Today was the final day of *Aza* in the Sharif family, a kind of open house for friends, relatives, and neighbors who drop by to console the bereaved. You walk in, quietly offer condolences, and sit in silence while the *sheik* recites verses from the Koran. The *sheik* stops for a break from time to time, and then you are offered cigarettes, sweets, and coffee, and may exchange a few words with the person sitting next to you. An *Aza*, like the death it mourns, is a democratic affair. Anybody—beggars from the neighborhood whom the deceased may have helped in his day, local vendors, shopkeepers, newspaper boys, and the like—can drop by. And they were all there—men of all classes, all ages; Moslems and Christians, rich and poor, secular and sectarian. Men dressed in their colorful national garb, others in Western clothing. Worldly men looking confident and self-assured, and villagers looking ill at ease and shy. All men, of course, for an *Aza* is strictly male. No women allowed.

When I walked in, with my leather jacket, beard, and long hair, all eyes fell on me. Everybody looked shocked, even angry. I could almost hear a collective sigh released by the group of two dozen or so. What on earth is this *American* doing here? Or, God forbid, what on earth is this *Israeli* doing here?

Hatem stands up and hugs me, which reduces but does not completely dissipate the tension. I don't look Palestinian. I don't talk or walk or carry myself like a Palestinian. Maybe I'm not Palestinian anymore. There is a way you have when you're a Palestinian, even one who grew up in Western exile, that gives testimony to what you have thought in the dark, that other Palestinians can sense. I don't have that way about me anymore. They all look at me as if to ask: What is your truth? How do you tell these people what your truth is? In my exile, I have suffered as much grief as you have. Unlike you, I addressed the world's emptiness with no homeground to support me. You can't imagine the barrenness of our dreamless life in exile, like a fire with no ash and no sparks. That's why I'm different from you. That is why I look and talk and walk and live differently. And that is why I'm back here, in this land, to confront you with my presence, to show you and myself that my reality is also real.

I sit quietly next to Hatem and listen to the *sheik*'s Koranic recital. Moments later, I feel a formidable urge, at once inexplicable and uncontrollable, to cry. There is something about that melodic voice and the onrush of words that seems to bespeak a time in my childhood—something I had distanced myself from, yet that had not distanced itself from me. And I had not listened to a Koranic recital for a long time.

As I sit listening to the *sheik*, a man in his early sixties with lizard eyes and a thick mop of gray hair, ululating the charged verse of the Koran and passing it over his tongue like a rare vintage wine, I become one with the enraptured gathering, feeling the flow between voice and ear, word and world, quietly regrouping my emotional resources, remembrances, self-definitions. (I have to confess that I also felt like smoking a joint.)

Leila waited outside. Despite the fact that Palestinians have been conducting daily transactions with history for the last eight decades and despite the resulting massive shocks to their social system, their traditions have remained unshaken. Regardless of how our cultural contradictions were sharpened by political struggle, these traditions proved resilient to assault. Leila, though more worldly, sophisticated, and successful than any of the men at the *Aza*, was still a woman. And a woman waits outside. The startling thing was that she didn't seem to think it inconvenient to submit.

Finally Salem, Leila, and I head to one of the very few restaurants still open at this hour. It's already 7:30. Soon all the service cabs and other public transportation will stop. Unless Leila can get a ride to Ramallah, a half-hour away, she'll be in trouble.

The owner of the Philadelphia Restaurant, a fellow called Walid who is thirty-six but looks twice as old, greets my friends, whom he knows well, and shakes my hand effusively.

"You live in America, brother?" he inquires after he seats us. "I say may the Lord pour acid on the soul of Washington and on the soul of the man who occupies the White House today, Mr. George."

"I never voted for him," I respond lightly.

"I am not against Americans, just against their government," he says and actually sits down with us at the table. "I love Americans. Especially Mr. Carter. Mr. James Carter and his wife Mrs. Rosalyn. They were here once, you know. They came here to eat. At my restaurant. At that table there."

He gets up and rushes to the wall to show us a framed picture of Jimmy Carter shaking hands with him, with the former president's wife smiling in the background. He proudly passes it around. "They ate at my restaurant. They were here . . . I'll tell you when they were here. March 21, this year. That's when they were here."

We show our appreciation and give him his precious memento back.

"I told the president," he continues vehemently, "I told him that we want peace. The Palestinians want peace, and when they, the Jews, cut the hand off, there will be no peace." He extends his right hand to us and with the other simulates the act of chopping it off with a knife.

...

Leila relaxes only after she is assured that Salem will give her a lift home *and* after she calls her parents to inform them that she was engaged in "an honorable encounter" with "honorable friends." The restaurant is full, but except for a foreign journalist or two its diners seem entirely Palestinian.

"Before the *Intifada*," Leila offers, "there would be a lot of Israelis here. But now they just don't come anymore. In fact, as you will see for yourself in coming days, they never come anywhere in East Jerusalem. In the past, there would be thousands of them shopping in the marketplace, walking around in the streets of the Old City, eating in our restaurants and so on. Today they keep to their part of the city, and we keep to ours."

I tell Leila that I am intrigued by the fascinating grip that this uprising has had on the imagination of the people and the massive support it seems to have elicited from virtually every sector of society.

"There is a simple explanation to account for all of this. And I guess it goes beyond the elation, the pride, Palestinians derive from knowing that they have initiated something called *Intifada*, a word that every language in the world has already naturalized," she says, eyeing a man who walks by our table before she continues. Living under occupation for so long and having to be wary of collaborators, even of individuals who refuse to get involved in the struggle, Palestinians are paranoid in public. They could be talking about the most innocuous subject, but they carefully look around before they voice their thoughts. You forget about things like that when you live in the United States, and you tend to see these gestures as theatrical. But here, where every family has had at least one member beaten, deported, imprisoned, tortured, or pauperized for the slightest expression of activism, real or imagined, I suppose being paranoid doesn't mean that someone isn't following you.

"The explanation," continues Leila, "is that people here have come to see the *Intifada* as an embodiment of every individual's malaise, a struggle that has originated from everybody and is about everybody. Being involved in the *Intifada*, whatever form that takes, is thus Everyman's concern. And that involvement finally exalts Palestinians, creates a world for them of self-reliance, healing celebration, and awakening. The *Intifada*, very simply, has connected Palestinians to the energy of their struggle for statehood. You see, before the uprising three years ago, we were, to put it bluntly, becoming progressively alienated by the corruption and incompetence of our leaders in exile; we were especially devastated by the disaster in Beirut in 1982, when finally our political leadership and all our military forces were kicked out of Lebanon. The tired cant and lame banalities of the PLO, issuing now from Tunis, seemed so mockingly remote from our reality here. The *Intifada* had to come. It was as if we had been waiting for it and knew all along that it was coming."

I am thinking, Yes, *this* is the new generation of Palestinians that was meant to come forward and declare its devotion to freedom. The children of the *Intifada* have made their struggle so hypnotically human that they appear to be asking us all, as they might of judge and jury, why the world should balk at their humanity.

Finally, the world did not. Nor did it balk, two decades earlier, when my generation of Palestinians, whose will to rebellion had been insistently at work since 1948, burst on the scene. To be sure, at the time of their emergence in 1968 at the battle of Karameh, they mouthed the same eccentric insights about freedom as their young counterparts around the world had done in the 1960s. But they finally made their point: Palestinians were very much a part of the global dialogue of cultures.

A struggle for freedom is a central, life-giving force in the life of a people. But there is a close relationship between a people's fitness for freedom—as opposed to that silliness we call "national independence"—and their responsiveness to humane being. The more organic that connection is, the steadier will be the mirror in which they see themselves, and the sharper the pen with which they write their names.

The Palestinians had to pick up their hats and leave the stage in the early 1970s because the mirror cracked and the image was fragmented. Their movement survived, having transplanted itself to Lebanon, but only as a ghost of its old self, now attracting the worst elements of society. Meanwhile, the doors slammed shut in the face of those who still retained a spirit of political idealism.

Yet those who lived the struggle in those few short years would glory in the knowledge that their contribution would surely one day animate new impulses in their society. Nothing goes forgotten into dust. People always knit themselves anew, instigated by the legacies

of feeling that they draw on from the rear. It was left to a new generation of Palestinians, marked by the scars of lost or betrayed
dreams, to surge forward again, with rage in heart and stones in
hand.

It is true that the *Intifada*, as Leila claimed, had been the embodiment of every individual's malaise and may have lastingly altered
the way the world saw Palestinians. But the hideous truth is that
the rules that govern both self and society here continue to hold
everyone, including those of Leila's intellectual calibre, prisoner.
Leila had spent four years in the United States yet she remained a
captive to the dictates of her culture. Along with the overwhelming
majority of her fellow intellectuals and activists, she has fallen easy
prey to the afflictions that ail Palestinian society.

One of these is the narrow inwardness that Palestinians retreated
to following their realization, after 1948, that the Arab world and its
peoples were fully prepared to stab them in the back, to mistreat
them and place them close to the door for eviction to another country, another refugee camp, another state of destitution. Arabs had
done that, and more, for their own selfish reasons. So Palestinians
withdrew into their shell and discarded the greater depth of their
Arab identity. All Arabs, and certainly all Arab governments, they
felt, were determined to co-opt their cause and finally sell them
out. The best posture to adopt with other Arabs was therefore a
defensive one. Palestinians are alone in the world. Which means you
do not criticize your own people, your own cause, your own movement, when with outsiders. In the end, this was inevitably to mean:
You do not criticize Palestinian society even when with your own
kind. This was to translate into a kind of resolute provincialism that
would make Palestinians turn a deaf ear to the attractions of another way of thought and social conduct.

Here is Leila at the dinner table telling me about how "trivial"
American culture is and how "frivolous" are its values. Never mind
that whatever intellectual depth she brought to her argument was
marred by the smug hauteur that Third World activists traditionally
bring to their criticism of the United States. The problem is that
she is unable to bring the same critical acumen to bear on her own
society.

"There are a lot of iniquities in America," Leila tells me, feeling,
like other Palestinians, most at ease when they criticize other cul-

tures, especially American. "I mean, look at the poverty, the way they treat blacks, the way they elect presidents, and the way they invade other countries."

"Okay, let me tell you this," I respond. "I have railed against injustice and racism and bourgeois smugness and a lot of the other iniquities you're thinking of. I have marched outside the White House and called a variety of American presidents, from Nixon to Bush, a variety of unprintable names. But I want to tell you that as I railed, I also marveled at the fact that I could do so."

"Do you mean," Salem interjects incredulously, "that you consider America a better place to be than your own country?"

Why should I tell him that I have long since dropped anchor in Western culture, where I truly feel I belong? So I respond simply by saying: "I'm equally and vitally at home in both."

I have no doubt that there is stringent honesty in Salem's and Leila's love for their people. There is love in me too for these people. And it is this love that justifies the scorn I pour on Palestinian tradition. I have, you see, known the punishing visitations of Palestinian tradition since my childhood.

Leila looks at her watch and says to me: "Oh, yes, it's already past nine o'clock. For you people in the States, this is when you think about going out. For us here, this is past our bedtime."

We say good-bye outside the restaurant. I shake hands with Leila. She still looks as young and as glamorously intense as she had done back in upstate New York, seven years before, except for a fold of skin at the corner of each eye. I hold her hand for a few seconds longer after the handshake. That was it. I was, after all, "honorable company."

I love this Palestinian woman. Today, basking in the southerly wind, my heart is full of love for all Palestinians. In this land, my homeground, I want to graft my being onto every other Palestinian and become irreducibly one with them, one with their pain. As Salem and Leila drive off in the dark, I wave, and I keep waving long after their car turns the corner. I am picturing myself as Holden Caulfield, standing in the field of rye, catching Palestinians who do not know where they are going. I come from somewhere else, like Holden Caulfield. I will catch them before they fall. Now I know that I am crazy too.

2
God's Backyard

I get up early and head down to the office of one of Faisal Husseini's uncles. This man runs an educational institution that offers grants to bright Palestinian students who want to study abroad. He is in his early sixties, with a harried look about him—the kind of man who frets that someone has walked off with his pencil sharpener. Nevertheless, I decide that I like him. I introduce myself and tell him it has been arranged that I meet Hatem and another friend here in his office. We were going to the Aqsa Mosque to pray and walk around the Old City together. The praying part, for me at least, had nothing to do with religious zeal or a sudden burst of piety. I just wanted to see the Haram el Shareef grounds and to visit a mosque that is not only architecturally exquisite but embodies so much of our history.

"Yes, dear brother," he says, shaking my hand with both of his. "Hatem told me you were coming. I'm truly honored to meet you. I'm familiar with your work."

Just then the phone rings and he picks it up. After listening a while, he begins to call upon Allah, His Prophet, the Prophet's Companions, and the Angel Gabriel to wreak vengeance on the Israelis. Then he hangs up, removes his glasses, rubs his eyes wearily, and says: "They've just given Ibrahim a green card!" I look at him blankly, and he realizes that what he has said is meaningless to me.

He rubs his ears, from which countless bristles sprout in all directions, and explains: "Ibrahim Jaber is one of our brightest students. The Israeli occupation authorities have just given him a green card. That means he cannot leave the West Bank. To a have a green card means you're a political activist and are not allowed even to enter Jerusalem, let alone travel overseas. They have just destroyed the boy's future. It took us over a year to get him a scholarship and an acceptance at UCLA."

A few minutes later we are joined by two visitors, a man and woman who are there to see about a grant for their son. The woman is wearing one of those exquisitely embroidered Palestinian dresses. Her husband is wearing a Western suit with the traditional Arab headdress.

"Tell them, tell them," the woman says earnestly to me. "Tell them in America when you return. Tell them my son Samir is eight years old, and they beat him senseless. Only eight years old."

"I'm sorry to hear that." I don't know what else to say.

"You people in America," she continues. "You don't know what the Israelis do to us. They're highwaymen. They're vagabonds. Thugs. No one knows that about them. Not the UN. Not Europe. Not America." She nods her head with outrage, her hair falling forward as if to complement her words.

I say nothing.

"Americans don't understand us. Perhaps they don't want to understand us," she announces, uttering the word *understand* as if it were an obscenity. Her eyes are as hard as flint, seeming at once to hold rage, defiance, and frustration.

I look at her, and she looks at me, without either of us saying a word, briefly silenced by our mutual agreement.

The woman is right. Americans do not understand. But not because, as she said, they don't want to; rather, because they cannot truly understand what Palestinians are going through and why they respond as they do to the challenges of their history. The fact of the matter is that no experience by one people is translatable unaltered into the language of another. When Americans read about the Palestinian struggle, they filter it through their own semantic and perceptual conventions, and it comes out very different from the one that Palestinians are living.

After my two friends turn up, and after drinking the mandatory tea, we take off.

How do you prepare yourself for a place like Jerusalem? Hatem, like virtually all other members of his family, was born here and left in his twenties. Akram, my other friend, *still* in his twenties, was born in Cleveland, Ohio, to Palestinian parents who had decided to "return to the homeland" four years ago. At first Akram and his four sisters didn't like it here, but now he tells me he wouldn't live anywhere else.

We walk down Ben Battuta Street (named after a famous tenth-century Arab traveler) to Saladin, the main street, and all the way down to Herod Gate, just outside the Walled City. This is going to be a wondrous place to visit, to be in, a place like no other. I have been to Benares in India and to Mecca in Saudi Arabia, to the famed pagodas of Rangoon and those in Bangkok. But Jerusalem has more to say to me than any other holy place that I have been to. Everywhere you go, everywhere you look, there is history. Already we have passed Tombs of the Kings, St. George's Cathedral, the Dominican Church of St. Stephens, Jeremiah's Grotto, the École biblique, and now we are at Herod's Gate. Viewing the ancient walls of the Old City, I am overwhelmed by emotion. I go to touch the stones as if they would speak to me, about me, revealing ancient memories, evoking scenes from our history—of men and women armed with brave dreams, with crazy visions, with yellowed birth certificates or testimonials from their God, attesting their right to be here.

An elderly Palestinian woman walks by balancing a jug on her head, a hand lifting her embroidered dress an inch off the pavement. The jug was made of plastic.

My two friends are smiling at my wonderment. If you have lived here, as they have, you turn a deaf ear and a blind eye to the diverse essences of Jerusalem after awhile, for Jerusalem has everything to saturate the hungriest appetite for the sonorous, the historical, the tactile, the religious. But seeing the city for the first time, as I am doing now, one cannot fail to feel an archetypal presence.

Inside the walls, as if to underscore how men would rebel, even in God's own city, against a stable, pluralistic incarnation of His word, there are the Moslem Quarter, the Christian Quarter, the Armenian Quarter, and the Jewish Quarter.

As we prepare to enter the grounds, surrounded by their own walls, where the Dome of the Rock and the Aqsa Mosque are situated, we are stopped by three burly Palestinian guards with walkie-talkies who ask my two friends what "this American" is doing here. Palestinians are still angry about the massacre of nineteen of their compatriots a few weeks back by Israeli soldiers who shot them when some worshipers, fearful that Jewish zealots were about to expropriate some of their holy sites, began to throw stones at Jews praying by the adjacent Western Wall. Nerves were still raw. No foreigners were being allowed to enter.

I affect a heavy Palestinian accent and tell them I am a Moslem. I even shake hands with them. They let me through.

Approaching the mosque, I see nineteen potted plants scattered over the grounds, placed where the "martyrs" had fallen.

We enter the mosque and proceed to pray. I stand a few feet behind my friends so I can emulate their kneeling movements. I don't know anything about this business—all this kneeling and bending and mumbling entreaties to God. So I copied my friends—that was easy enough—and for the prayers I sang, under my breath, some lyrics I remembered from the Sixties.

There is something special for Palestinians about being in a mosque at this moment in history. It is a more protective enclave than their own homes. After eight decades of living under occupation by the British, the Jordanians, and then the Israelis, the outside world to Palestinians became a place of gloom and even terror, while Palestinian homes became retreats of safety, not of ease and relaxation. The heavy curtains over the windows of virtually every Palestinian home give the appearance of being there to ward off threat. Inside, the furniture is functional, inelegant, and cheerless. The emptiness of the living rooms, notable for the absence of such objects as coffee tables, sideboards, bookshelves, and the like, conveys a sense of vigilant austerity. Pictures and other artifacts on the walls are hung helter-skelter, conflicting with each other in size, color, shape, design, intention, as if to advertise the turmoil and confusion that reigns in Palestinian life. Even outside the home, where Palestinians work, play, or study in enclosed spaces, there is no rest from this confusion, only variations on it.

When a home becomes a refuge from the outside world—a world assaulting you at every turn for the least infraction of its repressive rules—it acquires a disquieting air of secrecy, obsessiveness, conspiracy.

The one remarkable exception is the mosque, and particularly the Aqsa Mosque. To a foreigner, the inside of the Aqsa may seem bare and unsuggestive; but to a Moslem, particularly a Palestinian Moslem, the mosque's impact is visual, emotional, and acoustic. There, sitting on fine Persian rugs, surrounded by beautiful calligraphy on the walls, mostly in cheery red and blue, listening to a Koranic recital or to the imam reading his sermon from an exquisitely designed pulpit, the Palestinian—in an open, free, and seemingly imperishable monument to his own history—feels disentangled from the absurdities of occupation, inviolate as he sits close to his Maker. The mosque may affirm human weakness and the individual's fragility in relation to God, but it also affirms the justice due to the believer and the punishment He will assuredly mete out to the oppressor.

The helpless Palestinian unperson, who all week has walked the streets of Nablus, Gaza City, or the village of Abu Diss, experiencing the brutishness of an occupier who just will not go away, can now, on Friday, attend noon prayer, surrounded by fellow unpersons, and feel that his will to meaning is affirmed both by his own God and his own history.

...

My friends and I walk to the Dome of the Rock, the jewel in the crown of what is known as the Haram el Shareef, in the northern part of the grounds. To contemplate the beauty of the structure, its breathtaking architectural eloquence, is to understand why the dome has always been the defining feature of Jerusalem. Its uniqueness, along with the supreme status it has always had in Islamic mythology as the place whence the Prophet ascended to heaven, sets it apart with such an absolute finality as to make it dwarf everything else.

As we enter, I am overwhelmed by the way the dome seems to communicate, with stubborn mystery, energies of the religious psyche beyond our temporal sphere. These energies seduce you, enticing you to plunge effortlessly into prayer, as if only thus can humans find identity.

There are a lot of women praying there, quietly reading the Koran, or staring at the rock, as if entranced. I reach out and touch it. Then kiss it. I don't know why. Perhaps for those of us who no longer wish to listen to voices that speak with a ritual reference, an impulse to some meaningless, emblematic action like this must break loose from time to time.

At the Islamic Museum, situated at the southern end of the grounds adjacent to the Western Wall, we are greeted by the director, a simple man of about sixty-five who apologizes for not having been trained as a curator. His name is Hassan Mamlouk. Possibly his family could be traced to the Mamluks who ruled here centuries ago and, judging by his fair skin and blue eyes, to the Franks as well. He shows us his collection of old, handwritten copies of the Koran, some as large as four feet by three, in Kufi script, encased in glass cabinets. In another section of the museum, there are wooden doors on display preserved from the Islamic era, inscribed with Koranic calligraphy, as well as Crusader shields, swords, and the like. But there are no sculptures. The graven image is forbidden in Islam. Altogether, not a very impressive museum. But for an occupied people, with few resources of their own, it will do.

The building itself, erected by the Crusaders in the thirteenth century, looks forbidding. Mamlouk, who seems to love his work—he obviously has not had many visitors lately—informs us that the Crusaders built it as an arms depot and later used it as a dining hall for their garrison. And the place looked it. I could easily imagine Frankish soldiers in their medieval military garb conversing loudly in their various European dialects as they ate their meals.

Inside the walled city, Jerusalemites walked their ancient streets trying to get their shopping done before 1:00 P.M., when business is supposed to come to an end, by order of the *Intifada*. There is an hour to go, and the narrow streets are still crowded. Jerusalem has the feel of a Third World city and the sounds, images, and smells associated with a Third World city assault you from every direction. There is a refreshing breathlessness about these streets. These are streets that do not allow you to maintain your own island of privacy. Here everybody knows everybody else, and where they all stand in the social and political hierarchy. The fortune-tellers, the money changers, the vendors, the shopkeepers, the homeless, the hucksters, the black marketeers, the neighborhood toughs, the oral poets, the local revolutionaries—all fuse in a consensual amalgam. They all rub shoulders, recognizing no anonymity in their midst. The air is wracked by Arab music blaring from every shop and every home. The smell of spices mixes with the smell of uncollected garbage. The cafés are crowded with patrons reading newspapers, smoking water pipes, discussing politics, and sipping on glasses of tea. These streets have somehow acted to absorb the people's turmoil and brutality, their gestures of despair and destitution, and have diffused it all back to them. Perhaps it is this pattern of diffusion—from the people to the streets and from the streets back to the people—that has enabled Palestinians to widen their emotional resources and to sharpen their awareness of their place in historical existence. In addition, their collective fear—fear of the unpredictable, arbitrary, and often inexplicable actions of the occupier—has brought the people together and eroded their private identities as Moslems or Christians, rich or poor, and so on.

I have walked the streets of many cities in my time. I have felt happy only in cities. Having lived in Sydney and Amsterdam and Paris and Washington, and many other places, I am steeped in the urban life-styles of the West. I have lived with their realness, with the ash and grit of their cosmopolitan tensions. When I arrived in New York in the Sixties, fresh off the plane, I had no first impressions to speak of. I already felt that I belonged there. Not only could I affect the cocky, impious posture of a New Yorker, but going one step further, I could imitate the know-it-all hipness of the countercultural vanguard. This was the movement I felt part of. When millions of Americans felt their lives were not working because they had been despoiled of authenticity, and finally rebelled against tradition, I joined them. Those were my people. They too were exiles. And tellingly enough, when we needed inspiration for our values and ideas, our champions were European émigré intellectuals whose own culture had cast them out a generation before.

Today walking the streets of Jerusalem I feel my past is spilling out in my encounters with ancient stone. Yet I offer this past no meek apology for the rupture I had made with it. I am a Palestinian, but also one who has come to believe that the spirit of Palestinian society will not become hot to the touch until Palestinians escape the prison of their moribund cultural norms.

The hour, I know, will one day meet the people. The Palestinians are a human community, and like any other, it has the potential to break its traditional bounds and find its bearings in the modern world.

Everywhere the walls are covered with graffiti. When you are denied political expression in your media, your books, your lecture halls, your artwork (a Palestinian artist who once painted a rose with petals of red, black, green, and white, the colors of the Palestinian flag, was carted off and had his exhibition closed), then the walls are your only resort. All manner of slogans are splashed on the walls and splashed again soon after the Israelis paint them over, usually in the middle of the night. WE WILL NEVER KNEEL TO THE OCCUPIER, one says. Another states, WE WILL FERRET OUT THE COLLABORATORS FROM ALL THEIR HIDING PLACES. These two do not identify their authors, but most graffiti incorporates the name of the faction that has written it, such as HAMAS IS THE HOME OF THE STRUGGLE and FATAH IS THE ESSENCE OF THE REVOLUTION.

East Jerusalem differs from other Third World cities in one respect: it is under occupation. You wouldn't know or even see it if not for the border police and soldiers swaggering around the streets. Ordinary Israelis no longer come here, and foreign tourists wandering around with their maps of the city have decided this year that Jerusalem is not a place to have on their itinerary. These soldiers and policemen walk the streets in twos and threes, looking determined, solemn, angry: they never step aside. When people see them coming, even old women with children, they are expected to get out of the way.

Ariel Sharon, the ultraconservative former Israeli defense minister, had decided sometime back to move into a house in the heart of the Old City, to underscore his party's provocative contention that Jerusalem—Old and New, West and East—is eternally Jewish. The house is guarded by two dozen Israeli soldiers armed with Uzis, tear gas canisters, and hand grenades. They are youngsters with olive brown skin and olive brown uniforms, squatting on the ground outside the entrance. As we pass, one of the soldiers looks at me for a moment and our eyes meet. He looks so much like my younger brother Samir that I want to walk over and tell him. It does not matter who looked away first. We just did.

I wander around the city with Hatem and Akram. Soon the shops will be closed, the crowds will thin, and the tempo of Old Jerusalem will slow down. We stop by a fruit cart and talk to a vendor.

"Where is the brother from?" he asks my two friends, pointing at me. They tell him I'm a Palestinian who lives in America.

I pick up one orange.

"How much?" I ask.

"Come on, brother, take it. No money," he says smiling. "You're a guest here."

The man looks nice enough except for what appears to be a permanent snarl affixed to his lower lip. Then he adds, out of the blue, but still smiling: "America is filth."

The profound assertiveness of the remark shocks me. But I am startled less by the words than by the violent way they were uttered. I have forgotten how the bending force of politics in the lives of Palestinians here has distorted their views of the rest of the world. I am a Palestinian exile by upbringing and an American leftist by choice. I am here to be one, if only for a moment, with the Palestinians who have never left Palestine. But I have to admit that to be Palestinian, like them, is not like a glove that an exile can slip on at will. Nor can these people slip into my glove. How would this vendor, and other Palestinians, react to the news that my best friend, Tim Pascoe, is not only an American but is at that moment serving in the Gulf? They would think it outrageous—even more so if I told them that I had spent hours with Tim back in Washington, roaching out joint after joint, talking about whether Eric Clapton, John Lee Hooker, or Jimi Hendrix was the greatest guitarist who has ever lived.

Palestinians in the homeground are shaped by the irremediable suffering in their daily lives. I can no more pretend to feel the way they do about that suffering than they can afford a welcome to my way of being Palestinian. Our life experiences are simply too remote from one another.

Hatem, Akram, and I leave the walled city and decide, on Akram's recommendation, to walk all the way up to the Mount of Olives to view Jerusalem from there, in its entirety, its glory, spread below us.

"Once you see Jerusalem from the Mount of Olives," Akram says, "you'll never, ever forget the scene. It will be etched in your memory for as long as you live."

We pass so many historical and religious sites on the way that my mind grows numb. From the Golden Gate to the exquisite Gethsemane Church of Mary Magdalene, to the equally exquisite Gethsemane Church of All Nations; from the Tomb of Hulda the

Prophetess to the Chapel of Ascension; from the Tomb of the Virgin Mary to the Tomb of Zachariah; and from Lions Gate to Stephen's Greek Orthodox Church.

When I first saw Jerusalem, the whole of Jerusalem, from the top of the Mount of Olives, I had to clap my hand to my mouth, almost gasping at the sight. Streaks of bright afternoon light smoldered on it and made it look—encapsulated as it was within its ancient walls—like a giant pomegranate. If a city ever exuded a mysterious meaning, Jerusalem must be the one. For contemplating the city from the Mount of Olives, I feel that my senses are host to something more beautiful than beauty. The force of the obvious hits you: Jerusalem is the way it is because it is Jerusalem. We cannot—should not—ask, "What is Jerusalem?" or "What is like Jerusalem?" That is because the core of our identity as Moslems, Christians, and Jews was apprehended here. We are because it is. Our God may have created Himself through that cosmic scream known as the Big Bang, but we created ourselves right here, through the fiat of religion. When there was nothingness and void in their lives, Moslems, Christians, and Jews came here to define themselves, to affirm that there is being and substance and word. But self-definition and affirmation are acts of rage and repossession. And that is why Jerusalem became a site of endless violence.

There is animate logic in calling this land the Holy Land, and nothing else. To call it a nation, a state, a country, is like debasing a rose by using its botanical name. When this land is freed from the petty effusions of politics and the venomous fabric of nationalism and when we allow it, this little piece of land between the Mediterranean Sea and the Jordan River, to make accessible the magic of its metaphoric affinities with our being, then we have to call it simply what it calls itself: the Holy Land. No person who encounters this land, in this manner, could give to another so much of his love.

3

A Long Way from Home

At Salem's insistence, I leave Jerusalem and move down to Ramallah to stay with him at his bachelor apartment. He lives on the top floor of a five-story building a mere five hundred yards from the headquarters of the military governor.

The view from his sun-room is stunning. On a clear day, you can see Tel Aviv and the Mediterranean to the west, and right in front are these biblical hills. I say that because they have a curious timelessness, dotted as they are with shepherds dressed in rough robes, herding sheep; peasants riding donkeys down dirt tracks; and village women in traditional embroidered garb and headgear, walking sedately as they balance water jugs on their heads.

Salem's apartment is huge, and he pays the equivalent of two hundred dollars in rent, a lot more than an unskilled or semiskilled Palestinian worker earns in a month. But there is no central heating. The only room with heat is the living room, which has an electric heater the size of a shoebox. The rest of the house is ice-cold. That's how most Palestinians live during the wintertime—that is, most well-off Palestinians. Poor ones, especially those in the refugee camps, get no heat at all; where they do get heat, it comes from *kanoon*, a metal tray of burning coal on a stand, around which the family sits the whole evening. And a Palestinian evening is not much of an evening.

Even for Salem, a well-known activist with important connections, an evening does not amount to much. He is home by five o'clock, eats dinner, watches the news on television (with Israeli, Jordanian, and Syrian channels available), and by nine o'clock starts nodding and getting ready for bed. At times his activist friends drop by and they discuss politics or organizing work, but that is it. As a Palestinian living under occupation, with border police and soldiers patrolling the streets at night, you do what needs to be done during the day. Starting at dawn with the *muazzen*'s call to prayer, you come to life and start your day. By 5:00 P.M., and for many people earlier—because business in the territories comes to a standstill by early afternoon—you are indoors with your family. When there are curfews—and these can extend from a day to a month—they will be confined indoors for the duration.

These unnatural constraints have taken a heavy toll on the psyche of Palestinians, altering the very tenor of their sensibility. The open space of a town square, neon-lit at night, with cafés and traffic and pedestrians, does not exist here. Involuntary confinement during daylight hours to the shuttered home, the single room, has drastically altered the style, attitudes, and communicative patterns of Palestinians over the last quarter century. It is as if the rigors of that confinement had turned them introspective, driven them more to self-address.

On my first night at Salem's, two young fellows informally dropped by to visit my host. I guess that's the only way people drop by here. No one calls beforehand because few people have phones (an application for a phone can take eight to twelve years). These two young men—both under twenty-five—are union leaders. From the moment they walked in to the moment they left, they discussed politics and nothing else. They spoke softly and deliberately, in somber tones, as if at a funeral. No jocularity here, no emotions. In fact, when Salem said how much he hated Hafez Assad, the Syrian president, for adopting a "dirty" position by joining the coalition against Iraq, one of the fellows scolded him.

"These are subjective terms, brother," he said in protest. "These terms are irrelevant in the context of our discussion."

Like all activists in the West Bank/Gaza, they belonged to political factions—one to the Popular Front for the Liberation of Palestine, and the other to the Popular Democratic Front, both

Marxist-oriented. Together with Salem, who belonged to the mainstream Fatah movement, they represented the three major political factions in the PLO. Hamas, the influential Islamic group, which over the previous five years had gained many new converts—mostly youngsters alienated from the PLO—operates independently.

Unfortunately, when you belong to a political faction, the pressures of ideological conformity usually turn you into a bore. And more's the pity. These two fellows, with the interesting lives they had lived, could have conveyed their passionate convictions much more cogently.

Ibrahim had worked at a sausage packaging plant in Israel before taking recently to full-time union work.

"I used to get up at 4:00 A.M. in order to get to work on time. Though the plant was a mere hour away from my home, we used to get stopped at checkpoints so many times on the way that it took three hours."

Osama chimes in, with a shy smile playing around his mouth: "Hey, when I lived in Gaza, a couple of years back, I had a neighbor, Munzer, who used to get up at 2:30 in the morning in order to get to work on time."

"You're kidding!" I exclaim, genuinely amazed.

"Most workers from Gaza would get up at a similar hour."

"What kind of money would they get for that effort?"

"Twice as much as they would here."

"And how much is that?"

"From four to five hundred dollars a month," he says.

Ibrahim hastens to add: "Believe me, most of these people would kiss your hand if you could find them a job, any job, at home for half as much. But even if we can get hold of the $500 million we would need to create enough jobs here at home, the occupation government wouldn't allow it, under any circumstances. They will not allow us to become self-sufficient. Permits to start little industries here, even little cottage industries, were hard enough to come by before the *Intifada*. Now they are impossible."

The primary instrument for controlling, impeding, or blocking Palestinian economic growth in the territories has been the granting and withholding of building permits. All construction in the rural or semirural towns or villages, where 70 percent of the population lives, requires the approval of the Central Planning Department.

The process of obtaining a building permit is made so insufferably complicated that it sometimes takes years for an application to be approved, if at all. Projects have also been halted halfway through construction, *after* approval has been granted. Work on the Jerusalem Teacher's Cooperative Housing Project was ordered to stop, after a permit had been granted, because the proposed site conflicted with a regional plan. In another instance, the village council of Deir Ghusson, outside Tulkarem, applied in 1986 to build a village community center to house its offices, a clinic, a kindergarten, and a cooperative society, but the permit was later denied because the Israelis said that the site for the planned center "fell outside the building zone."

"Our house was demolished well before the *Intifada*," said Ibrahim. "My brother was accused of involvement in a military operation. He is still in jail. Sentenced to life."

"Have you ever been arrested?" I ask Ibrahim.

"Yes," he says quietly.

"Once?"

"No a few times."

"How many?"

He looks at me with a frank gaze, as if to study me, wanting to know what this exile is doing here, why he has come from America, where he lives in his comfortable middle-class dream, asking him to lay bare his grief.

"About ten times. I have a green card. I can't leave the country. I can't even go to Jerusalem, just up the street, because in their eyes Jerusalem is part of Israel. If they catch me there, they will lock me up again."

Ibrahim's quiet dignity impresses me. He shows no rancor, as if his personal travails are just another test to be endured in the long journey of his people.

"I have faith," he says. "I have faith in the future. We all have faith in the future. We will have our independence one day. We have to believe in the future because that's all we have. Our present is intolerable. Our past is irrelevant. Only the future matters. We are possessed by the need to be free, and I can tell you, rhetoric aside, there is no going back on that idea."

Ibrahim may as well have been quoting Alexis de Tocqueville, who observed in his commentary on the French Revolution: "So long as it appeared beyond redress, a grievance comes to appear intolerable once the possibility of removing it crosses men's minds."

Ibrahim continues: "As you can see for yourself, or will soon see, we here in Palestine already have an incomparable intimacy with pain, with daily destitution. But we look at it as a sojourn through hell, from which we will emerge in the near future, purified. See us as the stone that is being turned by a searing flame into ash, living ash, that will again knit itself into new stone, endowed with an even greater resilience. I have faith in the future. I have faith in the future because our sense of history is anchored in it."

Ibrahim's haunting optimism is as profound as it is unlikely. Without their capacity to generate a future image of themselves, unhindered by a backward look, Palestinians cannot survive. Suddenly it came to me—the difference in the mind-set of Israelis and Palestinians. If the future defines the Palestinians' perspective (because their present is intolerable and because, as Palestinians, they have no past to speak of), Israelis are possessed by the past. It is futile to attempt an understanding of the conflict without knowledge, however imperfect, of these private inner tensions that define it.

...

The morning sun blazed across the hills outside my window and drizzled into the living room. My host had left a note saying that he was going to be gone the entire day doing political work in Nablus and warning me not to wander around Ramallah on my own. A Palestinian artist named Issam, he wrote, would be coming around noon to pick me up and "turn his soul's concern in my direction," a Palestinian idiom that roughly means "to take me under his wing." I may be bound to English, but my idiom, along with my empathy for the culture that speaks it, is still with me.

There is no such thing as Palestinian fine art or fine artists. Palestine, like the rest of the Arab world, has no such high tradition. Palestinian culture, because of its Arab and Islamic heritage, has mainly expressed its creative impulses in music, dance, poetry, calligraphy, weaving, embroidery, and the like, in some of which forms the inner history of Palestine was genuinely recast. Fine art is a recent Western import, a mimetic bunch of candy floss produced by displaced, hesitant, insecure Palestinian "artists" who pathetically, and often comically, imitate their Western counterparts. Even an elementary art form like silkscreening is one that Palestinians had not known until a decade ago.

Issam is a man in his middle thirties with sickly white skin. He greets me effusively, his words tumbling out in rhetorical bursts.

"And may I say merry Christmas!" he concludes.

Heavens! I had totally forgotten that today is Christmas Day. It's an eloquent reminder of the state of affairs in this land, the birth-place of Christ, that Christmas would come and go without anyone taking notice of it in more than a perfunctory fashion.

"You can forget about Salem for a day or two," Issam tells me. "There is a curfew in Nablus. No one can leave or get into the city. There is no curfew here, but the road to Jerusalem is blocked too."

"What's the problem?"

"Israelis don't give you reasons," he shrugs. "We've long since stopped asking or reasoning with them about the why of it."

I guess there is no point in reasoning with an occupier. It is like reasoning with God: you can address Him in prayer, in plea, in peti-tion, but no response can really be expected.

Issam's wife runs a pharmacy in town, and like other pharmacies all over the territories it can, with the approval of the Unified Com-mand, stay open all day. He wants to be there to fill in for her while she takes an hour off for lunch. He himself runs a little workshop that employs half a dozen people in the production of pottery, most-ly ashtrays, mugs, candlesticks, serving plates, and the like. He used to export most of that to Saudi Arabia, Kuwait, and other Gulf states, he tells me, but now, in the last week of December 1990, with the Arabian Peninsula and the Persian Gulf on the verge of war, business has come to a total standstill.

At the pharmacy, Issam's wife, Jamila, is in a back room marked "laboratory." When we go inside, however, I discover there is no lab of any kind. It is a little family room of sorts where the couple's nine-month-old baby is sleeping in a crib.

The street outside is quiet, with few pedestrians and little traf-fic. Not so quiet a mere half-hour ago, however, Jamila tells us. A boy about twelve years old had thrown a stone at a passing Israeli army vehicle. By the time the soldiers reversed and went after him, the boy had melted into the side streets. So they picked up another kid, the first one they saw wandering around. The boy's mother, who saw the soldiers drag her protesting son into the jeep, came out of the house screaming, flailing her arms and trying to free him, but in vain.

Jamila tells the story, sighs wearily, and changes the subject, as though this painful episode was just another incident in daily life. After three years of an uprising that had seemed to get them nothing and nowhere, Palestinians in the territories were sapped of the capacity for any fresh response. They ran on empty—on the old ideas that the PLO leadership has cobbled together like a merchant of old metals who joins together salvaged scraps.

While his wife goes out for lunch with the baby, Issam bemoans the consequences, but not the act, of Iraq's invasion of Kuwait. "I don't mind losing my business because of this mess. But this Gulf crisis has affected the lives of well over a million, if not 2 million, Palestinians. Before the invasion, there were 400,000 Palestinians in Kuwait. Three hundred thousand have already left, losing their jobs, their livelihood, and their savings. Many of these people had relatives here or in Jordan or in Lebanon or elsewhere dependent on them for a living or for an education. Others who left Kuwait, from Bangladesh or Sri Lanka or Korea or Egypt or what have you, returned to their countries and villages, perhaps to an acre of land where they could grow their food . . . but Palestinians, well, that's a problem. Take my own sister. She was caught here when Saddam invaded Kuwait, and she couldn't return. She grew up in Kuwait, you know. She got married there. Her husband, who is a Palestinian, can't come here because he lost his residence permit a long time ago. Every time someone asks my sister how she's doing, she bursts out crying."

And yet to the Palestinians Saddam remained a hero. The simplest explanation is that to them, as to other poor Arabs in Morocco, Algeria, Tunisia, Sudan, and other Third World countries, especially Islamic ones, the Iraqi president had initiated a struggle between the rich and the poor, the powerful and the helpless of the world. Propelled primarily by their emotions, the Palestinians not only did not shed a tear for the Kuwaitis but actually cheered the destruction of their society. The Kuwaitis were seen as an arrogant, self-indulgent, exclusivist, and even cruel community who had it coming. Moreover, Saddam Hussein was a man who stood up not only to the Israelis but to the Americans as well. No Palestinian, no other Arab leader, had done that before. Saddam stood for status, for power.

And these are a weapon of vengeance in the hands of the weak. Moreover, by reverting to Islamic codes of reference, by appropriating Koranic lore and affirming the believer's duty to undo, to unsay, his vulnerable condition, the Iraqi president used the idiom that spoke most cogently to the destitute of the Islamic world. And the Palestinians were prepared to support him, cheer him, endow him with heroic attributes—even at the cost of their own interests.

After Issam's wife returns from lunch, we take off to the one art gallery in town, Gallery '79, where Palestinian artists display and sell their work.

The gallery is housed in an imposing stone building inhabited by a prominent Palestinian family around the turn of the century. Hanging on the walls are a lot of unaccomplished—some embarrassingly infantile—silkscreens, canvases, and lithos, along with political posters. The last are interesting more for their message than their quality. One says, "Don't Break Up Our Families," with an illustration of an ID card torn in half; this refers to a major problem afflicting Palestinians under occupation—families that are separated because a husband, brother, or father overstays his trip abroad and thereby forfeits his right to return. Another poster, showing a young woman with a confident expression, staring into the distance, as if at some vanishing point in Palestinian history, bears the nifty caption: "Your Liberation Is Through Your Struggle."

I ask Issam if he has ever been arrested. He says: "Oh yes, hell yes. We've all been arrested. The first time I was arrested was way back in 1968. I was a teenager then. I marched in a demonstration calling for an end to the occupation. We thought the Israelis had been there too long already. Well over a year." He laughs bitterly. "I was arrested again in 1980, a year after we opened here, and my gallery was closed by the authorities. The excuse they gave us was that we displayed provocative works."

Before we leave for lunch at a restaurant in downtown Ramallah, Issam produces a bottle of wine and asks if I drink. I say no. He doesn't know about my problem with alcohol and drugs, and I'm not going to tell him.

"Do you mind if I drink a glass of wine in front of you?" he asks sheepishly.

Drinking, even a little glass of wine, is such a big deal here. And to drink *in front* of someone who doesn't drink is an affront to good manners as well as religion. A man who drinks is, simply, a *sukarji*, a pejorative term connoting the most incorrigible kind of social degeneration. The worst you can say about someone is to identify him as "he who drinks *el cohol*," the Arabic expression from which English derives the word *alcohol*. "He goes to bars, you know!" is all they need to say about a degenerate no-good drifter.

"I only drink one or two glasses a month," Issam offers, by way of apology. "Some of the artists here, though, I tell you, they are scandalous. Once five of them came here with a bottle of scotch, bringing some visiting Italian artist with them, and they partied from six in the evening 'til as late as ten o'clock at night."

He stops for a moment. "I mean, I have a gallery here to run, not a bar. Hell, what if the Hamas people had heard about it? I tell you they would've burned the place down," he says, referring to the powerful Islamic group in the West Bank and Gaza that wants to run Palestinian society according to fundamentalist Koranic rules.

On that point, he may be right. "I mean the Hamas people have got a distorted image of Islam, but who wants to argue with them. Not me, brother, not me. Everyone is afraid of them," Issam tells me.

There is a middle-aged woman in the gallery who works there with her twelve-year-old daughter as full-time cleaners. They come from a nearby refugee camp. It is very cold today and the gallery is like an icebox, yet both are dressed in tatters. Here I am with my duffle coat on, and I'm still cold. I feel sorry for them and ask Issam if I can give them some money before we leave. He assures me it is okay. When I try to give the little girl the equivalent of twenty dollars in shekels, she looks at me sullenly, turns to her mother, and says: "Oh, may his imminent death be mourned by his family. He is a Jew. I cannot take a Jew's money."

Her mom assures her that though I look "like a Frank," a term that has persisted since Crusader days and connotes a hated foreigner, I am in fact a Palestinian. She takes the money. I remain a stranger among those I should know best.

On the way downtown, Issam tells me in all seriousness: "It's your hair, you know. It's your hair and beard. I know a good barber in town. He'll trim your beard, cut your hair."

Downtown Ramallah, as I was to discover of other Palestinian towns, is formless and boorish. It is haunted by the occupation and haunting in its dull stillness. The sense of helplessness, self-pity, and cultural isolation that afflicts Palestinians is echoed in the appearance of their dismal towns. The only sign of lively expression is the political graffiti. It is everywhere, calculatedly defiant in its message and optimistic in its spirit. In a way, graffiti in the territories has become like the cave painting of ancient peoples, intended to transform the menace of the beast around them into recognizable, and conquerable, forms. Ostensibly, graffiti here is used to exercise freedom of expression, but maybe that's what freedom of expression is all about: an attempt to exorcise the demons of our state.

Just before we get to the restaurant, we spot an Israeli army jeep carrying five border police, parked at the curb. They eye us as we walk in their direction on our way to cross the street. Issam suddenly freezes. I sense his fear, so palpable I can almost smell it. He looks down the bridge of his nose and walks on nervously, reaching out to touch his breast pocket to make sure that he has his ID. Woe to those caught by the border police without their identification.

"Hey you," one of them says to us, "come over here." His Arabic is fractured but comprehensible.

We go over. They start with my friend. They inspect his ID and ask him to open his shoulder bag in which he has a small computer. They ask him what it is, and he tells them nervously that it is a small computer that he owns. I can see how Issam adapts his manner of speaking, even his body language, to suit the occasion.

He is communicating with the border police with deferential propriety and imposed decorum. You exchange few words with your occupier. You don't argue with him, reason with him, converse with him, have anything to do with him. Yes. No. Maybe. I suppose so. Thank you. Goodbye. That's all. You hoard your own vernacular, sharing it only with fellow Palestinians. You guard your private spaces of identity. Only when Palestinians are out of earshot of Israelis do they erupt together, with torrential energy, into free speech. Their idiom, with its drift toward defiance, is the primary unit of social energy. Only through such talk, in privacy, do they allow themselves, in their politically oriented chatter, in their chaotic gush of words, to affirm their place in historical life. With Israeli soldiers you stand mute. In dialogue with them, you proceed from the humblest level of propriety.

"And you," the soldier says, pointing a finger at me. "Let me see your ID."

I tell him I don't speak Arabic and add that I'm American.

He turns to the guy behind the wheel sitting next to him and mumbles something in Hebrew.

The driver, who is in his mid-twenties, leans over and asks me in English if I am really American. I tell him I am.

"Well let me see your passport," he demands. The guy has a definite New York accent. What do you know! American like me.

I show it to him. He examines it carefully. "You sound American and look American," he says contemptuously, "but you're an Ayrab, ain't you?" He glares at me with hatred in his eyes.

Hell, I thought he might be glad to see a fellow American in this place. Maybe exchange a few words of common reference to acknowledge our relatedness. Instead he throws—actually *throws*—my passport back at me. It falls to the pavement.

I bend down to pick it up and say, looking up at him, "Fuck you!"

He stares at me for a long while, his eyes holding me captive. "Hey, do you have any idea what I can do to you if you give me lip?" he hollers. "Okay, get the fuck outta here, both of yous."

It is at moments like these, on a day like this, when my comfortable notions of identity are assailed and I am reminded of my otherness. To that kid from the refugee camp I had met at the gallery, I was a Frank. How could I be a Palestinian if I did not look like her, live like her, suffer like her? I did not project that aura of foreboding darkness that Palestinians instinctively seek when they meet one another. My blood is not theirs any longer. I am a stranger now to those I should know best. I am no less a stranger to that Jewish kid from suburban New York, to whom I remain an "Ayrab." He too, like that kid from the camp, has become captive to the preoccupations of his inner history. Declarations of loyalty to the one and of relatedness to the other would not save me from assault on either side.

...

The restaurant we finally arrive at, a dingy, functional hole-in-the-wall in upper Ramallah, is called something like the Freedom Café. It serves a basic menu—the Palestinian version of fast food, like hummos and falafel and stuffed cabbage leaves.

After we are seated, a boy of twelve or thirteen wanders in. His hands are deformed, and he is missing most of his fingers. He goes from table to table begging for change, and most patrons wave him away with the remark, "Not I, but God, will help you."

When he comes over to us, I give him a couple of shekels. He immediately takes the money—without a word of thanks—goes over to the counter, slams it down, and orders a plate of food with two loaves of pita bread. He wolfs it down, using, in the absence of fingers, both hands to put food in his mouth.

Palestinian priorities are truly screwed up. What is an *Intifada* if it has no institutions to care for the needs of kids like that?

I share my concerns with Issam.

"Oh, don't worry about him," he responds lamely. "The restaurant gives him free food when he's hungry."

When the kid is done eating, I ask him to join us.

"Are you a Jew?" he asks after he sits down.

"No, I'm Palestinian."

He looks suspiciously at me and says nothing.

"Where are you from?" I ask.

"Gaza."

"How did you get here?"

"I don't know."

"Did you come here with your parents?"

"I don't know."

"How old are you."

"I don't know."

"What's your name?"

"Omar."

"Omar, I want to give you some shekels. That might help you a bit," I say and give him about twenty.

He takes the money sullenly.

"Give me some more," he demands. The kid isn't even smiling.

Destitution, hunger, and isolation don't ennoble anyone. They brutalize.

To hustle a living, you must connive and thieve and lie and scheme. This Omar is not a nice kid. Who the hell said oppression makes anyone better?

"You're a Palestinian? You ain't a Jew?" he asks again.

"I ain't," I say, adopting his own shorthand.

"Where do you live?"

"In America."

"When do you go back?"

"Soon, I guess."

Then he says eruptively: "Give my love to Bush. Tell him we're going to fuck him up the ass. And tell him to tell his Arab friends in the Gulf we're going to fuck their womenfolk, burn down the houses their ancestors built, and piss on their graves."

With such violence in the soul is this kid growing up in the streets.

To him I was no Palestinian. It was a name I wore around me, like a cosmetic.

What is in a name unless it's *lived*?

But I *have* lived that name. And I, like Omar, lived it in the streets. I grew up with it there. I too suffered isolation and brutality, and endured their corrupting grasp on my humanity. I too, as a child, groped for words to express and experience my world. Forty years ago. In the streets of Beirut.

4

In the Streets of Beirut

The world of our exile that began around 1948 was so recent that, like some primitive society, we had not yet found words to describe it. I suppose that people need to have a mastering grip on their own lives before they can begin to put its manifold truths into words.

Some years into his exile, my father convinced himself that he had found that grip. He did what he had always done: he ran a little grocery store, which helped us move out of the refugee camp.

There he was, aged forty-six or thereabouts—I don't think he quite knew, or much cared, how old he was—shuffling around in his little grocery and vegetable stand in the Basta quarter of West Beirut. He bantered with the customers, bargained with them, teased them, discussed politics with them, and with those who owed him money, badgered them about their debts. That hole-in-the-wall store was dad's kingdom. In it he felt he was lord. In the brutal world that we inhabited, men valued whatever safety they could find in the clearing. At least until the day of the Return.

He would discuss President Nasser's recent speech with one customer, congratulate another on the birth of his son, berate a third for squeezing the pears too hard, and in between he would order me in distracted asides to get this or that done for him. With the women, especially those who were veiled, he would make sure that no hands touched when goods and money were exchanged. He disdained customers who were not astute bargainers, especially those who offered prices well below the value of his goods. He would remain seated as he addressed them, with one hand resting on his crotch and the other stroking his moustache—which was, like his hair, jet black—and stare haughtily into the distance.

Dad always wore an apron around the store. He had bought it, along with some towels, from one of the neighborhood thieves. It had some words in English printed on its lower left side, which remained a mystery to him until one day one of his customers translated them for him. The words, he was told, said: "Property of the British Embassy." Dad was excited by the revelation and never ceased to tell people about it.

"It's about time we started robbing *them* for a change," he would say.

It was determined that I help Dad in the store because he said so. That was it. Besides, at age 12, I could already read and write. There was no need for further education. You don't argue with *diktats* of a father or even an older brother. My brother Mousa, who was now almost twenty-two and worked as a mechanic, loved to issue *diktats* of his own around the house, especially in Dad's absence. The man was so insufferably dour that he never smiled. He was also a brute who pushed me around mercilessly. My sister, Jasmine . . . well, she was a female and not even a bread earner, and thus was expected to act like a slave to him. He would hound her about her outfits and demand that her breasts not shake visibly when she walked in the street. The girl was barely fourteen. And whenever she came home from her sewing and embroidery classes, he would question her interminably about whom she talked to, whom she walked home with, and whether any of the boys from the neighborhood had looked at her.

Jasmine was no pushover. She was a true rebel whose demeanor always leaned toward the adversarial, the scandalous, the revolutionary. Even at that age, she was an immensely sensual young woman who flaunted her femininity in a world that expected her to hide it and would brutally chastise her for even hinting at it. She would sometimes wear a velvet ribbon around her neck or just one earring instead of two and affect an air of vague, aloof impatience when she spoke to her elders. The insolent, sardonic tones she used with Mousa did not go down well around the house. He was the kind of guy who expected you, when he said jump, to jump through flaming hoops. Maybe it was because he had no authority of his own at work, where he was pushed around by his boss. Maybe it was because he'd had ambitions of being an accountant and working in an office, where he would wear a suit and tie, but was rejected by the accountancy school. Maybe it was because he was so short. Or maybe he was just born that way. What kept him off the edge was his pigeon coop, which he kept on the roof of the house. That's all he cared about, the only thing he loved. He would be up there after work, and on his days off, waving a white shirt nailed to a pole at his pigeons, directing them to return to the coop or behave however else he wanted.

Our culture has its ways, and you don't argue with them. Their origin, their justification, buried in time, is beyond recall and certainly beyond challenge.

I worked six and a half days a week. On my half-day off, I would go off to downtown Beirut with Adnan and some of the other boys from the Basta quarter. These were tough fellows molded by the instincts of a tough neighborhood. They lived by their wits, disdaining school and those who attended it, and carried switchblades. Adnan in particular was a role model, not only for those who went around with him but also for those other kids from the Basta who knew him but whom he would not have as friends, only using them to further his growing career as a huckster. He was only in his late teens, a couple of years older than me, yet he exuded a primitive, unrestrained élan, an irrepressible charisma that embodied and expressed the rough rules of the Basta.

"There is treasure, a fortune to be made, dealing in smuggled goods," he would tell me, "so give up your job at your dad's store."

I told him I could not.

"Only a son of a whore would work for his dad," he would joke, ruffling my hair.

When, on my half-day off or after work, I would walk into a Basta café with Adnan, the fellows would see him coming and make room for him. It would feel good, for a moment, to think that they were making room for us, not just for him.

Soon after we were seated, these young people—mercurial, glib hustlers—would sidle up to Adnan and unload their stolen or smuggled goods. If there was a raid, he wouldn't care. "I've got them in my pocket," he would say, referring to Basta cops. Mostly he dealt in watches, cigarettes, and scotch, whose heavy import duty made its list price prohibitive, like an illegal drug. He would bargain haughtily with his contacts, and if he didn't like them or their bargaining style, he would just sit there and look straight ahead, refusing eye contact.

The first time I went to *souk sharameet* was with Adnan and his buddies. The *souk*—the Arab marketplace—was a six- or seven-block area in downtown Beirut where prostitution was legalized. You walk into one of the houses, inspect the girls, pay for the service, and do your thing. To have a *souk* like this in an Arab capital was scandalous at the time. Red-light districts are not exactly part of traditional Arab culture. But in those days Beirut was the Paris of the Middle East and a major exporter of VD to the Gulf, whose denizens would go crazy in the *souk* when they flocked to the Lebanese capital during the tourist season, between June and August.

Despite Adnan's genuine toughness, he lived at home with his parents. His dad, known around the neighborhood as Abu Adnan, worked as a storyteller at the Hurriah Café in the Basta. He was there every night between 8:00 and 10:00, sitting on a kind of dais at one end of the café, telling stories about Antar, an Arab Robin Hood from the ninth century, who like his Western counterpart robbed the rich and gave to the poor; but he was also a mean, tough warrior who waged a constant struggle against established authority. Every tale had a simple beginning, an exciting middle, and a suspenseful end—always culminating with Antar's defeating his enemies.

The café patrons loved listening to the stories, sipping tea, smoking their water pipes, and stringing their prayer beads. As the storyteller neared the end of his tale, the audience would be on the edge of its seat. Afterward, the suspense dissipated, the patrons returned to their normal café pursuits—talking politics, playing cards or backgammon and conducting business deals.

One day, Abu Adnan had a bad sore throat, but he still came to work, mounted his dais, and proceeded to tell another Antar tale. Halfway through his voice gave out, and he told his audience that the story was "to be continued tomorrow," leaving Antar captured by the emir's soldiers who were about to cut his head off. And he went back home to go to bed and nurse his sore throat. Around one o'clock in the morning there was a violent knock on the storyteller's door. It was one of his fans, a neighborhood peddler who had been to the café that night.

"I cannot sleep, oh Abu Adnan," the peddler explained plaintively, "unless I know what has befallen Antar after his capture by the emir's soldiers, and may the lord curse their fate and banish their dead ancestors to hell."

Abu Adnan took pity on the man, invited him in, made him a glass of tea, and gave him an abbreviated version of the happy and heroic end of Antar's latest escapade.

If you live in the Basta, you grow up in the streets, you work in the streets, you learn in the streets, you find your self in the streets, and finally you come to love the streets, and they love you back. I am acquiring a past of my own here, in the Basta, in Beirut, in the land of others, a land that, now in my middle teens, I am beginning to feel close to. Haifa is a distant memory. When you are a child, you live with the abandon of an animal, in the eternal present.

At that time, people my father's age would not accept the present, regardless how fulfilling its rewards. They came from a place that had made them and where they wanted to return. They believed only in the past, an arrested past that in their minds could be bettered neither by the actuality of the present nor the potentiality of the future. What *was* is best. They wanted to return. Never mind that the world had changed. To them it hadn't. They were like men who had gone blind years before and continued to imagine their environment in terms of remembered images.

Me, I didn't care. A child will not care—until something happens, as it always does, to remind you of your otherness and shock you into seeing that you have framed the world mistakenly.

•••

In the middle fifties a new government was elected in Lebanon, if that is the term one may use to describe the transfer of power in an Arab capital that was fiercely anti-Palestinian. In time the president, Camille Shamoun, pressured the Lebanese parliament to bar Palestinians from employment, "whether paid or unpaid," without a work permit. These permits were made so difficult to obtain that Palestinians did not, after a while, bother to apply for them. The government was hoping that the Palestinian community in Lebanon, which was then being held responsible for every ill in the country, from communist plots to unseasonable weather, would move out and find other places to live.

Thus Dad had to surrender his grocery store, his little kingdom. There was no way out. We could still eat because Mousa was able to keep his job. The body shop where he worked was owned by a Palestinian who had bought a work permit (paying a year's income to a bureaucrat at the Alien's Department in order to get it), and he allowed my brother to stay, though illegally. I immediately found work with Adnan and quickly began to earn twice Mousa's salary just being a bum.

My father was desperate at the loss of both the store and his sense of worth as a provider. He could not bear to walk around the streets of the Basta anymore, especially where his grocery had been situated. It was now taken over by a man called Abu Rustum, a neighbor of ours. Abu Rustum was one of those few Palestinians who had become a naturalized Lebanese, married a Lebanese Christian, a nurse at the Makassed Hospital, and affected a Lebanese accent. For many years he had worked as a postman, but he was fired by the authorities when he was discovered tampering with the mail and stealing whatever valuables and cash he could find.

His route was downtown, which also included the *souk*, where he delivered mail to the various brothels. As a kid I remember him boasting about the "freebies" he got there. In fact he boasted also about how "I get to fuck some of the boys as well." Passive homosexuals were considered the scum of society, the lowest form of life; those active ones who gave it to them were tough guys who publicly advertised their "conquest."

Abu Rustum was a tall man, well over six feet, who always wore tight clothes and sweated profusely, even in wintertime. The hair on his face was so thick that when he shaved—almost all the way up to his eyes—his cheeks took on a greenish tinge. At one time he sported a Hitlerian moustache, but when one of his friends, a fellow communist, pointed out the resemblance, he took to wearing a Stalinist one. When Abu Rustum was not putting down an adult, he would be tormenting a child with questions like: "What is heavier: a kilo of wool or a kilo of iron?" If the child fell for the trick and said iron, Abu Rustum would berate him for stupidity and say that when he grew up he was going to be a *kondorgi*, a shoemaker. Shoes in our culture were base objects, and those who made or mended them were considered, next to passive homosexuals, the meanest of God's creatures. Sometimes when Abu Rustum saw a group of girls jumping rope, he would deliberately put his foot in to break its swing, and walk off laughing.

Abu Rustum boasted that he was a committed Communist and claimed that the Palestine Communist Party had sent him to Moscow, where he allegedly stayed for a number of years, and met all sorts of high party officials, even marrying a blond Russian giant "whose tits were *that* big, I tell you."

My father's greatest grief was that Abu Rustum had turned the store into a watermelon shop. Mountains of watermelons—and nothing else—were piled up inside and outside in a manner that offended my father's sensibility and broke his heart.

"How could that son of a whore, that *ben sharmouta*, that scum whose mother's pussy is on sale at the *souk*, do that to me?" my father would ask, looking at the ceiling as if to seek his answer from Above.

When he could no longer bear being unemployed, sitting around the house snapping at people, he decided to look for work in Kuwait. Employment agencies in Beirut, working for the Kuwaiti government or for independent contractors, did not want him. But this did not deter him. He was going to go there anyhow and look for work when he arrived. When he discovered that the Kuwaiti embassy would not grant him a visa unless he already had gainful employment awaiting him, he made up his mind to enter the country illegally. His intention was to travel through Syria and Iraq, then south to Basra, and enter the country on foot through its desert approaches.

My mother's entreaties came to naught. There was no dissuading him.

He borrowed money from every friend he had in the Basta, and one morning at dawn, after morning prayers, with a *boaji* under his arm containing his few belongings, he was off. We did not see him for a year.

When he reached the Kuwaiti border, it seems, he had already teamed up with a half a dozen other illegal immigrants like himself—Palestinians, Lebanese, Egyptians, Jordanians, West Bankers, and the like—and together hired a bedouin guide to take them across. It was their misfortune that this was the fiercest, most merciless summer on record in that part of the world. Three of the men perished in the desert. The survivors returned to Basra, and a few days later one of them, a young Egyptian peasant, had the idea of hiding in a van, driven by a friendly fellow Egyptian, that was transporting spare parts to Kuwait. Locked inside during the long trip, he suffocated and died. The Kuwaitis instructed the driver to return the body, which had already decomposed in the intense summer heat, to Basra.

Despite this, Dad was still reluctant to come home, not only because he had failed in his efforts but because he owed money to people in Beirut, which he now had no way of repaying. But he did not find work and finally had to return.

Soon after, he hit on another idea. He would make the *hajj*, the annual pilgrimage to Mecca that Moslems were encouraged to make at least once in their lifetime, and stay in the country illegally to look for work.

"Once there I could look up Yacoub and he would help me," he would say, referring to a relative of ours, as he busied himself getting the easily obtained pilgrimage visa from the Saudi embassy.

It did not occur to him that Yacoub, who worked for Aramco, was up north in the town of Rass Tonoura, a thousand miles from Mecca.

Dad's idea of course, was not original. Tens of thousands of Arab workers from economically depressed countries had attempted it, and each year the Saudi authorities rounded up these illegals at the conclusion of Hajj and sent them back to their countries of origin.

So Dad came back again, crushed, humiliated, crazed by his failures and mortified by his inability to repay his many debts. He had always been an independent man who was proud of his accomplishments as a bread earner. He was respected around the Basta. When he walked into the Hurriah Café to smoke a water pipe or play backgammon, everyone shouted the familiar greeting: "Hey, Abu Mousa, father of all youth, how are you?"

Now he found himself having to enroll us in the United Nations Relief and Works Agency program, which doled out food to destitute Palestinian refugees, and there was a danger that we all might soon have to move back to the Borj el Barajni refugee camp, since there was not enough money to feed us and repay his debts.

Now Dad just sat around the house and mumbled incoherently about how soon—for surely it must be soon—we would all return home to Haifa and no longer be subject to the dictates of others, in the land of others. His hair turned gray, then white, and his voice began to lose its edge. He walked hunched over, and when he moved his limbs, he moved them with great effort.

He fought with my mother relentlessly. He called me a vagabond, a hoodlum, and a worthless son. And he slapped Jasmine around for the least infraction, real or imagined.

One day Jasmine came home and declared that she had been offered a job as a waitress in the coffee shop at the St. George Hotel. The money was good, and there was a chance she could become a waitress in the restaurant where the tips were even better. That's where Salwa, one of Abu Rustum's daughters, worked, Jasmine hastened to add, and she had been assured that the environment was "honorable."

"You are not associating with the daughter of that son of a whore, Abu Rustum, I say," he thundered.

"Abu Rustum has nothing to do with this, Dad."

"May the lord pour acid on his soul, and on his name and on his honor."

"May it be thus, if you wish, Dad."

"How much money is involved?" he asks.

Jasmine tells him and his face lights up. Perhaps it would save us from having to live in the refugee camp and even help repay his many debts. Perhaps he could discontinue the unbearable practice of going to the depot each month to pick up our rations, for he hated that more than he hated anything else—standing abjectly in line for powdered milk, dates, flour, and canned meat.

Soon after Jasmine became a bread earner, she became a changed woman, throwing her weight around the house, complaining loudly if Mother did not have her dinner ready when she came home or hadn't ironed her blouse before she needed it. If Mousa was listening to a program on the radio that was not to her liking, she would turn the knob without asking his permission. She even took to going out with Abu Rustum's daughter Salwa, with whom she worked at the hotel, and with Samar, Adnan's plump sister, doing what independent, bread-earning girls did on their days off: walk up and down the streets of the Basta or the Corniche, where boys their age would follow them, making remarks about how cute they were, while from time to time the girls would throw glances over their shoulders and giggle.

Jasmine even took to coming home after dark following these outings. And when Dad asked her where she had been, she would retort that it was none of his business.

"I buy the bread you eat, Dad," she would proclaim confidently. "No one gives me a hard time around here, do you hear?"

Jasmine had changed, and so had Dad. He had become a decrepit, confused, uncomprehending old man who wanted to die before more disasters overtook his life and destroyed the system of meaning that had governed his life and his people's from time immemorial. He no longer exercised his authority around the house. He surrendered that to Mousa. And Jasmine had jumped from childhood to adulthood, skipping adolescence on the way—an independent woman who was not going to let meaningless custom smother her life at the root. By the sweat of her forehead she earned her bread. And bread is *nimeh*, the most sacred of all God's bounty. She could fill her own cup when she was thirsty, unsay what was said about the Way of His creation, barter tradition for dreams. No one would gag Jasmine anymore.

But our society, our culture, our time was not ready for that kind of independence. There is a line you do not cross. Tradition is tradition. It takes as long to remove as it had taken to create. You challenge tradition, you pay with your life.

One day Jasmine kissed a boy. She was seen by a friend of Mousa, and he reported the sighting to my brother. When Jasmine got home, Mousa pointed at my sister and howled like an animal: "She soiled our honor!"

He turned to my dad. "She soiled our honor," he screamed triumphantly. But Dad had already abdicated his power to Mousa. Mousa then proceeded to pummel Jasmine until she was semiconscious. Even after she cowered in the corner, he still kicked, slapped, and punched her.

Such is the power of tradition, so pervasive in its grip on our instincts that no one in the house, including my ten-year-old brother, Samir, who was terrified, moved a finger to help her. She had, after all, kissed, actually *kissed*, a boy! No one delighted in seeing a sixteen-year-old girl, one's own sister, one's daughter, get savaged this way, but then she had it coming, didn't she?

Within less than ten minutes, Jasmine's face began to swell like a balloon. Bruises showed all over her body.

What had to be done was done. Nothing unusual here.

Then we sat down to have dinner. Samir refused to eat. Jasmine remained cowering in the corner. During dinner, mother explained that Aunt Hanan, who lived in Damascus, was going to visit soon. Dad grunted his approval. After the plates were cleared, we listened to the radio for an hour and drank tea in small glasses. Then, as if on cue, mother proceeded to take down our mattresses, pillows, and blankets, stacked neatly in a corner and spread them on the floor. By 11:00 P.M. we all went to sleep.

Things were expected to return to normal the following day. For the rest of us they did, but not for Jasmine. Something had snapped loose in her. To be sure, she returned to work and continued to go to her sewing and embroidery class, but her movements were increasingly inert and automatic. Still, the rebel in her had not been entirely crushed, for she now sought an instrument with which to avenge herself, to express her refusal to accept her world's traditions—even at the price of her own ruin.

So one day, less than three months after her beating, she went to bed with a boy from the neighborhood.

When Mousa found out, we all knew what drastic fate awaited her. Her punishment was going to be a terrible, terrible one indeed. It was just a question of the manner in which she would receive it. My sister had committed an unspeakable act beyond all understanding. Since time immemorial, women guilty of it were returned to their Glorious Maker, for presumably only He knew how to deal with them. Even Jasmine herself seemed to see no injustice in the fate that awaited her. At the time, even I saw nothing despotic or venomous in the verdict passed on my sister. I did not turn away in nauseated disbelief. I did not flinch with horror. I did not try to stop it. Tradition had long since devoured our autonomy. We could no more get outside it than we could jump out of our own skin.

Mousa chose poison. He handed it to Jasmine in a cup.

Jasmine stood by the dining table assuming the bored stance of someone standing in line at a movie theater, and drank the contents.

Then she lurched forward and staggered around like a bull gored by too many picks and fell dead on the floor.

Dad was the first to react. He knelt over his daughter's body and howled: "I'll join you, I'll join you soon, Jasmine, I'll join you soon, my lovely darling."

Mom started ululating those God-awful Koranic incantations of distress. And Mousa went out on the balcony, took out a gun that he had acquired for the occasion, and began to shoot rounds in the air.

Now the whole neighborhood knows that we have redeemed our honor, just as tradition dictated. And just as tradition dictated, the judge in whose court Mousa was tried gave him three years in jail. "This young man," the judge intoned, "saved his kith and kin from disgrace." Those are the brute workings of our way of life.

I intended to kill Mousa as soon as he was released from jail.

The memory of my sister preyed on my soul long after her death. I remembered when she was eleven, when we were all still in the refugee camp and she worked as a servant for a rich family in Hamra Street, the fashionable street in the Lebanese capital, and how her employer's kids, knowing she was afraid of the dark, used to lock her in a room and turn out the lights as they stood outside doubled up with laughter.

Above all, I remembered when she and I would go up to the roof of our house and watch the Shoof Mountains east of the capital and play games with each other imagining what lay behind them. It was like a secret that we shared, what we imagined. "There is a land beyond the mountains where boys and girls run the government," she would say, and I would counter with: "I know what lies behind the mountains—a big country where people go where they please and they have no parents, no jobs and no rules." Once she told me: "When I grow up, I want to go there and find out what lies behind the mountains." Even into our teens we continued to play our mountain game. When Jasmine was angry at the world, she would say to me, in shared secrecy, "I want to go live behind the mountains," or "Let's you and me run off and live behind the mountains."

Now I can no longer look at the mountains without thinking of Jasmine. I cannot understand Mom's babble about how God surely has already forgiven Jasmine, because I cannot understand who is going to forgive God. Sometimes I would be at the Corniche, sitting on a rock, watching the sea, where I would go to take my failure to understand, my call for an explanation, and the sea would thunder back at me with mute indifference.

Even after I destroyed Mousa's coop on the roof while he was in prison, and released his miserable pigeons to find their own freedom, they kept coming back to perch forlornly on the ledge, as if they too were captive to the workings of our way of life. They kept coming back, week after week, looking for their old home. And then one day they stopped coming. Maybe they found a different home behind the mountains.

Where is Jasmine?

I will live forever tangled in my sister's memory. I will forever remember that day at her burial, with the earth slit open like a kiss, poised for the timeless taste of her dream.

I curse God and His world. I want to set fire to His universe. It is only my word, not his, that can feed life into a stone.

...

Soon after Jasmine's death, I felt a new consciousness grow in my mind. I wanted to distance myself from the moronic serenity that characterized our culture. I would swagger around the Basta with Adnan and his friends at all hours. I carried a switchblade. I took up the local argot. I affected, with impressive ease, the gestural repertoire that defined the young neighborhood toughs. I was making a lot of money working for Adnan, and I was feeling independent. In short, I was being, for the first time in my life, the only determining force of my destiny.

I wanted no part of this world I inhabited. I was to make a cult of the idea of independence. My identity would be a product of personal discovery, and my life would be lived by a different perception.

Like most other Palestinians of my generation, I was experiencing, if only unconsciously, the emotions unleashed by the disruptions that occurred following the exodus of 1948. More than that was the alienation we felt in our host states, where we were constantly criticized by fellow Arabs for having "sold our land to the Jews." Not yet having experienced any of the humiliating defeats that they were to suffer at the hands of the Israelis in subsequent years, most Arabs disdained Palestinians for having "run away." Though Arab culture in the Fertile Crescent was only marginally different from ours, Palestinians in exile were forever made to feel like outsiders.

Palestinians of my father's generation had long since been inject-

ed with the torpor of helplessness and figured that they were going
to be around for too short a time to change their condition. With my
generation, it was a different case altogether. Our alienation in the
Arab world was a storm in the center of our communal experience—
and different Palestinians sought shelter from this storm in different ways.

Many young Palestinians were convinced that they could gain
mastery over their lives by becoming political activists (and politics
then was as much the milieu of a thirteen-year-old as it was of an
adult). What better way to gain acceptance in a society that scorns
your Palestinianness than to invest in the creation of the "Arab
Nation," the most popular movement of the day? What better proof
can a Palestinian give of his earnestness as an Arab than to be active
in the Arab nationalist movement, thus subsuming his Palestinian
identity in the greater Arab struggle? Nothing was more rooted in
the collective Arab psyche, nothing more closely related to its quest
for meaning, than the call in the 1950s for the unity of the Arab
states and the emergence of the New Eden of Arabism.

Propelled by turbulent energies from within and a perverse long-
ing for acceptance, Palestinians joined the nationalist struggle in
droves and in later years even came to lead it. Souls barred from
finding a counterweight to a profound loss in their center sought
release in political action—action that, considering the constraints
then placed on free expression, was often covert, conspiratorial, and
at times violent.

The powers that controlled the Arab world, however, did not
want such a unified nation. So as the fifties dragged on, thwarted
dreams of Arab unity created a void that only the advent of a purg-
ing fire, such as a military conflagration or a revolutionary upheaval,
could fill. The fire came again and again, but these Arabs remained
unpurged because they continued to think in Formal Arabic, a language whose constraints contributed to regimenting personal
behavior and helped to systematize the rules and corruptions of the
Arab establishment. No Arab activist could have hoped to transcend
his time or place unless he went beyond his formal language.

Here is Abu Jamal (Father of Beauty), a well-known Palestinian
figure in the Arab nationalist movement, at home, having invited
Adnan and me there for lunch. He wanted to buy a Swiss watch, and
we had acquired one for him. Not only was Abu Jamal an Arab

activist, but a Marxist intellectual as well, with several published pamphlets to his name.

"Oh, ye women," he shouts in the direction of the kitchen, where his wife and sister-in-law are cooking lunch. "Get me an ashtray."

A short while later, he hollers again, this time addressing his sister-in law: "Oh, ye Kadija, bring us some water."

The girl obliges by bringing a tray with three glasses of water.

"What is this?" he thunders. "I want water with ice in it, ye daughter of illegitimate birth."

The girl sheepishly looks down the bridge of her nose and, without uttering a word, takes the tray away and returns with three glasses of water with ice cubes.

Father of Beauty gulps down his water, belches, and smiles at us. "Thanks be to Allah," the Marxist intones.

Lunch is finally served and the three of us sit down to eat. His wife and sister-in-law do not join us. They wait until we have finished and retired to the living room before they sit at the table to eat our leftovers.

Other Palestinians of my generation escaped elsewhere. They retreated into a world that defined them as "more Palestinian than before," their crippling sense of loss of home and homeland nursed by a messianic vision of Return. They lived, as my parents lived, sheltered by the refugee camps or the isolated ghettos where they were less vulnerable to daily assaults on their identity. They too were activists. There was no escaping politics in those days; even the air was tainted with it. But these people cared only about Palestine. To hell with the Arab world, they said; it is Palestine that matters, and only Palestinians will liberate it. If the Algerian people can stand up to the might of the *colons* in their country, so can we resist the might of the Israelis. Awareness of one's national name is the principal validation of one's identity. We are Palestinians first and foremost, they asserted, and proud to be so. Soon we shall return, with or without help from the Arab armies, and show the Arabs that what is yet to come, not what is now, will validate our being and identity.

Other Palestinians changed their accents and adjusted with unseemly haste to Lebanese life; or, wanting nothing to do with Palestine, politics or activism, strove to emigrate—at worst to the Gulf states to make their fortune, or at best to America, where the streets were allegedly paved with gold.

And then there were the kids like us who did not go to schools or universities like other Palestinians. We grew up in the streets, where life fostered the free development of our own Palestinian voice and the flowering of individual identity through the struggle with daily existence. We did not speak Formal Arabic. Ours was not only the zestful idiom of Oral Arabic but an Arabic that the streets were reinventing, with the audacity that only the streets can project. Our language knew no structure, our grammar no constructs, our idiom no limits. Our speech was so dense with the subversive energy of the streets that it was all but impenetrable to those who did not live there. We had our own rules of utterance, perception, and response, and we delighted in the way we spoke, flaunting our lack of respect for traditional culture. If we were political at all, ours was a politics that embodied the integrity of rootless nihilism. The branches of our idiom, along with its stylized imagery, were nourished by the roots of every negative tradition in our culture.

One night Adnan and I, along with another Basta kid, were hanging around the *souk*, drinking beer at a small bar called Abu Hanna. It was a Ramadan night, when it should have been unthinkable for a Moslem Arab to be seen drinking alcohol. We were, of course, unconsciously mocking the very sanctum of Arab culture and, by doing so, striving for a kind of personal style and originality.

We were still in the *souk* district at 2:00 A.M.

"Soon the sons of whores in the Basta will be woken up by the *mossaher*," Adnan said, looking at his watch.

He was referring to the man who goes around from street to street, each night of Ramadan, waking the faithful by beating his drum and hollering Koranic incantations. Whole families would come to life, eat a *tassheer* meal to tide them through the day of fasting, and then go back to sleep. It was a tradition that had outlasted its practical use, since the invention of alarm clocks surely made the *mossaher* redundant.

"Let's go wake them up," Adnan offers drunkenly.

"We need drums," I offered readily.

"I have two at home."

The three of us started at Sidi Ibrahim Street, off which branched many of the minor streets of the Basta.

"Wake up all ye hypocrites," we shouted, beating our drums.

"Wake up all ye Arabs, pestilence of the world," Adnan called out.

"Wake up ye Arab scum and do unto your history what your ancestors had done to theirs."

More drums and drunken laughter on our part.

"I say wake up, ye miserable dogs," I hollered with all my might. "Wake up all ye who are repudiated by Allah and his prophets."

"Wake up, wake up, wake up," the three of us now screamed in unison. "Wake up and slam in kind him who slams you in the face. Wake up to the word of God."

In no time, there were people in pajamas standing on their balconies, calling out to each other about who we might be.

"That is the son of Abu Mousa," one identified me.

"And that other one," another exclaimed, "that is the son of Abu Adnan, the storyteller."

"Go away," they were now shouting at us all at once. "Go away before you all get banished to the hell of *jahannam*. Have you no respect for the Word of Allah?"

But the fact is that we, the street kids of the Basta and other poor neighborhoods in Beirut, scorned both the idea of respect and the Word of Allah.

It would remain to be seen which of these various Palestinian legacies would be resurrected and which would be eclipsed when the fighters at the battle of Karameh in 1968, and the stone throwers of the West Bank in 1988, emerged on the scene. In the meantime, most of us Palestinians, young and old, radical and conservative, activist and apolitical, still had to make a living. We still had our problems as Palestinians who had no passports, no work permits, no peddler's licenses, no recourse to justice. In the end, scraping enough money together to buy a child a warm winter coat is more important than grappling with existential issues about who you are in the scheme of things.

I was a street kid. I cared about survival too, but I sought it with the primitive ardor of a Basta tough. At least I thought I was a Basta tough.

One day, Adnan was arrested and went to jail. And when I tried to branch out on my own as a dealer in smuggled goods, I discovered that I was not really tough enough for the rigors of the street. I was being ripped off often and did not know how to be ruthless in defending my rights (the only way to survive in the Basta). Finally I had to give up dealing.

Over the next two years I took on a variety of jobs, all self-employed. I was a peddler for a while, but life as a Palestinian peddler without a permit was hell. I had to avoid the cops at every turn. And when they caught up with me, they confiscated my goods and slapped me around. Sometimes they took me to a police station, slapped me around some more, and called me "a two-bit Palestinian son of a whore who sold his land to the Jews." Then I became a carrier, a job unique to Beirut in the winter. Beirut, despite its reputation as the Paris of the Middle East, still had a medieval sewage system; the streets would become unpassable rivers of filthy mud and water whenever it rained. Carriers stand at a crossing on days like this and carry well-dressed Beirutis on their back, from one end of the street to the other, for half a lira. When it didn't rain, I worked as a reader. I hung around cemeteries clutching a Koran, and when I spotted a grieving family at the grave of a relative, I would offer my services. I would read for them, as I knelt before the grave, appropriate *suras* calling on Allah to show mercy for the spirit of their deceased. I liked being a reader. Unlike my fellows, who used to read their *suras* in rapid, dry, and enervated monotones, as if they were reading some legal deposition, I affected a sonorous voice that tried to communicate some of the energies in the idiom of the *suras* and to exploit the theatrical qualities entailed in my work.

In all these capacities I worked for myself, and I liked being self-employed. Only the last job I had in Beirut before I left the city, not returning for another twenty years, was working for someone else. The Canon Match Box Factory was situated in a vile district by the Beirut River inhabited by the poorest Beirutis, Armenians, and Shiites. The people who worked at the Canon were almost all children and teenagers. The conditions there were truly medieval, and the wages we were paid for the interminable hours we put in were those associated with slave labor. Sulfur and other noxious fumes got into our lungs and kept us coughing all day. In summer, when the heat was hellish, we would faint with fatigue, our eyes would droop, and sweat would pour down our faces, soaking us to the bone. Perspiration clung to our lips, eyelashes, and ears. Even the metal machinery we worked seemed to perspire, as if it too was being pushed beyond endurance. That was bad enough. But the supervisors, who were almost all relatives of the owner, went around accusing the workers of being *tanbal*, slacking off, or of *yilaab*, horsing around, and arbitrarily subtracted ten piasters, twenty piasters, or sometimes as much as fifty piasters from their wages. Some boys would go to pick up their wages at the end of the week only to be told that there was nothing for them because they had been *tanbal* or *yilaab*. And there was no recourse to justice.

I worked at the Canon with my younger brother, Samir, who was now almost thirteen, and his friend Omar, who had lost a couple of fingers in an industrial accident some years before. Omar's father had recently died, and he was now considered "a widow's son." A boy without an older brother, raised by a woman, is considered a lower species of being. You are "a branch cut off the tree." You don't belong.

Omar's mother was now supporting the family, including his two younger sisters, by working as a fortune-teller. She went around from door to door offering her services for a few piasters or for handouts of food. She knew nothing about fortune-telling, but she soon taught herself the tricks and was helped along by her hoarse, raspy voice and the outfit she wore. In addition, ever since her husband's death, Omar's mother had acquired the aura of a person who had suddenly made some kind of relevant discovery about life. She was actually elated at her husband's death, and now, being independent, she carried herself with abandon, even unrestrained joy. Once, after his death, she described her husband as a toothache. It pained you so much, she said, that you were prepared to have it yanked out just to end the misery it caused you. Her husband had been a brute and a wife beater, and—like all other brutes and wife beaters—a weakling.

I had first met Omar's mother back in the old days, when she knocked on our door to offer her mystical services. Since her accent gave her away as a Palestinian, my mother asked her in, and instead of fortune-telling, they fell into a long discussion about Palestine, what families they came from, and how beautiful Haifa and Acre were, the twin cities in "the usurped homeland" that they each came from. They talked and talked and talked, warmly and in animated tones, about how the land, the weather, the water, the fruit, the schools, the oranges, the olive oil, and virtually everything else was better there than in Lebanon, or for that matter anywhere else in the Arab world.

"I should go back to work," Omar's mother finally said.

"Why don't you go read the fortune of Rustum's wife," my mother offered, with a hint of mischief in her voice, and then proceeded to tell her guest everything about them—how many children they had, the watermelon store Rustum owned, the job he had had before that as a postman (from which he had been fired) and their one retarded son.

Armed with all this information, Omar's mother knew how to dazzle Rustum's wife and greatly enjoyed watching her subject stare with disbelief, her shoulders stiffening with every revelation, especially her predictions about how she could expect a son soon, this one normal, and a killing in a watermelon deal that Rustum was about to conclude.

At the Canon Factory, Omar was a good worker, despite his missing fingers. However, like everybody else, he hated his job and wanted to save enough money to buy a cart one day and become a vendor. But even when the supervisors did not deduct money from his wages for "slacking off" or "horsing around," what he made all went to his mother.

If Omar hated his job, Samir's contempt for it went to lunatic extremes. For a Palestinian kid growing up in the ghetto in those days, Samir had bizarre expectations. His ambition was to become a wine expert, learn French and other languages, and become an accomplished tap dancer. I don't know how he came by these notions, but he never stopped talking about them.

"What kind of sissy calling is that, you donkey?" I asked him once. "A wine expert? A tap dancer? A speaker of the languages of our colonizers?"

"It's un-Arab, ain't it, Blondy Boy?" he responded, calling me by my nickname.

Samir hated Lebanon and the Lebanese, as he hated the whole Arab world. He despised their lives, their values, and their politics. He described the Arab world as a whorehouse (*karakhani*), and President Nasser—the most revered, beloved Arab leader at the time—as a dick head (*rass air*). Yet Samir loved Islam and the ritual of prayer. At times he even went to the mosque on weekdays, after work, to lock horns with a *sheik* with whom he would argue some pedantic point in the manner of a man taking pi to the last decimal. But he avoided going on Fridays, the official day of prayer, when the mosques were like a circus, filled with Moslems who wanted to fool God into thinking they were devout or to scam their way to paradise by being seen giving alms to the poor. And the poor, with their servile looks, quivering lips, and whining voices, would always be there, assembled outside after prayer. Those non-Arabs among them from Sudan, Senegal, and Somalia, who were excluded from the favors of the devout, could be heard muttering under their breath: "*Arab jarab*." Arabs are scum. When Samir was eight years old, I remember him asking Dad at the breakfast table what the Aliens Department was after Dad had mentioned that he was going there that morning.

"The Aliens Department is the Aliens Department," Dad responded impatiently.

"What is that?" Samir persisted.

"It is the place where Palestinians go to get permits to work, to travel, and so on."

"Why do they need to get permission to do that?"

"Because we're considered aliens here."

"What are aliens?"

"Be quiet, oh son of legitimate birth," my mother chimed in.

"What are aliens, Dad?" Samir asked again, this time more earnestly, not even looking in mother's direction.

"You, for example, are an alien," Dad said, with an edge to his voice.

Samir, as if sensing the term's sinister connotation, said, with an equal edge: "I don't like aliens."

Samir concentrated on his breakfast of dried yogurt, black olives, and thyme pastries. Then, as if he had mulled it over and was still not satisfied, he asked: "Why are we aliens?"

The question seemed to be addressed to all of us this time—not just to Dad.

"Because we are not Lebanese," my father said, affecting a pedagogical manner.

"What are we then?"

"We are Palestinians. You know that, Samir. We are the other people living here. We are the others."

Samir dropped out of school at age twelve. His teachers were particularly cruel, more so than authority figures traditionally are in our part of the world. But he continued to read whatever he could about wine and had collected a thick file with photos of wine bottles clipped from various papers and magazines which he would spread on the floor to examine carefully and methodically. He listened to radio broadcasts in French, mimicking the accent and memorizing whole phrases with natural ease. And he was always tap dancing around the house to a music of his own making that none of us could understand. Above all, however, he disdained the way the Palestinians were resigning themselves to their lot.

Once after work, Samir, Omar, and I were on our way home, riding the tram from the River District, and a Lebanese boy from the Basta waved at us, singling out Samir.

"Hey, Samy, father of all youth, how are you?" the boy said cheerfully.

"I am here," Samir answered flippantly.

"What does that mean, Samy?"

"It means this: how the fuck should a Palestinian feel?"

It was getting increasingly difficult to put up with conditions at work. One day when one of the supervisors came round and told me that he was deducting twenty piasters from my wages because I was horsing around, I told him his mother was a whore from the *souk* whose pussy was on sale to American sailors. So he and a couple of other beefy supervisors dragged me to the office of the factory owner for instructions on what to do with me. Abu Iskandar, a Maronite who lived in Junieh, had framed pictures of his yacht hanging in his office, some of them showing him and his family and friends drinking champagne on board, along with various pictures of the Virgin Mary. He told me I was a two-bit Palestinian piece of scum, that I was fired, that now *all* my wages had been deducted, and that I should get the hell out of his factory, and the River District altogether, before he had his men break every bone in my body.

I knew he meant it and walked out quietly.

I sat outside the factory for a while, feeling a formidable desire to hit back at Abu Iskandar and at his supervisors and his family and his entire class, to inflict violence on their soul and their name and their reason. My hatred for them welled up like the taste of vomit. I could feel the uncontrolled jabs of this hatred driving my whole being. Suddenly something snapped, and I picked up some heavy stones and started hurling them with all my might at the windows of his office, which was on the ground floor, smashing them and no doubt causing havoc inside. As I hurled the stones, I shouted obscenities at the top of my voice: "We shall fuck your womenfolk and burn down your land and banish you to die in the land of others. Bastards. Germs. Filthy pimps repudiated by the Prophet and His Companions. We shall destroy you and shove shit down your throats." When Iskandar's henchmen came out, I stood my ground, hurling more stones until they retreated into the factory. Every time they tried to put their heads out the door, I hurled more stones at them, still shouting obscenities and abuse about what their mothers did at the *souk*.

"Come out, you bastards," I kept shouting. "Come out. Come out, I tell you."

I was like a man demented. I even took out my switchblade and held it over my head, showing it to the whole world to advertise my serious intent.

"Come out! Come out, I tell you," I hollered, jumping up and down like a *dabki* dancer in a trance.

"We will get you," I screamed. "We will get you all. One day we will get you."

For me, then in my late teens, living in the heartland of a world brutalized by its history, enfeebled by its tradition, life nonetheless still stretched ahead. For my father, Palestinian exile par excellence, inhabiting the land of others and tending the ashes of his past, nothing now stood between him and death. His world and its ways, once as familiar to him as the wince of his own muscles, were now a profound mystery.

One morning he woke up with a cold, and my mother asked him how he felt. He looked groggy and weak, his skinny body formless under his disheveled pajamas.

"When are we going back to Haifa, oh Um Mousa?" he asked wearily.

"Abu Mousa, father of all youth," my mother responded impatiently, "you know the answer to that lies in the mind of God or in the heart of the poet."

He looked at her, his thin arms tugging at the covers, and said: "Listen to me, oh daughter of legitimate birth."

"I am listening to you."

"I wish I were dead."

"Those are not, Abu Mousa, blessed words to utter."

"I want to penetrate His blessed words as men penetrate the women of the *souk*."

Mom said nothing.

"I wish I were dead," my dad repeated plaintively. Soon after that his wish was granted. And soon after that I escaped to Australia.

5

A Heart of Darkness

So I am stuck here in Ramallah for the next three days. A curfew has been imposed, and the residents are expected to remain confined to their homes. My host, Salem, is in Nablus, which is also under curfew. He will remain there for the duration.

Curfews are a way of life here, and Palestinians have long since learned to live with them. Now that the glow of the *Intifada* has faded and defiance receded from the national sensibility, they stand helpless before the manic agencies of occupation. They do what they are told, muttering grimly to themselves.

I don't understand how people can put up with this. Palestinians have lived, generation after generation, under the Ottomans, the British, the Jordanians, and now the Israelis, held in place finally not by their oppressors or even by the way they have internalized oppression, but by their own tradition. Generation after generation they repeat themselves, by sexual vigor and peasant toil, with tradition standing guard over the locked gates of their consciousness, preventing the entry of any new kind of awareness. I am not one with this way of life. The experience is too radically different from anything I now know.

What conceit I bring with me to this place. Who am I, after all, to come here from my comfortable exile, to foist my fancy musings on the homeground? The wine simply will not travel.

I sit in the sun-room and look out on the street. There is not a single human being in sight. There is no traffic, except for military vehicles heading to and from the military governor's headquarters a few hundred yards up the street. When I passed the building for the first time a few days ago, upon arriving with Salem in his car from Jerusalem, I was saddened and enraged by the spectacle—feelings that increased whenever I passed it going to or from Salem's apartment. For every day, from 6:00 A.M. to 6:00 P.M., there would be a crowd of about two dozen elderly men and women standing outside waiting to visit, or *trying* to visit, their sons and daughters who had been arrested and held for questioning before being charged (thence transported to a regular prison to await trial) or held under preventative detention (and transported to the prison compounds in the Negev Desert for terms of six months, renewable at the whim of the military governor). When I first saw the scene, I was touched by its unendurable sadness. Here were elderly mothers and fathers, with swarthy Palestinian faces, quietly looking into the distance, thinking Palestinian thoughts—and there are thoughts that are uniquely Palestinian—about their endless pain and the pain of their nation. In this shared moment they say not a word to each other, communicating only in silence. Some pain is unspeakable. They stand shrouded in the early morning fog, in front of the gate and the barbed wire leading to the governor's headquarters, watched by occupation soldiers chewing on watermelon seeds.

Around lunchtime, there is a knock on the door. It is Um and Abu Muntasir with their son, Victor, neighbors from the apartment below.

I let them in. They introduce themselves. "Well, brother," Abu Muntasir says, "we heard that you were here on your own. We don't know about your food situation, so we brought you some eggs, some vegetables, and some bread."

I tell them I am grateful. They say that people have to look out for each other during curfew and share what they have.

Abu and Um Muntasir are a couple in their late forties. They are plain-faced and sad-eyed, though they smile readily and cheerfully enough. Victor, who wears glasses, is a fair-haired boy with a bony, handsome face. Like many other folks in Ramallah who have lived in the United States for many years and made their money there, they have returned here to live. Victor, who was born in San Diego, is a regular American teenager who is still, after two years, learning to speak Arabic.

"He is all we've got left," Abu Muntasir says, lovingly ruffling Victor's hair. Their nineteen-year-old daughter Samira died in a car crash before they moved back.

I make them tea and we talk awhile, somehow drifting into English.

"Are you back here to live?" they want to know.

I tell them I am merely visiting.

"You don't like it here?"

"Oh I do, I do," I lie.

"Are you married?" the wife inquires with friendly interest.

"No, I am not. I'm divorced."

"Were you married to an American?"

I say I was.

"Oh that doesn't count," she says seriously, waving a dismissive finger. "Come and live here, and we will find you a wife."

Palestinians talk like that to a stranger anytime. In their isolated world, assaulted from every direction, they come closer the more they are attacked. Over the years, all private sanctuaries of identity have been broken into. Your age, your income, your profession, your marital status, your social and family background, everything about you save your sexual life, can be explored by a stranger without the slightest embarrassment.

"We are here to invite you to have lunch with us," says Um Muntasir, so confident of my acceptance that they all promptly stand up and wait for me to walk out with them before I can voice my agreement.

"Okay, I will. Thank you," I say.

"You'll meet my dad," she offers uneasily. "He lives with us and you, I mean, he, would like to meet you, I'm sure."

"Look, I want to warn you about my father-in-law," Abu Muntasir puts in gingerly. "He is old, you know. But more than that, he's a bit eccentric. He has a temper and at times tends to be, well, shall we say, sort of, you know, eruptive. He is eighty-two, you know."

Downstairs in their apartment, we are met in the living room by Mr. Muntasir, Sr., who is seated in an overstuffed armchair puffing happily on a water pipe. Mr. Muntasir is gray and grizzled, with an intemperate face that has fallen into woebegone lines. He does not stand up to greet me since I am expected to walk over to him and not only kiss, Palestinian fashion, both his cheeks but, in deference to his age, his hand as well. I do just that.

We all sit down.

"God bless you, God bless you," he says to me repeatedly. "Salem tells me you are a son of the camps and a member of the crowd of '48." The term refers to the Palestinians who fled their homeland that year and became refugees in the surrounding countries.

"Yes, *zeidi*," I say respectfully, using the appropriate title expected when addressing a grandfather.

"And you have come back to the homeland!"

"Yes, *zeidi*."

"God bless you, God bless you, father of all youth. God bless you, my son, and may your hands always be safe for the struggle."

He puffs on his water pipe, looking content, confident, unworried. He crosses and uncrosses his legs as he studies me with a smile on his face. There is assertiveness in the smallest physical gesture. That's the way my father was before he became an exile in the "land of others" and, stripped of the sanctuary of his ancestral home, was also stripped of the will to live. He had aged before his time. But this old man—well, he may be eighty-two, but he does not seem old. There is a verve about him, a dramatic irrepressibility. Unlike my father's, his is not a haunted life governed by unreason and torn by emotional violence.

Victor brings us syrupy-sweet tea, and we sip it in small glasses.

"Welcome, brother, welcome," Mr. Muntasir says. "And God bless you."

"You honor me, you honor me, *zeidi*," I reply.

And then we plunge headlong into politics. There is no respite from this when you're with Palestinians. That's all they do. And when they tire of talking politics, if they ever do, they play music. There is nothing else in their lives. Politics and music. Music and politics.

"It's obvious to you, brother, is it not, why Syria has joined the enemy camp and opted to fight alongside the Americans against sister Iraq?" he asks me bitterly.

He seems so sure of my answer that he goes on before I can speak. "That is because the Syrian regime, like all Arab regimes, is a lackey of American imperialism."

He then extends his hand to me, palm up, and expects me to slap it. I do. I have forgotten that what is known in the United States as the "give me five" gesture of solidarity has been a common practice here for centuries.

Mr. Muntasir loves to hold center stage, and he now regales us with recollections of his days of struggle in Palestine in the 1930s and 1940s. He had actually been a member of the executive board of the Arab Higher Committee (the Mandate-approved organization that represented Palestinians when the British ruled Palestine) and, after the committee was outlawed, a member of the *Mojahedeen*, the Palestinian underground.

"During the General Strike," he narrates, referring to the eight-month strike that Palestinians staged in the late 1930s to pressure the British into granting them independence, "King Abdallah wrote me a letter, which I still have, and in it he said that we should work for peace and that we should get our *thowars* [revolutionaries] to lay down their arms and, as he put it, trust in our friends the British to correct the wrong committed against us. I toyed with the idea of writing back to the son of sixty whores to ask him since when have the British been our friends. But I did not."

He tells us about his contacts with the *thowars* all over Palestine and how, in the absence of easy access to telephones and wireless, he always sent his letters to field commanders by messenger. He dwells on a story about the time he dispatched a letter by a trusted messenger to a unit commander just outside Jerusalem, in an area infested with British troops. He says that if his messenger had been caught, he, Mr. Muntasir, would have been condemned to death. His style is purely anecdotal, telling stories within stories, digressing from his narrative to tell us his messenger's name, the name of his wife's family, and how many children they had.

"But brothers, I want to tell you that before sundown, I had received a response from the *thowars*, and their commander wrote to say my instructions on the national struggle were being followed to the letter."

Of course, he had to tell us who the commander was, where his father came from, what family had accepted his offer for their daughter's hand, and which of his offspring were now recognized members of the PLO.

When he describes the Jordanian delegation that came to Nablus in 1943 to ask the populace to stop their demonstrations, he sniffs as he identifies its members as *iwlad kalb*, sons of dogs.

"The Jordanian officials were chased out of town by stones, I tell you," he says, laughing loudly and slapping his knees. "After 1948, when Iraq and Jordan sent representatives to us here in the West Bank, I told them, *ya ghawadeen*, you pimps, Palestine fell the moment the Arab armies entered it. I wouldn't have any dealings with them."

Neighbors are wandering in and out of the Muntasirs' home every few minutes. Some join us in the living room. Others visit in the kitchen with Um Muntasir, who is cooking lunch. Children are wandering around as if they lived there. A couple of teenagers arrive to visit Victor, who takes them to his bedroom.

When it is time to eat, there are seven adults sitting around the dinner table, and probably seven kids in the living room eating lunch there. Seated next to me is a youngish man from Gaza called Adli who works on the premises as a live-in janitor, maintenance man, and building supervisor.

Mr. Muntasir concentrates on his food. It appears that he's the kind of man who does not converse while eating.

Adli—like me, a son of the camps, which after 1968 became a mark of status in Palestinian society because most Palestinian fighters came from there—views me as a kind of soulmate.

"Brother, I want to ask you a question," Adli says, as he grabs my arm earnestly. "Have you written about the camps? Someone has to write about the camps. I don't trust writers myself, Palestinian writers; but you're different. You come from the camps. Our regular writers, especially those who live there with you in the United States, are chicken shit. Writers write books *about* us, about what *we* do. They live secondhand. They're parasites. They live by the grace of what *we* do. They feed, like vultures, on what *we* do. I'm not a very well-read man, and I don't want to be. What gives vitality to our history is action, brother, not words. Look at the Koran, look at Moslems. Look at those helpless thousand million Moslems around the world. Do you think God will accept them in paradise when they die?"

I suspect the question is rhetorical and do not respond. Adli looks at me with a somber gaze.

"God will not accept them because they have not accepted *Jihad*.

That is God. And today's Moslems, may the Lord pour acid on their souls, are not responding to the essence of God within them. They are distracted by their oil dollars, their imported material goods from America—may he who laid the first stone in that country's foundation be struck down by pestilence—and by their reverence for everything Western."

Then Adli asks me, with momentous gravity and a hand on my shoulder, almost benedictory in his solemnity: "Why don't you write about that?"

"I hope to be able to do that one day," I say flatly.

Now, during the fruit course, Adli reaches for an orange, peels it, and, as is expected of him, offers me and the guest on his other side a slice each.

"Oranges from Palestine are the best oranges in the world," Mr. Muntasir, who has finished eating, says, and proceeds to burp loudly. "Thank Allah for the blessing of his *nimeh*." He is referring to a term that simply means food, considered in Arab culture a sacred expression of God's bounty. Everybody mumbles in unison, under their breath, the same thanks to Allah.

"If it were not for the Arab regimes, we would not have been robbed of our homeland, and the *nimeh* it could produce, by the Jews," he proceeds.

Here we go again, I say to myself. Palestinians blaming others—world, fate—but never themselves, for their failure to meet the challenges of history. But Mr. Muntasir is off on a different tangent.

"Arab leaders are pimps," he continues evenly. "Their masses are whores. They care only about their own interests and are not beyond prostituting their own people."

"Dad, please," his daughter pleads.

In response, Mr. Muntasir purses his lips and looks at her angrily, as if searching for the right word to express his distaste at being interrupted. Happily he does not find it. So he continues: "The Arab leaders are pimps, I say. Look at that son of sixty whores, Saddam, and what he's doing. He lies to the Arab masses about his intentions, like every other Arab leader before him, from Nasser to Arafat, and he wants to sacrifice the Iraqi masses to further his own personal designs."

He picks up a dessert plate and passes it to me.

"No thank you, I'm really full," I say.

"You will take one piece. You *must* take one piece. I, Misbah Muntasir, demand that you take one piece now."

"Yes, *zeidi*," I say.

"They are pimps, I say," he repeats. "We have not had a single dedicated Arab leader, a single dedicated Palestinian leader, who has not abused his power, his people, and his mission, ever since I came into the world and opened my eyes to look at the face of God. And you, all of you here, children of Adam, you are letting them do that to you?"

"Dad, please, must we go through that again?"

Mr. Muntasir gazes at the space above his daughter's head, eyes burning with rage, his voice palpable with impatience.

"Silence!"

"Dad, look," his son-in-law pleads, "you must lengthen the rope of your self." The phrase, as I understood it, means something like: Cool it, we have guests.

"Silence, I say, son of legitimate birth."

Abu Muntasir holds his words, presumably afraid, like a skier who communicates in whispers lest his voice bring down an avalanche, that his father-in-law may erupt into one of his famous outbursts.

"I would like everyone here to understand that I am not a man driven by reason, like your generation of Palestinians are. Let it be known that I, Misbah Muntasir, father of Muna and grandfather of Victor and the late Samira, am a man of emotion."

He passes me the dessert plate again. There is no chance I am going to decline.

"And look at what the Jews have done in the village of Beita," his voice rises in ornate mockery. "They went there and killed people *and* uprooted the olive trees. If they want to kill people, that is their problem, a problem between them and their God. But the trees! The trees! What have the trees done to them? The Jews make a mistake if they think trees do not have a mind, a will, of their own. If you hurt trees, they will curse you. The Jews who came here can fight the people and the land and the soul of Palestine, but not the trees. The United States and Europe and the UN and the Arab regimes and other powers may allow it, but God will not. He is all knowing. He will punish them, they who destroy His trees and tamper with His creation."

We all then retire to the living room, and Mr. Muntasir retreats to his bedroom for his afternoon nap.

In the living room, I'm sitting with Um and Abu Muntasir and their son, Victor, discussing politics. There is no respite from it. The Palestinian experience has been so conditioned by occupation, under the British, the Jordanians, and now the Israelis, that Palestinians find it difficult to think of any other way to siphon off their malaise. Theirs is the quintessential political life.

I ask Victor if he likes being in Palestine.

"I'm learning to like it," he offers, adjusting his glasses, "but the occupation soldiers are making it difficult. You know, when I was in San Diego there were a lot of Jewish kids in my school, and some of them were my friends. I didn't think much about the problem then. I mean Mom and Dad talked about it at home, and I knew that I was Palestinian and all, and that I should support the Palestinian struggle and that kinda thing, but I didn't feel strongly about the issue either way. In less than four months after I arrived here, I was arrested twice. The first time, we were just being let out of school that day, and there was a demonstration up the street. I didn't join it or anything. I mean I didn't know anything about demonstrations or politics. In fact, I even decided to take a side street to avoid being near it. Well, when I got to the other end of the street, there were these four soldiers blocking the exit and arresting anyone and everyone there. Students and nonstudents. They dumped me in a jeep with four other kids whom they had arrested earlier. My Arabic wasn't that good then, and I was trying to tell them, in English, that I was an American, but they wouldn't listen to me. Then I took my passport out and waved it at them and said, 'American, American, I'm an American.' That was it. That was a big mistake. I guess they hate Americans," he says evenly.

Victor's father chimes in. "No! I think they admire Americans. What they hate is that we, who are in their eyes despicable, dirty Arabs, could be American."

"I mean there is hatred in their eyes, man," Victor continues. "They hate our presence. They like to kick and punch us. They feel good when they know they made us feel bad. I mean on quiet days, especially on quiet days, when there are no demonstrations, no stone throwing, nothing, patrols of five or six soldiers drive up and down the streets of downtown Ramallah and el Bireh—the twin towns here—and just out of the blue, they stop, get out of their vehicles, walk over to a vendor and kick over his vegetable stall. Just for the hell of it. Even those soldiers you see on roofs, I guess when they get bored, or despondent, or angry that there is no action, they start throwing stones at the people below, or firing in the air to scare the hell out of them. At any rate, when I waved my American passport at the soldiers, it was as if I had waved a red flag at an enraged bull. They pulled me out of the jeep and beat the hell out of me. My elbow got broken. I was hit on the back, on my shoulders, legs, chest, face. Three of them were doing it. Then they pushed me to the ground, face down, and one of them placed his boot on my back and just stood there, talking to each other in Hebrew about some trivial thing. We were taken to the military governor's headquarters just up the street. I was there for six hours. During that time I was punched and slapped around some more and then released."

"Just like that, hey?" I ask, morosely. Sometimes you can't help asking the obvious question.

"Yeah. Just like that. Just for the hell of it." His casual, offhand, disdainful arrogance is so American. "I was in pain for a week after that. I had bruises all over my body. But I still have the shirt I wore that day. I haven't washed it yet. The boot marks are still on it. I don't want to forget the incident. Nor will I forget what happened to my friend Anis Hussein. He's older than me, a freshman at Beir Zeit College. One day there was a demonstration on campus, on campus mind you, and the soldiers barged in, picked him up, and beat him senseless. I mean he lost consciousness. When he arrived at the headquarters, he came to, so they beat him some more, and again he lost consciousness. Then they took him to the hospital, not out of compassion but because they thought he was already dead or dying. But instead of taking him to the emergency room, they just dumped him, like a sack of potatoes, on the steps leading to the entrance to the hospital. That was about two years ago, but he still had to go to the hospital repeatedly at least once a week after he was released. I don't know what the soldiers did to his leg, but it's going to be amputated, you know. They can't save it."

Victor falls silent. I say nothing.

"It's worse than you can imagine here," Victor's father says somberly.

"Well, didn't you go to the American consulate to complain?" I ask.

He laughs contemptuously. "Are you kidding? The second time my boy was arrested, less than five weeks later, I did, and it was a waste of time. I talked to this idiot there, who distractedly filled out a form and, in effect, said don't call me, I'll call you. I said is this all you're gonna do, and he goes yup, there is nothing else I can do about it, still as distracted as ever—as if he'd filed so many of these complaints that his eyeballs were popping out with boredom. And I go, that's it, that's all there is to it? I fill out a form and go home? He says yup. I say, Jesus Christ, my son is an American citizen, born in San Diego, California, for heaven's sake, an all-American fifteen-year-old kid dumped in jail and beaten up, and you tell me there is nothing you can do about it? And he just nods. And I just leave. To hell with him, if you'll pardon my language. Who needs him? I mean I was in Vietnam, and I served my country and this is what I get."

Later Victor tells me about a friend of his from school who was being driven by his dad to Jerusalem and the border police stopped the car, asked the father to pull his window down, and slapped him on his face twice—all without saying a word—and then waved him on.

I am taking notes.

"Brother," Victor's mother admonishes me jokingly, "if you're going to write down every one of these stories, you need as many volumes, and as many words, as there are in the *Encyclopedia Britannica*. Besides these are insignificant, exceedingly trivial incidents compared to the stories you hear from the people of Nablus, say, or God forbid, Gaza. That's where hell is. That's where reason stops."

How could people live like this? How could the occupied sustain these conditions? How could the occupier impose them? It's a mystery to me that an Israeli soldier, or border policeman, would beat up a child, break his bones, then dump him unconscious at the entrance to a hospital, *and* later that day go home, kiss his kids, and read the Torah before going to sleep as if nothing extraordinary had happened. It says something about our human psyche. Perhaps within us coexists the capacity to enact the monstrous and the humane. If man has not made of his humanity an impediment to the inhuman, what right has he to this humanity?

One might ask why the Muntasirs, and other Palestinian-American families like them, have returned here to live. The notion must seem absurd but is perfectly understandable.

The fact is that for most Palestinians from the homeground, America is a means to get an education, make a fortune, establish a name, acquire a passport. They do not go to America to become

American. They do not, and finally find that they cannot, cross the divide to American culture. The freewheeling social, sexual, and linguistic norms of American society are at the furthest remove from the internal climate of the Palestinian soul. Americans fiercely assert individual freedoms and a right to privacy that Palestinians find not only strange but threatening. Palestinians like the Muntasirs, who may have arrived in America when they were young, cling to their close-knit family (whose members never stray far from each other), social community, and religious values. If they were to surrender these as the price for becoming American, they would never gain as much as they had lost. They leave it to the second generation to assimilate. To feel at home in America, they would have to bring about a profound reordering of their cultural consciousness and stifle the emotional and social claims to which they remain heir. When they decide to return, it is because back in the homeground everything is safe, enfolded in shared recognitions.

Palestinians are conservative to the core. It is more difficult for them than for other émigrés to open themselves to the solicitations of another culture and effect a break with primary ties to their past. They are the product of a society that for five hundred years has moved around the treadmill of immemorially divined truths. The notion that American culture is wicked and is corrupting their children is woven into the temper of Palestinians living in America. They will see to it that their sons do not go to mindless rock concerts, that their daughters do not go out on dates, and that the corrupt Western values that destroy other families do not destroy theirs.

In the end, however, these families return, feeling exulted and consoled, after they have "made it"—that is, amassed what to them is a modest fortune. If the price they have to pay to live again in the homeground is to endure a foreign occupation, then so be it. After all, life under occupation may be harsh, but it is no better for Palestinians living in host states in the Arab world. More than that, they will live in their own homeground, in their own piece of Palestine, though it may be governed momentarily by a foreign occupier.

The tug to return always lies at the center of a Palestinian's identity. If you live in the homeground, you are made more compact yourself by that fact. If you die in the homeground, you are all the more prepared to meet your Glorious Maker. It's as simple as that.

I understand this tug, and at times I feel it in my own heart, but it is alien to what I believe. It would be absurd for me, a person who has railed against nationalism all these years, to imprison myself now within the boundaries of one nation. I belong to a small group of Palestinians who see a large gap between their experience of being Palestinian, with its countercultural rhythm and its stress on personal discovery, and that of Palestinians whose lives are penetrated, rendered safe, and finally standardized by shared national recognitions.

The Muntasirs, like Akram's parents, the Mahers, have returned to their roots, their culture, the land of their birth. They were not born in America. Their kids, however, were. And I predict that these children, who grew up American, cut from the same cultural cloth as other American children, will one day return to their roots, to their culture, to the land of their birth, just as their parents have done.

Just then a neighbor wanders in unannounced. (Unannounced is the name of the game during curfew.) He is a smug-looking man in his late thirties dressed in a suit with a button-down shirt and tie. He greets me by my first name.

"You don't remember me," he says, slapping me on the back. "I am Raymond." The name here is pronounced the way it is in French, a hangover from our Crusader days.

"Good to see you again," he says cheerfully as he sits beside me in the living room. I don't remember him, and I say so.

"Of course you don't," he says. "I was sitting in the third row, and after the lecture we only shook hands."

He explains, his face fluttery with smiles, that we had met at Yale University eight years ago when I gave a lecture he'd attended while a student there. He reminds me how the Jewish Defense League had threatened to blow up the lecture hall if I turned up and how the publicity given the threat in the campus paper had attracted three times as many people as would otherwise have attended.

"You never know with these Jews," he says simply. We are conversing in English.

I am taken aback by his bigoted tone. Palestinian intellectuals usually never throw the word Jews around like that. He could feel my discomfort.

"I mean that's what I call them," he says. "What do *you* call them?"

"I call them what they call themselves, Israelis," I respond.

"Israelis, Jews, Zionists, who cares? They're the enemy, all of them."

Mrs. Muntasir can see this conversation is going somewhere unpleasant. She passes around a plate of fruit and Raymond grabs a banana, peels it, and bites into it.

"What you've just said is bullshit," I say.

Raymond's jaw stops in mid-bite. He does not mistake the tone in my voice for anything other than insolence.

"I will never accept these people," he goes on, undaunted. "Why should I? Palestine is our country. The whole of Palestine, from the Mediterranean Sea to the Jordan River. The Jews here are intruders. They are usurpers. The only language the damn Jews understand is force. So we throw stones at them, and they shoot bullets at us. What's the point? We *should* use violence. Guns. That's the only language they understand, the only language they respond to," he concludes, his words tumbling over each other in an impassioned flourish.

I look at this man, and he just doesn't fit the picture of a terrorist, revolutionary, or underground conspirator. He is a middle-aged man with a lot of baby fat on his face, thinning hair, feminine features and gestures, and a sonorous voice that somehow does not carry the fury and venom he is trying to project.

I'm wondering if he's one of those many Palestinians who has been arrested, interrogated, beaten, tortured, and the rest, which may account for—if not justify—his stance. So I say: "Have you been arrested . . . and you know, sort of beaten up and stuff?"

"No, not me."

"Maybe, you know, humiliated and all?"

"Well, yes I was dragged out of a service cab by the Jews once," he says triumphantly. "No, twice!"

I want to change the subject.

"So where did you finally do your dissertation? At Yale?"

"No, actually I did it at En Why Jew, get it?" he offers, laughing at his own ready wit. "You know, NYU. I don't trust the damn Jews. You can't trust them. They are violent and wicked. Do you see my point?" He sits back in his seat, his arms held wide.

"I sure do," I say. The tone in my voice is level but does not hide my distaste. "As a matter of fact, Raymond, my daughter happens to be Jewish."

He looks at me blankly as I continue. "You see, her mother, my former wife, is Jewish, and Lisa, my daughter, is being raised Jewish by her. So your description of Jews fits Lisa all the way."

Raymond's face flushes crimson, and he responds meekly: "I didn't know."

An uneasy silence descends, as if my shocking revelation needed time to be absorbed.

"Are you married, Raymond?" I ask. I can pull some Palestinian banter too *and* change the subject.

"Yes, oh yes, I am," he hurries to respond, grateful I have deflected the conversation to a harmless tack. "I'm married to a Palestinian girl. Genevieve grew up in Haiti with a Palestinian father who left Bethlehem when he was fifteen and a Palestinian mother, also from Bethlehem, who grew up in Cuba."

"Any kids?"

"Oh yes, I live in the apartment on the third floor with my wife and two children, six and three, and a six-month-old baby. And oh, I mustn't forget the dog, Hunter. He's sick now, really. I think he's got pneumonia."

"How awful," I say, trying not to gag.

"You must come down and have dinner with us soon, before you leave," he says.

Yeah, sure, I'll even bring a date.

I take my leave of the Muntasirs and go back to my apartment.

•••

It is late afternoon. I sit in the sun-room and reflect on how differently people here live and think. Palestinians in the homeground have their own voice with its own particular timbre, and it is alien to me. Its hauntingly plaintive sounds hammer in vain on the locked gates of my psyche. I hear direct echoes, at times fierce in their clarity, but they are mockingly faint. Dealing with the savage agony of Palestinians here is for me like dealing with a new word that has just been added to the lexicon of the street; it has a tentative meaning still. I am a stranger to the homeground. I no longer feel the anguish and the tensions and the uncontrollable rage that Palestinians feel. I was afflicted with them too at one time, but I have long since gotten rid of them, throwing them away like broken toys. The mask I have worn all these years has become one with my skin.

I put on one of my tapes and listen to Jane's Addiction singing:

Motherfucking bad wind came

blew down my home

Now the green grass grows

Goddamn goodness knows

Where the green grass grows

There can't be wrong

Bumped my head, I am a battering ram

Goddamn took the pain

True leaders gone

of land and people

We choose no kin

but adopted strangers.

When I was in Haifa two weeks ago, aimlessly walking the city's streets, I felt, in a momentary eclipse of reason, that if I looked hard enough at the faces of men my age, I would spot Uri, the Jewish kid who lived on our street before we left in 1948. Hey, what's up, man? How you been, dude? Isn't it a damn shame they didn't leave us alone to grow up together, to go to each other's weddings and end up in a bar one night, smashed, drunkenly asking each other how the hell we had gotten so middle-aged all of a sudden. Instead, look at us, look at us. We've been doomed—by history, by nature, by God, who knows?—to parade our ethnicity around and to flaunt it through "national struggle." We've become so intoxicated by the rush from this shit called "national struggle" that—as my druggie friends in the District would put it—we're so up we can't get down. And look, Uri baby, don't pull rank on me with this pain shit. Your people suffered. My people suffered. So what? Let's form a secret cabal of sufferers and spout off at each other and the world. How about it? Look at how my people—oh, what a cold and intricate term this is—have allowed the politics of their present to master and corrupt their lives—at how your people have allowed the private anguish of their past to become ingrained in their habit of feeling. You want to know what happened to my people, or those I grew up with in exile? I'll tell you.

When I returned to Beirut in 1979, after a twenty-year absence, I met an old friend and asked what had become of the kids we had known in our teens.

Adnan, the kid whose dad was a storyteller, died on the streets—where else?—in one of the battles of the Lebanese Civil War, when he stepped on a live wire from a fallen lamppost. Walid returned from a Moscow University to join a PLO student brigade and was killed during an Israeli incursion into Lebanon. His body was never recovered. Salwa, Rustum's daughter, who was then living in Kuwait with her traditional Palestinian husband, a vicious brute, committed suicide by blowing herself up with a hand grenade. Massoud made it to Seattle, Washington, with a Ph.D. from Columbia University, got married, divorced, became an alcoholic, lived in an empty house in the suburbs—after his wife took away their kids, furniture, and savings—and was finally fired from his job as a professor. A fellow called Guy—there's a typical Palestinian name for you—went into partnership with a friend, opened a women's lingerie store (Victoria's Secret it wasn't, but it did well as a business) and, during an argument with his partner, was shot dead. Abdel Razzak spent twenty years in the Gulf slaving to make a fortune; finally he went to live in Geneva and married this gorgeous French woman who turned out to be a hooker. (When she came to divorce court to claim half of Abdel Razzak's fortune, the cops greeted her with: "Hey Maxine, haven't seen you around lately!") And me, well, *my* people's tradition followed me relentlessly even to the United States, to my exile within my other exile, demanding tribute for my wayward life. I was expected, like my sister Jasmine, to drink my poison. I did, but it didn't kill me. I had been too abused by time, I had been blunted at the whetstone of experience.

And look at *my* people here, Uri; just look at them. Their lives are not much better.

...

The sun had journeyed a great distance in the sky since I came back from the Muntasirs, climbing down to the horizon to sink in the Mediterranean. As dusk comes to these biblical hills outside my window, they begin to assume a bleak strangeness. A kind of lethargy arises from the land, even the trees, which lean inertly in all directions, as if mourning their surroundings or advertising how they too were fatigued by the rigors of life under occupation. A flock of birds gracefully circles in sweeping arabesques, up there in God's free sky, soaring and swooping, rising and falling, with dizzy abandon.

Outside, there is stillness. Soon the lights of Tel Aviv began to glitter in the distance. It is a different world there. Here, the people are about to go to sleep. No one defies the curfew. A few dogs bark in the distance. No other sounds. It seems like the end of the world. I think it one of the saddest scenes I have ever seen. I am reminded of the lyrics to Jim Morrison's song "The End," which so poignantly evoke the confusion and darkness in the human spirit.

Just then an army truck comes lumbering down the street, horn blaring—the sounds ringing out with frightening force in the stillness of the Palestinian night—on its way to the military governor's compound. As the truck passes, its headlights shine on the two-story house across from mine, illuminating a slogan on the wall: BURN THE LAND UNDER THE OCCUPIERS' FEET.

What an improbable outcry! The Palestinians barely possess a damp match! What they possess is merely a summation of meaning. Weighed down by tradition, however, this meaning is at once anarchic and helpless. Palestinians live constantly under its debilitating shadow. Yet some, like my sister, Jasmine, paid dearly for the encounter; others, like Randa, stepped outside its circle of damnation and were able to live defiantly, if only for a moment.

In Beirut, after my return in 1979, I had occasion to be at the Palestine Research and Arts Center (PRAC), a kind of Palestinian Smithsonian-in-exile that houses the largest collection of out-of-print books on Palestine, along with ancient manuscripts dealing with the country, samples of Palestinian silk embroidery from the eighteenth century, and the like. My business there was to see if an officer of the PRAC would help me with a book I was thinking about writing, which was to be an oral history of the 1936–1939 uprising in Palestine. The director of the center assigned me Randa, a thirty-one-year-old Palestinian woman, who was to work with me on the project over the next four weeks.

Randa had dark hair, smooth and shiny, and hazel eyes fringed with heavy black lashes. Her face was pretty, but it was a Palestinian face, with a hard, uncompromising edge to it. Palestinian faces, like the faces of other people, reflect the lives they live. During the first few days, Randa displayed a kind of invincible shyness around me, and in deference to social norms, I treated her with frigid gallantry. The decorum with which men and women interact here creates a necessary distance, and the words they use to speak about their feelings resound with the dread of the forbidden. Everything is forbidden here, including laughter, love, and revolution. If you dare to laugh and love and to revolt, tradition will drag you, feet first, to its inquisitors, who will honor you with their vengeance.

By the end of the week, we had both relaxed enough to deal with each other like two polite strangers meeting over a stalled car. By the middle of the second week, she started having to come to my hotel to inspect my documents, and we actually began laughing together. Of course, we worked in the lobby (where else?), but one day we ventured to my room on the top floor and found ourselves sitting there for as long as an hour. From then on, we worked only in my room. At times she would be so shocked at being alone with me, or so ashamed at having involuntarily touched my wrist, that she would suddenly retreat into the pose of a demure, blushful Palestinian woman comporting herself with sexual reticence and social propriety.

One day as she stood up, about to leave, I caught her looking at me. Rather, she gave me a look. A look that welled with deep reserves of feeling. A look that shimmered with erotic meaning. I pressed her to me, and she stiffened for the longest time.

"Please," she said simply, but her body relaxed. "Please. They will kill me."

For the next two weeks we made love every afternoon, but she always left in time to be back at her parents' place by the hour she was expected after work.

Our sex was not, as would have been prudent, stealthy and silent. Instead, it was brazen. It was as if we were in a placeless place where lovers were fearless and threw not a single furtive glance over their

shoulders. Ecstasy always came in torrents. The sighs she uttered—
even after our lovemaking was over—were violent and wild and with
a meaning all their own—sighs that broke the silence in the heart
and unmasked the darkness in tradition. Every time as we gathered
to a climax, she was like an incensed beast, thrusting and tossing,
grasping and hitting, ablaze with a long-dormant carnality.

One afternoon, she settled down on the rug, naked, her chin resting on her knees. "I love that," she said. "I love you."

"I love you too."

Making love to Randa was, well, different. I felt like a man who,
blind all his life, had suddenly regained his sight. The women I had
dated, made love to, and lived with in the States were, well, ordinary. They were like rest to a man who was not tired.

"I'm engaged to be married to a first cousin of mine who works in
Kuwait," Randa says, her chin still on her knees, looking straight
ahead through the window, as if at a world too far away to affect her.
"You see, I'm thirty-one and unmarried. My family and relatives and
friends and neighbors and colleagues all think I'm *maskeeneh*, over
the hill. So they got this cousin of mine. He's almost fifty."

Randa laughs bitterly to herself.

One afternoon, after making love, I dozed off for a minute and
woke up to find her stroking my face.

"Hi," I said.

"Hi," she responded cheerfully. "I have often wondered what it
would be like to watch a man sleeping beside me."

"Watch all you want."

"I want to dance."

"You want to dance?" I asked, looking at her quizzically.

"I want to dance," she repeated. "I want to dance now."

I chose a tape at random. Wilson Pickett sang, "I'm gonna wait till
the midnight hour, till my love comes tumbling down."

There is Randa, beautiful in her nakedness, dancing all by herself. She dances like a person whose body is permeated by music
and the drama of its language. There is Randa, beautiful in her
nakedness, I say, throwing off the constraints that tradition has
placed on women's sexuality, in her part of the world, stomping her
feet in vigorous motion, as if to crush a force dragging her to the
floor, and bending her body lustily backward and forward.

"I love this. I love you. I'm gonna wait till the midnight hour, till my love comes tumbling down," she howls, affecting a charged pause while she looks at me, her arms flung sensually over her head, and then jumps up and down again, as if in celebration of the sudden soaring of her spirit.

"I love this. I love you," she sings, puffing out her chest erotically, her breasts heaving up and down.

"They will kill me," she says before she leaves. "I'm terrified."

But Randa came back every day so we could be together, despite the terror—or maybe because of it. Terror has a kind of magnetism. It draws you seductively, and if you're crazy enough to respond, it will welcome you to an encounter with a logic other than that of reason.

On our last day together, I am wrought with grief.

"Come home with me," I plead with Randa. "Marry me. Come to the U.S. with me."

She sits on the edge of the bed, already getting dressed. Tears spill from her eyes and trickle down her cheeks.

"They will kill me," she says faintly, a wave of dizzy fear seeming to rise in her throat. She is now sobbing, and her shoulders lift and fall with every sob. "They will kill me."

They. They are the guardians of tradition. Our repellent tradition. *They* are the sleepless guardians that deny us sleep, with eyes that see without being seen.

"Please come with me. Today. Come with me now. Let's get you out of this fucking hell now. Let's fly outta here this minute."

More sobs.

She adjusts her skirt around her waist. Her waist is a mere trifle.

"Come with me!" I'm almost shouting.

"They'll kill me. You don't understand Palestinians. You've been away too long."

"Fuck Palestinians. I hate them."

God, what was that I've just said? Was that me who just uttered these words? Yes, it was. It was from my own lips, my own heart, that the resounding indictment had come.

Leave me alone. You have taken my little sister away from me because she was a dreamer, and now you want to take my love away because she's a freedom fighter.

Leave those of us who want to be dreamers, who want to be free, alone. Leave us alone to go behind the mountains searching for our dreams and to dance lustily to our songs.

"Goddam it, Randa, come with me."

"You don't understand," she says, now soberly, wiping away the tears. "You don't understand. You've been away too long. I am engaged. I'm already engaged. I'm engaged to be married to my first cousin. There is no question, no question whatsoever, that I could break my engagement. I'm engaged to my first cousin. My first cousin is my first choice for a husband. That's the way it is. Moreover, the donkey is coming from Kuwait soon for the wedding, and he's bringing gold with him. He has a lot of gold." She laughs at that.

"Randa, please listen to me."

She pauses. "What do *you* have?" she asks mockingly, bitterly, pitifully.

"Randa, please."

"What do *you* have?"

"Randa." My voice is a resigned whisper.

We hug tearfully in the middle of the room. Then she walks to the door, opens it, and leaves without looking back.

I notice later that she has forgotten to take her black silk scarf with her. There it is, clinging to the chair by a thread. I look at it for the longest time, waiting for it to fall any second. When it doesn't, I walk to the door and close it quietly, afraid it might fall off.

I left Beirut the following day without finishing my project. I had no connection to this place, not even to members of my family, whom I didn't see. My younger brother, Samir, was now living in France. And my mother, whom I would have wanted to visit, was living with my older brother, Mousa, and his own miserable family. And I'm not so sure that I wouldn't have killed Mousa if I came face to face with him. He may have been a victim of his own culture, and he may have done what he did to my sister because that's what tradition has dictated since time immemorial. But there was no forgiveness in my heart.

However, I did speak to my mother on the phone.

"How you doing, Mom?"

"Oh, my son, I miss you so. Come and see us all."

"I can't, Mom."

"What are you doing nowadays, my obedient son?"

"Mom, I'm a writer."

"Oh, I know, I know, I saw your picture in that American magazine, and we're so proud of you," she gushes. "But what do you do for a living?"

Other than stringing words together, I do nothing for a living. But I don't tell her that.

"Did you visit Jasmine's grave?" she wants to know.

"Yes, Mom, I did."

"And your dad's grave?"

"Yes, Mom, I did that too."

"Did you read the proper *suras* from the Koran?"

Yes, whatever *suras* referred to a poor man who never knew what had hit him.

"Are you keeping yourself warm in America, my son?" she asks, genuinely concerned. "Most illnesses are caused by the cold, you know."

"Mom, I gotta go now, bye."

I have not seen or spoken to my mother again.

Mother was right. Most illnesses are caused by the cold.

And when Betty Clark and Ray Charles sang, *baby it's cold outside*, they weren't talking about the weather.

...

Outside, inky blackness has come to another Palestinian night under curfew. Ramallah is asleep. Am I the only person still up in this town, pondering things Palestinian? The heater in the sunroom gives a strange buzzing noise. I still feel sadness about Randa. Your cousin has gold, my love, but I have words. Goddamn it, I have words. Gold, like war, eats men and the soul God gave them. Words show us how to reach for our image in the cracked mirror of creation. Randa. I continue, in vain, to shake my head with mute revulsion at tradition. Jasmine. My lovely little sister. I see you in every screaming horse in *Guernica*. I derive meaning so rich and cruel from what you both have done—from your rites of defiance, your commitment to freedom.

Fuck this land and its bruised spirit. Fuck its pack of misery. Its authority. Its reason. Its history. Fuck its flamboyant gestures of nobility. And fuck its name. For behind that elegant name, this land has concealed all that is shallow and murderous.

I get rid of myself for the next eight hours by going to sleep.

...

By the second day of curfew, I am tired of being lost in my morbid reflections on the meaning of occupation and the impressive ease with which the occupier can impose curfews. I turn on the television. I get an Israeli soap opera, which, of course, I don't understand. I switch to another station and get Damascus. A plump, scantily clad lady, with layers of flesh dangling over her lacy chiffon, sings lustily about love. Behind her are three equally fat, scantily dressed ladies doing the old belly twist to the accompaniment of sonorous tablas and oud. I switch again and get Amman, and there is this little, bald twit reading poetry. Fine, I like poetry. But I discover that his poem, recited in the manner of a song, is about his love affair with his city of birth, "my Amman." In a voice choking with emotion, drama, and pathos, he recites, "the rose of my heart, Oh Amman, you are the moon that does not sleep." The oud music in the background gets louder. "The birds fly," our poet, whose name was given as Habib Zay Wadi—literally, Lover from the Valley—is singing, "carrying with them my sadness when I'm away from you, Oh, Amman." The poem goes on in that vein, mercilessly with no commercial interruptions, for well over twenty minutes. I loved it. The whole thing was so bad that it was good. And imagine, all that panegyric was for Amman—the armpit of the world. After our Lover from the Valley is finished with his recital, the evening news comes on. The broadcast is as comical as the poem was. The news is, all in all, twenty minutes. The first seven, always, are devoted to what the king and other members of the royal family have done that day, complete with the full title of each member. Here is "His Royal Highness, Prince Hassan, Crown Prince of the Hashemite Kingdom of Jordan, and may the Lord Almighty Allah in Heaven safeguard his health and well-being," having a good time sailing on his yacht in the Gulf of Aqaba with his wife and children (each one of whose titles is given); the queen receiving representatives of the Boy Scouts of Zanzibar visiting Jordan; the king hosting a dinner for the ambassador from Malawi; some other obscure prince being greeted by Jordanian dignitaries at the airport upon his return from an overseas trip. Only when this is over do we get the news about the

Baker-Aziz meeting in Geneva. For the forecast, the weatherman predicts rain the following day, "God willing." No wonder Jordanians—tuned-in Jordanians—never tune in to that nonsense but instead listen to the Arabic broadcasts on the BBC, Radio Monte Carlo, or the Voice of America.

•••

Before the curfew was lifted, I was to meet most of my neighbors, who dropped by (often laden with food) to visit or invite me to their homes for dinner. (During curfew, there was no danger, living as I did in a building with ten apartments in it, of spending lonely, dull, or uneventful days.) I was also to learn what it was like to be a Palestinian living under occupation: I would experience the hysterical, raw fear of soldiers breaking into my apartment in the middle of the night.

The next day of curfew was sunny. The winter morning light glinted on the timeless hills. There was insouciant calm everywhere. Deadly, stultifying calm. How could people live like this, I keep asking myself, locked up in their homes like tormented vermin?

•••

Akram, the Palestinian-American kid I toured Jerusalem with, also lives in the building with his parents and four sisters. His dad, Karim Maher, is a prominent psychologist—or is so recognized in the West Bank—and has just returned from South Africa, where he participated in a conference attended by Third World psychologists. Maher's paper on the psychology of the oppressed had been eagerly awaited by his fellow psychologists, who are struggling to find—as the theme of the conference called for—a new paradigm for dealing with the mark of oppression in the postcolonial world that will depart from the cant of Western scientific materialism. They felt that they could learn from the Palestinian experience.

Tonight I'm invited for dinner at their home. One of Akram's four sisters, Jamila, twenty-three, married to a fellow of twenty-seven who looks like a teenager, is also there with her husband. They live in the building. (That's how it is with Palestinians. They don't stray too far from kith and kin.) Ibrahim Mousa, a man in his seventies, is there with his bride of twenty, and his thirty-year-old son from his first wife—to whom he is still legally married. Mousa is dressed in the traditional attire of *shirwal* and the *hatta* headdress. He has an improbably huge, jet-black moustache. Even Raymond, that pompous little racist, is invited along with his wife, Genevieve, and their two older boys.

When I walk into the Mahers' apartment, everybody is already there. The seductive odors of Palestinian cooking waft through the entire place.

"You'll have dinner with us, my son," Mrs. Maher says to me in the way of a greeting, "and may it be one of many you'll share with our family."

The Mahers' apartment, like most other Palestinian homes, is furnished tackily and haphazardly. But the energy, the energy of a people who feel—temporarily—safe inside their shuttered home, is evident everywhere. Everybody here, all the people in this living room, seem genuinely happy, secure, free. There is shared laughter and a sense of intimacy. This sense of an enfolding nexus binding these Palestinians together is brought here, as if by magic, from another place, another time. It stands in stark contrast to the social and cultural chaos outside—all the pain that is endemic to native life.

At the dinner table, everybody is talking at once. At home, or wherever Palestinians are out of earshot of the border police and occupation soldiers, they erupt into speech. Torrential speech. Words are the only property the occupier cannot expropriate, their only inviolate sanctuary. The gush of words is chaotic. It comes from every direction. No one is listening to anyone, and everyone is interrupting. Words are hurled back and forth across the table with abandon, laughter, and wild gestures. I find I cannot plunge into it, as I honestly want, heart and soul, even for a moment. I don't want to be a stranger among those I should know best. But I can't. The words are stringently idiomatic. I understand them. I can even say them. But I cannot affect their penetrative cunning, their laconic hilarity. In the West Bank, this type of environmental vernacular, with its emphasis on defiance, constitutes the prime unit of a social energy that remains alien to me. The charged vitality of this vernacular, which Palestinians display sparingly when foreigners are around, has organized and shaped their inner history. It is as if they don't want any outsiders to be privy to its semantic conventions. And the manners of ceremonial exchange at a Palestinian social gathering like this! These are forcefully drawn in accordance with primacies of age, class, social status, gender. Only if you have grown up here and absorbed it all, as it were, by osmosis, would you know who can interrupt whom in a discussion, who is addressed by first name and who is not, who reaches for the first cup of coffee off the tray, who brings an evening to an end, and the rest of it.

Over sweets and coffee, Jamila, who like Akram himself and his three other sisters was born in the States, and whose Arabic is almost as bad as mine, is explaining bitterly how her husband, a bio-chemist, was offered a Fulbright scholarship for the second time, and how for the second time the Israelis refused him permission to leave the West Bank.

"How come?" I ask, in English.

"How come! How come!" she demands, responding in English, in wild anger, pausing for a moment, as if shocked at the harsh tone in her voice. "Because the pigs arrested him once."

I haven't heard that term since my hippie days in the Sixties.

Jamila's husband, it seems, had belonged to a political faction—as most Palestinian activists did—and on a visit to Amman once in 1987 had met and talked about the situation in the West Bank with certain PLO leaders. Upon his return, he was "arrested by the pigs."

"I was locked up for eight days," Jamila's husband takes it up, his voice strong but matter-of-fact. "I was made to stand naked in my cell. There was no toilet in there. There was shit all over the floor. I had my arms tied behind my back. I couldn't sleep. And I was con-stantly being punched and kicked in the balls. I had no food or water the first twenty-four hours. After the first eight days I was sent to a comparatively better cell. I was there for three months. And they would knock on my door at 2:00 A.M., at 2:00 P.M., and any time between—any time they felt like it—for interrogation. Then I went to trial, accused of meeting with a proscribed group. I got one and a half years in jail. My uncle on my mother's side went on trial that same day, in the same court, for the same offense. He got twelve years."

I sit there stiffly, dully, looking at this youthful-looking old man, being so matter-of-fact about his pain, and I realize how mockingly remote my own Palestinian experience is from his.

"Hey, that's nothing!" says Ibrahim Mousa, the old man, whose name translates as Abraham Moses. He lets the observation hang in the air until he reaches for his cup of coffee and takes a sip, a smirk appearing behind the fierce moustache. Mr. Moses, who owns a large orange grove outside Ramallah, is dark brown, with a bronzed face. The color of his skin appears to be the result of constant exposure to the elements.

"You want to see what they do to the kids they catch on military operations," he thunders, between aggressive puffs on his cigarette, looking like the angered Moses he was. "One of them is my sister's son, Rustum. They tortured him with electric shock. No sleep for days on end. With a hood over his face. For months on end, they did that to him. And may the Lord pour acid on their souls and banish them to the hell of the devil's *johanam*. The boy was a vegetable when they released him. He was clinically catatonic. And may the Lord burn down their religion, their land, and the house their ancestors had built. He could no longer function as a human being. He would eat if you fed him. If you gave him a cigarette, he would smoke it until it burned his lips or you took it away from him. He would go to the toilet only if you took him there. Otherwise he would do it in his pants. He is no longer with us as Rustum. Before his arrest, he had shown such promise as a scholar. He was engaged to be married. He had such a future before him. The Israelis inflicted so much pain not only on Rustum but, by extension, on his parents, on his brothers and sisters, on his friends. Well, I for one, I, Ibrahim Mousa, will never forgive them. Not as long as I live. And though I know that I cannot punish them, I know God will. For He will see to it that in their next life, they will be born Palestinian."

"Well, that's the Jews for you!" Raymond puts in vehemently. "They're all like that, I tell you. Barbarous, they are, that's what."

"That's not true, Raymond," Akram's other sister, seventeen-year-old Jawhara, says. *Jawhara* means "diamond," which I find a cute name, befitting this cute girl from Cleveland.

Jawhara tells us the story of three teenage Palestinian girls, friends of hers, who had been arrested and beaten up by occupation soldiers in a demonstration. Since the girls were discovered under interrogation to have belonged to political factions, they were tried and each sentenced to one and a half years and placed in a prison where there were also Israeli women prisoners. One of these was an eighteen-year-old Israeli girl who had been given a long sentence for stabbing and killing her boyfriend. Ironically, her boyfriend was a soldier doing his stint in the West Bank at a base outside Tulkarem, the very town these three girls were from. She came from a well-to-do Israeli family and hadn't done anything illegal in her life. Her boyfriend used to beat her up every time he came home on leave, so one night she couldn't, or wouldn't, take it anymore. She pulled out a kitchen knife and stabbed him to death. Somehow the Israeli girl, and the three Palestinian girls, who were the same age, became friends.

"This Israeli girl used to cry all the time," Jawhara says, "and every time she cried, our girls cried right along with her. I guess they became bosom buddies. They would console her. Put her to bed. Even tuck her in. My three friends are out now, but they correspond with her."

"Well, when she's out," again Raymond butts in with one of his infantile observations, this one mercifully not racist, "she'll become one of our supporters."

"May you be damned by both your parents, Raymond," Jawhara responds flippantly, using a typical Palestinian expression of chastisement. "Leave politics out of this."

"I agree," says our host, Dr. Maher. "I feel the Israeli girl and the Palestinian girls became friends because they shared each other's humanity, and they shared it at a level that transcends politics."

Suddenly, Ibrahim Moses says loudly: "Okay, let's see the kids dance!"

Singing and dancing are an indispensable part of a successful evening like this. It is almost inconceivable in a family gathering of this kind, bringing together friends and neighbors, children and adults, not to have at least one person performing, even if it's only a poetry recital. So Dr. Maher puts on some folk music, and suddenly at least five people are up, holding hands in the folk dance circle, and stomping their feet to *dabki* (folk music) tunes. Jawhara sings lustily. And then everybody is singing along. It is as if where the occupation devours, music exalts and heals. Where occupation dehumanizes by the formality of its rules, music liberates by its form. Where politics merely unites Palestinians in community, music brings them together in communion. *Dabki* and *mawal* (the Palestinian equivalent of the blues) are a genuine lingo that speaks against, denies, the silence imposed by successive occupiers. Their rhythm is as much a part of Palestinian life as the smell of the crops is part of the rhythm of the land.

I join in. And I dance. And I sing. And I no longer feel, if only for a moment, a stranger among those I should know best.

...

When I return to my apartment, it is already close to eleven o'clock. That's a late evening. Ten minutes later, the power goes off. I think it has gone off in my apartment, or in my building, but when I look out the window I see that the power is off all over town. With the heat off, my apartment gets to be like an icebox within half an hour. It is a bitterly cold night—the coldest night on record in a decade, as I was later to discover. Outside, the wind howls with fury. Inside, the cold begins to slice to the very marrow of my bones. I'm freezing. I haven't been this cold in a long time. And it keeps getting colder as the heat, which had been diffused by the shoebox heater during the few hours I spent at the Mahers', is sucked away every minute. I put my duffle coat on. I put my gloves on. Then I throw two blankets over me. Now I begin to shiver less. I use my lighter to look for candles but can't find any. So I just sit in the sun-room, waiting for the power to come on again, and watch the lights of Tel Aviv twinkling in the distance. Again I'm reminded of how there is another world out there, and this world here. I don't know if the twain shall meet. I belong to neither world. Now I know it. I am not, or at least no longer am, part of the Palestinian world. Exile and the homeground speak to each other unintelligibly. I am a stranger to those I should know best. Palestinians here are in search of a homeland. I already have one. My search is for a sense of at-homeness, a connectedness to my roots. Though my identity had long since connected itself to new circuits, this passion to return had wound itself in dizzy patterns all around that new identity. Like other exiles, I was driven from one language to another, from one culture to another. The transition brought deep shifts in my sensibility that cannot be corrected. You cannot think in one language and feel in another. And yet there is identity and meaning in our world because there is shared being. Without responding to its summons, if only once in a lifetime, we stand shattered, alone, disconnected.

...

On the third and last night of curfew, I was woken by violent sounds in the street. I had been dreaming I was caught in the streets of

London during the Second World War in the midst of a German bombardment. Bombs were falling all over the place and buildings blowing up all around me. People were running into shelters to escape the carnage. Every time I went to a shelter to seek refuge, the guards at the entrance would tell me the place was full. I kept going from one to another, increasingly petrified, until I discovered I was standing alone in the street, the only man denied access to a shelter. The feeling was terrifying.

When I woke up, this feeling of terror clung to me as I looked out the window and saw army trucks parked outside the building, with lights and loudspeakers and armed soldiers.

Inside the building, soldiers and plainclothes police were knocking on doors, and my neighbors were standing around inside and outside their apartments in their pajamas, clutching babies and holding on to children. Suddenly there was violent knocking on my own front door and the back door leading to the kitchen.

I felt my skin creep, not with the cold, not even with fear—that was to come later—but with the dreadful abruptness of it all. Why would they want to knock on *my* door? What do *I* have to do with any of this tiresome nonsense going on in the West Bank? It was truly unnerving because the knocking on both doors was simultaneous, and I didn't know which door to open first. Jesus—and this was happening in an upper-class neighborhood in one of the most prosperous, least pugnacious towns in the West Bank, whose population had shown a limited confrontational posture with the occupation. What do they do in refugee camps?

So I'm looking for the keys to open both doors. In the West Bank, for reasons known only to local locksmiths, you need your key to open doors to your apartment from the inside.

All of a sudden, I can't find the keys. Where are the keys? Where are the fucking keys?

There is bang, bang on my front door. And bang, bang on my back door.

Okay, okay, I'm coming, I am coming! I shout from inside my apartment, after I find the keys and go to let the soldiers in, my hands trembling all the while.

Two soldiers come in through the front door and another two, accompanied by a plainclothesman, from the back. They are, of course, armed. They converge on the living room. There are other soldiers in the other apartments in the building simultaneously doing the same thing. I don't know if any of my neighbors were experiencing the terror I was. I am told that they are used to it by now. They see it all, I'm told, as an inconvenience—unpardonable to be sure, but an inconvenience nonetheless. Palestinians tell me they have become immune to fear. The bestial element in their lives has become routinized. It exacts from its victims nausea, disbelief, and anger, but not fear, they say. I don't believe them.

Palestinians have developed a habit. It's like an itch. When you're with them in the street, you see how, every five minutes or so, they reach into their pockets to check for their ID cards. If you're caught without one, you're dumped in jail and stay there until someone notices you're missing, locates you, and returns with your ID. I would be in a service cab, or a private car, with five guys and I would see them, from time to time, feeling in their breast pockets, hip pockets, back pockets, inside jacket pockets for their IDs. After a while I started doing that too.

Under occupation, notwithstanding what Palestinians tell you, you feel fear. It's so palpable you can almost see it. At times you can almost smell it. I've never been in a place like this before. I've never known a place like this. I've never heard of a place like this. It is a place whose very soul is so subverted by incessant terror, by the anarchy of limitless fear, that you watch over your own thoughts lest they be heard by an omniscient occupier.

That is what the experience of having armed Israelis break into my home in the middle of the night is exacting from me now. Absolute fear, coupled with a flash of controlled hysteria.

The four soldiers and their Shin Beit or secret police escort are doing a kind of wolf's prowl around me, circling, mumbling to each other in Hebrew. A chill comes over my body. They are all young, in their early twenties. One of them, surprisingly, is a woman. I was under the impression that women soldiers did not serve in the West Bank. I didn't know whether she was there for the ride or whether women soldiers did in fact serve in the occupied territories, at least in this capacity. She is dark and oriental looking, probably from Morocco, with an angular face that is at once handsome and plain. The soldier next to her, apparently the leader, has a tuft of blond hair over his lip.

He addresses me in Hebrew, and I respond in English, controlling the sound of my voice, which I disguise by a calm I far from feel: "I'm American, okay? What the hell is going on, man? I mean this is a goddamn outrage."

"Please?" he asks.

My palms grow damp. I put my left hand in my pocket and the other on the knob of the glass door leading to the dining room, for it was a matter of great consequence to me that I not be seen trembling.

"You are from America?" he asks.

"Yes, yes I am. I am American," I say, feeling a new strength coming to me uttering the word, as if it had some healing effect on my nerves.

"Please, I see your passport?"

I show it to him.

He looks at it and his eyes narrow. "This, this here," he points to my place of birth in the passport, looking genuinely puzzled. "This Palmyra Atoll where you are born. Palmyra Atoll, is this a country or a town?"

Palmyra Atoll is the State Department's code name for Palestine or, for all I know, for countries that, like Palestine, no longer exist as states. When I first saw it on my passport, I was incensed. How dare they? Born on a goddamn atoll? What am I, a fucking seal? But in later years, I actually came to like it. When I traveled overseas and had to fill out forms that included a question about my place of birth, I came to love putting down Palmyra Atoll.

"This is a town in California," I tell the soldier.

He seems satisfied and returns my passport.

"Okay now, so what can I do for you?" I ask.

"Please?"

"I mean, like, what do you want?"

"Inspection. We inspect."

"Can we get this over and done with fast?" I demand gruffly. I'm beginning to feel much better now. This kid looks harmless. He might have been one of my students at SUNY in Buffalo when I was there as a writer-in-residence.

But the Shin Beit guy thinks I have an attitude problem.

"Inspection. We inspect," he says imperiously, his words menacing, threatening dire retribution. "We inspect all the time. Every time. Anytime. Inspection."

Inspection? Who gave you the right to inspect our homes on whim? How about less inspection and more introspection? How about that?

"Okay, inspect all you want," I tell them impatiently.

The Shin Beit guy goes off with the three male soldiers to rummage around in my host's drawers, closets, and bookshelves. And I'm standing there in the living room with the woman soldier. For about five minutes we confront each other in electric silence.

"Hey, do you speak any English?"

"A bit," she says wearily.

"So what's your name?" I ask, after I give her mine. That's what we do in the States, right? Introduce ourselves when we meet.

"Zahra," she offers sluggishly, not wanting to converse. Then she adds, as an afterthought: "You're an Arab."

"I am a Palestinian."

"I thought you were," she says in a voice like ice with a self-satisfied finality. When I try to engage her in further banter, she does not respond.

We're standing in the living room, just the two of us. There is a sensuousness about her that I find both explicit and menacing. The rawness of it plays directly on my nerves. For just a moment, my imagination obeys the impulse in me that her sensuousness has triggered. I'm dazzled by the cruel magic of it.

When the soldiers are gone—they were not really there with the expectation of finding subversive literature or deadly weapons but simply to harass and intimidate—I go back to bed.

Before I fall off to sleep again, I wonder to myself if this society, after such a long and numbing encounter with horror, will ever acquire a vigorous sense of equilibrium.

6

The Stones in the Wall

When the curfew was lifted on the third day, my host, Salem, returned home early that evening, clutching a bottle of Johnny Walker Black.

"I intend to get smashed," he announced with finality.

"It's nice to know that *someone* drinks in this country."

"You'll have a drink with me later?" he asked.

"No man, I can't," I said with equal finality. "As we say at AA, I'm now clean and sober. I'm an alcoholic and an addict, you see. One drink of that stuff and I'm history."

"What is that, AA?"

I explain, but I'm not sure he gets it. People who have a problem with booze and drugs are not a social phenomenon here.

"I haven't slept for two days," he says, looking and sounding as if he hadn't. "I'm off to bed."

In less than ten minutes, he is snoring contentedly.

At dawn, I am up with the *muazzen* calling the faithful to prayer. I open my eyes and find Salem standing in his pajamas in the sunroom with a blanket draped over him, staring into the distance at Tel Aviv and the Mediterranean, on which a half moon blazed. He is holding a glass of scotch.

"What the hell!" I hear myself saying, for no apparent reason, as I come out of a deep sleep.

Salem must have heard me, for he suddenly turns and walks a few steps toward the living room where I slept on a mattress on the floor. He stands for a moment in the dark before he says: "Watching that sea, brother, watching that Mediterranean. Always instills wonder in me. This ancient sea of ours has a magic to it. It is as if it has a soul, an ancient soul, all its own. Do you have the same feeling about it? You were born in Haifa and grew up in Beirut, so the Mediterranean must say something to you."

It does! It does. Our sea says more to me than the land. I never knew the land of Palestine, but the Mediterranean Sea was in me. I remember how, after I left Beirut and went to live in the Australian bush, I would think about it from time to time and would feel a sudden urge to be by the water, just to watch the waves and smell the salt and see the sun set and stare at the horizon. And so I would find myself, like an aboriginal Australian going on walkabout, dropping everything and running to the nearest coastal town.

When I left the Arab world in my late teens, I had given up everything, even my language; but what stayed in me was the Mediterranean. I left it, but it didn't leave me. It has had a way of storing and responding to our memories. That's how it has always been, as the waves fought the wind, and the wind fought the earth, and the earth fought man, and man fought man, and short wars followed long wars, and aggressive societies followed docile societies, and night followed day, ever since the first human culture sunk its roots here. Just as we have often spoken of our self and willed it on reality, so has our sea projected its self on our destiny and slowly, like the coming into form of a poem, given us more than just our name.

We sit there in the sun-room, Salem and I, and watch the sea as he gets progressively smashed.

"It's very difficult to explain, even to myself, why I came back here to live," he says. "I could've stayed in the United States, gotten a good job as an engineer, and lived the good life. But I prefer to be here, and I can't explain it. It's like trying to explain to someone from New York why you prefer to live in Kansas. I run around the West Bank helping the families of prisoners—the families of the martyrs, as we call them—and the families of those whose land has been expropriated. I get to save 2000 *dunums* here, 500 *dunums* there, from confiscation by the Israelis. I get experts and lawyers to testify in court that the land truly belongs to those who are cultivating it—

that it is not so-called state land—and that it is arable and productive already. If I save just a few *dunums* of land every year that's enough. That's important to me. I don't care about the PLO leadership outside anymore. I don't care about their corruption and their ineptitude. The mother of a boy who had been shot comes to me for help, or the wife of a man, a man who is the only bread earner in the family, comes to me for help—well I help them by dipping into the Fatah fund that I have access to. That is important to me."

Five minutes after all the *muazzens* had finished their call to prayer from various mosques in town, our local *muazzen* starts his call. He must have slept in this morning. Moreover, as if feeling guilty about his tardiness, he turns up the volume on his loudspeaker to the max. The sound is deafening. Salem and I can't talk until he finishes, so my host goes to the kitchen for another hefty refill of his scotch.

I admire Salem's idealism, his decision to return. I cannot be like him. To begin with, my sensibility is centrally conditioned by a transnational view of the world and of my place in it. My imagination, my use of metaphor, my emotional reach, may still be rooted to this place, but my mind has freed itself from whatever rational bonds it may have had with it. For those few Palestinians who have refused to be blackmailed into silence by traditional values in our culture, our struggle can be waged only from the periphery. The center will not tolerate an adversarial current. There is no chance that I would return here to live. In fact, there is no chance that I *could* return here to live. In the eyes of the Israelis I am part of the crowd of '48 and have no rights beyond those accorded a tourist, since I am a Palestinian who was born in a town that, after 1948, became part of Israel. The million or so Palestinian refugees who fled their homeland that year have no right of repatriation whatsoever. Palestinians from "the crowd of '67," however, that is, Palestinians from the West Bank and Gaza, are able to live here and can leave and return when they please.

•••

"You know I spent two years in Beirut in a Fatah cadre," Salem continues after he returns. "That was in 1980. The PLO pretty much controlled Lebanon, except for those areas already dominated by the Syrian army and the Phalangist militias. We controlled the whole of West Beirut and the South, all the way from Damour to the Israeli border. I saw enough in those two years to turn me off everything we call the movement, the resistance, the revolution, the organization—the lofty names the PLO loves to be called by. It was none of these things. It was a racket. Or at least it had, by that time, degenerated into one. When I was a teenager in 1968 and our local guerrillas would mount a military operation against Israeli soldiers, all of us kids used to go to the spot and go down on the ground and kiss it, because that was where our resistance fighters had left their footprints. We all wanted to be fighters. All of us kids wanted to join the resistance and struggle for freedom. As it turned out, most of us did. I sure did. I joined a Fatah underground cell. We were all dreamers then. We really believed we had a genuine liberation movement and that it was our duty to join, even die for it."

Salem goes for yet another drink. Outside, the streets are already full of traffic.

"What I saw in the South was revolting. Most of our top PLO people—and I say most but not all—were involved, very simply, in rape, smuggling, even murder. I'm talking about military men, political commissars, bureaucrats, officials, you name it. Everybody. There was this one guy, Abu Zaim, which means father of all leaders, and may the Lord curse him who gave him the name. Well, one day he raped this girl. I forgot whether she was Palestinian or Lebanese. And for some reason, the news leaked out, and a scandal erupted. So Abu Zaim was called to Beirut to answer charges leveled against him by the Fatah Central Committee. The man was so arrogant, or so stupid, that when he was questioned by journalists, he laughed uproariously and said: 'Imagine, the whole Central Committee of Fatah is meeting to discuss my dick!' And mind you, Abu Zaim was the first to desert his post, leaving his men behind, after the 1982 invasion of Lebanon by the Israelis. Around the time I was in Lebanon, there were 60,000 *motaferegheen*, that's full-time PLO officials, functionaries, clerks, bureaucrats, journalists, on the payroll. And these people, whether in Beirut or the South, cared little about the cause. Or if some of them started out caring, they no longer cared. The good guys, the true revolutionaries and patriots, had long since left the movement in disgust or withdrew into cynicism and alienation. And the armed militias in the South, well, they were just as bad. I can tell you what used to happen in Sidon. You know Sidon, right?"

Sidon is a town in the South, halfway between Beirut and the Israeli border. Populated predominantly by Sunni Moslems, it has a long history of being a Nasserite, pan-Arabist town whose politically involved population actively advocated the integration of all Arabs, regardless of their regional backgrounds, into one united Arab nation. Its association with Palestinians goes back centuries to the time when people in the coastal towns of Haifa, Acre, and Jaffa in Palestine, and Sidon in Lebanon, thought of themselves as one people. They traded with each other, traveled freely to each other's cities, and intermarried constantly. During the struggle for Palestine in the 1930s and 1940s, a lot of Sidonites joined their Palestinian cousins in the fight against the British, and later the Zionists. So when the Palestinian exodus took place in 1948 and the refugees from the north of Palestine began to arrive in Sidon, they were received with open arms. And when Palestinian fighters began to arrive in Sidon in the middle of the 1970s, after their expulsion from Jordan, they found a town wildly supportive of their cause. It didn't take long for that sentiment to shift. In 1980, there were violent demonstrations in Sidon calling for the expulsion of PLO cadres. More violent demonstrations followed, and continued until the week before the Israeli invasion.

"There was no law and order in the town," continued Salem. "The armed men from the various factions, well, they wrote the law, which was no law at all, and they defined order, which was disorder. That's all they were, outlaws, or at least that's all they had become. Those armed men would go into restaurants and expect to eat for free, go into a tailor's and expect to be clothed. When they went into a grocery store, they would tell the storekeeper, after they picked what they wanted, 'I'll pay you later, brother.' Of course the man knew no payment was to be expected. And those fellows manning checkpoints, in both the South and Beirut! Whoever recruited these people was determined to alienate the Lebanese from the Palestinians at any cost. They were there merely to harass and intimidate. They would stop drivers and demand to see their ID, be rude to them, push them around, call them names, and so on. You do that repeatedly, day in, day out, and you're going to earn the resentment, if not the enmity, of the people.

Salem sips his drink and stares into the distance. "I mean, who the hell are Palestinians to push the Lebanese around in their own country?" he asks vehemently. "A joke went around that the Lebanese needed a green card—like alien residents in America do—to live in their own country, and needed to get it from the Palestinians. I remember this little pimply-faced kid, sitting on top of his jeep at a checkpoint in suburban Beirut, waving drivers on with his foot. Well, you know what it means in our part of the world to wave your foot at someone, especially with your shoes on. That's the biggest insult. The main problem here was not these kids but the guys from the PLO who recruited them. These guys, not being the trained, informed, sophisticated revolutionaries they claimed to be, did not realize that before you arm and send out a guerrilla into the streets you have to educate him about the awesome responsibility that comes with the privilege of carrying a weapon. These fools didn't realize that sending armed men into the streets should have been an opportunity for them to make friends for the cause they were serving. They should've trained these fellows to be pleasant, friendly, helpful to drivers, to act as if they were there to protect them, not to act like overlords. I could see the writing on the wall, brother. I could see it all. The whole system was disintegrating. Chaos reigned supreme. Law and order were nonexistent. There were people, including guerrillas, breaking into empty houses and apartments and squatting there. There were feuds erupting all the time, often resulting in shootouts between the guerrillas over turf. The *massouleen* of the guerrillas, as their commanders were known, were just as bad. Indeed worse. They had no morals. No revolutionary ethics. They were thugs. They were not above abusing the mothers, the daughters, or the wives of our fallen patriots who would go to pick up their monthly pensions at their offices. They were not above using their authority to pressure these poor women into going to bed with them. The bastards. The *bastards*. May the Lord take away their honor and destroy the houses that their ancestors built. Those bastards didn't care that the women, the poor refugee camp women, had given their sons, their husbands, their brothers for the cause."

He falls silent for a moment as he sips his drink. "What did *they* give?" he asks rhetorically. "What did *they* give, I ask you? They didn't give, I can tell you. I was there, man. I saw it all.

"I leave our cause now in the hands of God, or in the hands of the devil, or in the hands of others. I leave it there because when it was left in our hands, it disintegrated. The first lesson a guerrilla must learn, the first role he must play, is that he has a duty to gain the love, the trust, and the respect of the people in whose midst he's operating. Once he loses that, he is lost. His cause is lost. And that's what happened in Lebanon in 1982 on the eve of the Israeli invasion and our expulsion from the country. By that time, the very structure, the very function, of our movement had become so rotten that the South was a walkover for the Israeli army. To be sure, there were a few pockets of heroic resistance here and there, mostly in the refugee camps, but that's where the people, left leaderless and fragmented, were defending their homes and their womenfolk. And the military commanders—may the Lord curse those who gave them that title—just ran off and left their own people to fend for themselves.

"We made the same mistakes in Jordan in 1970 where we were just as haughty, just as arrogant, and just as stupid as in Lebanon. You will remember that by 1970, directly after the battle of Karameh two years before, a pivotal event that had given us the takeoff, and earned us the popularity, for our movement, we had become literally a state within a state. But instead of using that power to gain the support of the Jordanian masses, we did everything in our power to alienate them, to turn them against us. Again the checkpoints! Foolish armed men at checkpoints stopping cars and harassing pedestrians. They would stop a Jordanian soldier, ask for his ID, intimidate him, and on some occasions take his weapon away from him. You don't take a soldier's weapon away from him, especially a bedouin soldier. A soldier would rather you took his pants off than take his weapon. The Popular Democratic Front for the Liberation of Palestine, or so they called themselves as a Marxist group—Marxist my foot, they didn't know anything about Marxism—would hoist red flags over the minarets of mosques as a way of advertising their intention to turn Jordan into a communist state. These idiots were so ignorant of the ways of their own people that they had no inkling of the profound role Islam plays in Arab culture. They didn't know that that was one sure way to turn the people against them. Once they actually demanded that the Amman government declare Lenin's birthday a national holiday!

"So in Jordan the people finally, predictably, inevitably, turned against us. Our *own* people. Keep in mind that out of every five Jordanians, three are Palestinian. And our political leaders from the movement, ignorant as ever of the hostility they were generating by the irresponsible behavior of their cadres, would be up there giving speeches in Formal Arabic about liberation and struggle and sacrifice and martyrdom and the rest of it—speeches that would go on for two, three, or four hours. I remember on my occasional visits to Amman in those days—I was barely twenty then—I would attend these gatherings and listen to these damn speakers, and in the end I would wrack my brains trying—honestly trying—to fathom what had been said. They said nothing. Absolutely nothing. It was all like poetry, bad poetry to be sure, but like poetry. Meant to entertain. They would use these damn long words, and meaningless phrases, about the heroism of our fighters, the honor of our Arab nation, the imminent liberation of Palestine. I can't imitate the comical way of these rhetorical speakers, but you know what I mean. They would shout and scream their rhetoric at the audience and then bring their voices to a hush when they talked about the memory of this martyr or that. And the people, brother, the people loved it all. They loved the theatrics. The acting. They loved the action on the stage. For that's all it was. The people just sat there and applauded madly, having a great time. All they were missing were their water pipes. For hours on end, speaker after speaker would hurl words at you. Words flew all around you, wastefully, senselessly. How could our language, any language, sound so ugly and meaningless and sterile? I can't believe that we speak the same language that the Koran is written in, the same language that Ben Khaldun wrote *Makadamat* in." Salem is referring to an elegantly written, seminal work on the philosophy of history by Ben Khaldun, a classical Arab scholar, whose contribution continues to be recognized by modern historians.

Salem's capacity to hold his liquor amazes me. The man has demolished three-quarters of his fifth of scotch, and he's still coherent.

"We screwed up in Jordan," Salem continues. "We made so many mistakes there. Basic, elementary mistakes that we insisted on repeating in Lebanon. The same mistakes. The chaos. The lack of discipline. The irresponsible disregard for mass sentiment. The blind obedience to the word of your *massoul* [political commissar] and that of the *tanzeem* [political factions]. The authority we follow, the language we speak, the backwardness we are mired in and can't get out of are all issues that are important to an understanding of why we have repeatedly failed to score one single political victory during the last eighty years of our struggle for independence. We Palestinians like to think of ourselves as more progressive, informed, educated, heroic than other Arabs. That's a joke. We are straitjacketed by obedience to authority like other Arabs. We speak our language as wastefully as other Arabs. We are held back by our backwardness—a backwardness whose existence we refuse to admit—like other Arabs. When we burst on the scene in 1968, after the battle of Karameh, the Arab world saw us as its revolutionary vanguard, but we turned out to be its jerks. And it took the Palestinians, our generation of Palestinians, a quarter of a century to acquaint the rest of the world with our identity, and through that mutual acquaintance the world discovered that we are not worth knowing."

Salem stands up and says: "I think I want to go back to bed."

He is not staggering one bit. Between the effusion of emotions such as these and one's intake of alcohol must lie a special zone of awareness that refuses to be destabilized.

•••

What is it about Palestinian history that has made failure to meet challenge preordained in it? Why has failure constantly dogged us? What's wrong with us?

Palestinians, like other Arabs, suffer from a multiple personality disorder. People who live in the Arab world have not yet resolved whether to call themselves Moslem, a name that their history gave them; or Arab, a name that their secular ideologies of the *nahda* movement—the nineteenth-century awakening—chose for them after the First World War; or names like *Lebanese, Palestinian, Jordanian, Kuwaiti*, and the like—the national names that colonial overlords had thrust upon them. To this day, the overwhelming majority remain locked in combat with themselves—and in places with each other—over what their name should be.

It all started with the *nahda*. The figures who dominated that era were so gifted with self-deception that it was then believed that to break with the past, and thus effect a leap into modernity, the Arabs simply had to take Europe, and secular nationalism, as a model. The problem with the leaders of the *nahda*, who came from the three centers of activism in the Arab world at the time—Cairo, Damascus, and Beirut (Palestine has always been a marginal province in modern Arab history)—was that they were a mimetic Westernized elite who lacked intellectual dash and operated outside the orbit of mass sentiment. They failed to grasp that the European ideas that they were so voraciously imbibing and transplanting to the Arab world—in politics and literature, in science and technology, in law and education—were rooted in the material conditions of European history. The European leap from medieval backwardness to the modernity of the Renaissance had occurred in response to decisive social changes triggered by internal and spontaneous forces. Aped by this Westernized Arab elite, these became tawdry ideas that *impeded* the Arabs' drift toward genuine social reform.

To be sure, in the global dialogue of cultures, no idea can remain the exclusive property of its creators. Ideas are cultural goods that travel and are exchanged like other goods. Any viable social system must be able not only to lend but to borrow. Borrowing ideas, however, is more complex than lending them. Not every nation can borrow wisely and put an adopted tool to as good a use as its original owner.

The *nahdaists* borrowed ideas freely, imported them voraciously, and applied them senselessly. The advent of these ideas in the Arab world was all the more strongly felt—in the form of lopsided development—because they were mediated by an elite who, as the intellectuals, the nationalists, the theoreticians, the ideologues, the belletrists, belonged to a class with a leading position in society. What they finally succeeded in doing was to rob their world of its teleological spirit and deny it that inward sense of self that had held it together for centuries, even during the darkest days of Ottoman rule.

Arab culture did not become totally pulverized, however, until the era of French and British colonialism. In less than fifty years, between the First World War and the late 1950s, the colonial powers managed to force upon the Arab world a system of social, political, educational, and economic relations, mediated through the Westernized Arab elite, whose grip even the coming of "independence" could not loosen. What we call the Arab states today are, in the common sense of the word, artificial creations of the Western powers. National boundaries were established by Britain and France with no consideration of a national will or of a demographic, ethnic, or political reality. As a result of their incorporation into the European orbit,

Arabs had become so feeble that they acquiesced to the foreign overlords in drawing up the internal structure of each of their states, along with their judicial, constitutional, bureaucratic, political, military, and economic systems. Above all, the system of education foisted on Arabs, patterned on Western models and calculated to disseminate Western ideas (and the notion of Western superiority) continued to produce generations of servile Arabs who not only copied the West but saw its ways in literature and the arts, in music and dress, in style and ideas, in government and politics, as superior to their own.

...

The crisis created by a European-imposed form of modernization is visible everywhere in the Arab world today: in the hegemonic hold of the West on a society whose resources have been organized in response to Euro-American interests; in a culturally dependent elite that can't think how to wear a dress or build a nation without reference to how it is done in the United States or Europe; in a people who, after 150 years of borrowing, still have to import their technology and science and send their children to study abroad; and a world whose social conditions have encoded a dynamic that, far from ending cultural dependency and backwardness, will only provide new means for their expansion.

The legacy of Western penetration of the Arab world thus not only consolidated Arab backwardness but guaranteed its transformation (through the introduction of bastard modes of social existence) into a more subtle expression of backwardness—what I like to call neobackwardness. We see it in the spectacle of an Arab who seemingly possesses all the attributes of modernity—who has a university degree, works in a high-tech office, speaks several languages, travels extensively, and appears normal to the naked eye—but once you scratch beneath that veneer, you find him infected with the germ of traditionalism. He is convinced that he has made the leap to modernity already; that his transformation is not shallow and superficial; that he is not a mere caricature, a Westernized Arab. His peasant counterpart, confronted by the fact of his backwardness, will admit it and ask you gratefully for ways to overcome it. Neobackward Arabs, like alcoholics, will continue to deny their affliction as long as they can.

Today neobackward Arabs rule the Arab world, direct its destiny, and define its identity. The Arab world has failed, once again, to find its anchor.

In modern Arab history, the call for the ideal—the summons for coherent self-definition—sounded three times. First was the Arab struggle to rid themselves of the yoke of Ottoman rule, which began around the middle of the last century and ended with the Great War. Next was their struggle against colonialism, which ended, for most of them, around the middle of this century with the coming of "independence." Last was the coming to grips by the Arabs—between that time and the present—with the realization that they inhabit a world that boasts twenty-one sovereigns but no sovereignty.

We grow incredulous when we confront the fact that with each of these phases, distorted social change has become more aggravated, backwardness more acute, and the spiritual exhaustion of the age more complete. The Arab heritage over the past 150 years has proved too fragile to stand against assault and too empty to produce the spiritual resources we need to revitalize Arab society.

The Arab world—which the national movement had sought to unite by one secular ideology within a single territorial homeland—is today a collection of disparate entities ruled, for the most part, by authoritarian regimes that rely on coercion, violence, and terror and demand from their people unilateral submission, obedience, and conformity. In the Arab state, state power is absolute. The various agencies of that power—the military establishment, the police, the secret service (known as *mokhabarat*), the bureaucracy, the various government agencies (including government-controlled media), and the so-called state party—all work together to crush creativity wherever it may be found and to silence the voice of dissent wherever it is heard. The authority figure representing state power is not answerable to anyone. He demands and will ostensibly receive respect from the citizen.

But the Arab is not in fact a citizen in his own country. He is an object that lives within a regimented social universe where the word of the authority figure has acquired attributes beyond those even of the Word of God. The individual's process of socialization reinforces this system of terror, for the various subsystems of society—the family, the school, the neighborhood, the ethnic milieu, the worship center, and the cultural environment—are microcosms of the vertical relationship that exists between the state and the individual.

The practitioner of authority in the Arab state delights not only in the exercise of power but in the spectacle of its diffusion to every level of society. In this sense, the power of the authority figure is expressed both through its traditional vehicles and as a set of relations of force. The objective of this set of relations is to ensure that the conduct of the citizen—his private life, his daily existence, even his thoughts—does not extend beyond the rules of domination. These relations of force support the power of the Arab ruler by ensuring, for example, that the family system is a reflection of state rule. Thus, the father is the state's representative at home, raising, disciplining, and punishing children as authority does its citizens; the male is equally the state's representative in his interaction with the female; as is the teacher with the student, the adult with the child, the religious figure with the believer, the employer with the employee, the *zaim* or local thug with the neighborhood poor, and so on.

The typical Arab regime is thus both a source and a confluence of power whose diffusion dominates, coordinates, and defines social relations at every level. It is the kind of power that can truly boast omniscience as well as omnipotence. Not only has it been able, over the years, to invade every form of social behavior, but also, through the coercive means of the *mokhabarat*, to conduct exhaustive surveillance of individuals and groups and to exact as well as advertise its threat of terrible punishment for recalcitrants.

In the various Arab countries, the *mokhabarat* are the eyes of the state, the eyes that see without being seen. Its officials watch for potential deviation, document cases of radicalism, anticipate disorder, dig for expressions of political discontent, and inflict appropriate punishment, including death under torture, all in the name of law and order.

Living in such an environment of constant terror, generation after generation, has had a corrosive effect on the constitution of personality and national identity in the Arab world. Not only does the individual Arab live in fear of retribution for the least infraction; he lives with the knowledge that the country he inhabits does not belong to him, nor is he considered by its rulers to be a citizen, but simply a denizen, of it. If he lives in Jordan or Saudi Arabia, he is constantly reminded that he should disabuse himself of notions that the country is his own. The Hashemite Kingdom of Jordan and the Kingdom of Saudi Arabia are named, in the manner of medieval fiefdoms, after the ruling families of Hashem and Saud.

Fear of retribution by the state and by the social milieu contributes to instilling in the individual, even encoding in his consciousness, the need to accept orthodoxy, dependency, and submission. This in turn triggers in him a permanent sense of fear—fear of originality, innovation, and spontaneity, fear of life itself. The Arab thus actively participates in perpetuating a broken-down society by accepting its stringent rules of self-discipline and its definition of him as a bane of creativity, not its source. Traditional social values, in effect, end up creating an individual who fulfills the basic needs of the power structure: absolute obedience to state authority, the sole arbiter of his allegiances, loyalties, and sentiments. A mass of people are socialized not only to believe in the supremacy of established power but to believe that they can be governed by a handful of rulers.

The Arab thus lives in a mutilated, broken-down society in which the coercive power of the state allows him no way out of his malaise, a society blindly opposed to change and relentless in its repression. The family system of which he is a member is engaged in the production of personalities subservient to authority, responsive to domination, and fearful of innovation. Arabs cannot even question, let alone challenge, established norms. Theirs is a consciousness based on an ethic of fear.

A whole people have, in effect, quietly acquiesced in the forfeiture of their powers of self-determination.

All the while that Arabs called themselves Arabs, their identity as Moslems was surreptitiously outflanking them, and their national names—Lebanese, Palestinians, Jordanians, Kuwaitis, and so on—were bedeviling them. They belonged to all three names—Arab, Moslem, the national name. They belonged to one. They belonged to none.

The Arab peoples' linguistic currency today also expresses the temper of their age, for they communicate in three different tongues, three tongues that, though derived from the same source, are as different as Chaucer's, Churchill's, and African-American English are from one another. These are Classical Arabic, the language that Islam bequeathed; Formal Arabic, the one invented by the age of neobackwardness; and Oral Arabic, the language of the masses, whose vocabulary, chaotic grammar, structure, and tonality reflect the mutilated world Arabs inhabit.

Classical Arabic is a great language that drew on and was energized by the intellectual resources of a commonwealth of nations noted not only for the intellectual coherence of its Islamic heritage but also for the innovative weld of sensibility that characterized its Abbaside, Ommayad, and Spanish eras. Classical Arabic, at the height of its inventiveness between the ninth and twelfth centuries, was a living, breathing language that reflected, and helped create, the emotional intensities of the age. To the modern Arab, however, especially the Oral Arab, Classical Arabic is as mute, as incomprehensible, as the hieroglyphics in an Egyptian tomb. That is why modern Arabs always listen to, rather than read, their Koran: they have a limited perception of its symbolism and are totally disconnected from the verbal consciousness of its text. Differences in idiom, in resources of social feeling, between the world of classical Arabs and the mutilated world of modern Arabs render impossible any communication between the two.

Now enter Formal Arabic, whose emergence and development have taken place, significantly enough, roughly over the past 150 years, coinciding with the *nahda*, Westernization, "independence," and neobackwardness. The exclusive lingo of the ruling elite, the Westernized intelligentsia, representatives of state power, the bureaucrats, the *mokhabarat* sadists, and the effete literati, Formal Arabic (sometimes known as Media Arabic) is a kind of secondhand derivative of Classical Arabic, replete with pretensions and artifices imported from the West.

Unlike Classical Arabic, a tongue that derived from specific historical springs and unlike Oral Arabic, an adventurous creature, Formal Arabic is a bastard, the offspring of the times of neobackwardness. Its ambiguous jargon, stock similes, mechanical habits of expression, and complex rhetoric—not to mention the Western intrusions—lend it no sense of spontaneity or style. It lacks directness and intensity of feeling. Like the ruling class that uses it, the language blunts and stultifies. It communicates but creates no communion. Formal Arabic neither lives nor is lived; rather, it is a lingo reflecting the deadness of spirit of a society and a class that possess formality but no form, rhetoric but no style, dissimulation but no grace.

It was in Formal Arabic, for example, that Nasser and Voice of the Arabs Radio from Cairo spoke to the Arab masses in 1967 on the eve of the June War, as did Saddam and the Voice of the Mother of All Battles Radio in 1991 on the eve of the Gulf War. If these broadcasts made absolutely no sense, that is because Formal Arabic has totally absorbed, and been absorbed by, the hysterics and buffoonery that characterize the Arab world today. It has the function of perpetuating the backwardness of Arab society, enforcing the brutalities of the regimes, and justifying the debauchery, waste, corruption, and decadence of its ruling elite. Used generation after generation by the ruling elite to intimidate, deceive, and control, its syntax has long since come to interact with and support the various instruments of domination in society.

This is apparent in the features of its verb system and in its repressive use of gender. The simple future exists in Formal Arabic, but the future perfect, with its exhilarating sense of forward motion, as in history, does not; or where it is used at all, it is resurrected from Classical Arabic. The mind of Formal Arabs cannot conceive of working from within a verbal structure that preempts, or wills an action, on tomorrow. The future perfect is proscribed for the simple reason that its use entails social change.

The use of the masculine gender likewise asserts the unlimited power wielded by the male in Arab society. The nation conceived as a family in which the patriarch exercises unilateral power is a favorite metaphor of Arab rulers. Thus, King Hussein of Jordan, whose family members believe they own the country to the extent that they have named it for themselves, continues to address the nation as *el osra el ordenia*, the Jordan family. Similarly, Nasser and Sadat, and Saddam Hussein today, always referred to themselves as *kabir el osra*, the eldest of the family. And in the Arab family, no one argues with the patriarch.

The Formal Arab idealizes, in his writing, the *zlam*, or true men, and dismisses the *harim*, or true women, who go beyond the simple future in their speech or beyond the soft, the sweet, and the chaste behavior expected of them. Conventional rules of propriety in discourse are enforced on the female and a dialectic of verbal tension habitually prevails between men and women that cannot be discarded. In the presence of men, women are confined to harmless verbal expressions. More often than not, their communication is expected to be gestural rather than linguistic.

The controlled puritanism of Formal Arabic, whose goal is standardized mediocrity and boorish conformity, has imposed substantial limits on the Arab libido.

It is not surprising, then, that Formal Arabs, whose language possesses no apparatus for swearing, obscenity, sexuality, or the merely sensual, often resort to the novel vocabulary of Oral Arabic. The balance in Formal Arabic is therefore constantly being shaken by inventive compositions imported from Oral Arabic that mock conventional constraints.

The relationship between language and sexuality in Arab society is a mirror of that between authority and freedom. Thus, the right to be loud, enjoyed by men, is denied to women when they are in the presence of men. Obscenity is profuse and condoned between men; but the sexual act itself, even in its privacy, is mute. Overt sexual expression in the conjugal bed is proscribed for the same reason that free discourse is proscribed between the rulers and the ruled in Arab culture. And just as the father, the teacher, the policeman, and the clergyman are socialized to represent state power in the home, the school, the street, and the mosque, so is the male its representative in bed. Thus, the repression of sexual fulfillment in Arab society is as much physiological as sociolinguistic.

It can be argued that individual freedom is either enriched or diminished by the quality of linguistic and sexual interplay. Take the youth revolt of the late 1960s in the United States. Recall how its primary aims were sexual and linguistic. The young assaulted social taboos by creating their own argot that was all but incomprehensible to the rest of society, and they created what came to be known as the sexual revolution. They were there "to do their thing" and "tell it like it is." Although the Sixties movement died, its legacies are still evident in American culture, and its impact on language and sexual mores is equally clear.

In the Arab world today, public discourse remains the domain of Formal Arabic. Embodied in the cant of this dead language, much of social and cultural reality exists as a set of obscure, irrational notions. There is an established set of rules beyond which nothing is admissible. How could a society produce a literature when it does not allow anything adversarial, critical, or innovative to be said? In other words, how could the language of the police bully, the government bureaucrat, and the mimetic intellectual, a language that demeans ideas, debases labor, and cheapens the value of human existence, produce a body of elevated thought and expression?

Much of what passes for Arabic "literature" today should be remaindered as quickly as it is published.

The repressive constraints that Formal Arabic places on the soul of Arab culture are reflected in the flight of high school and university students to foreign languages, mostly English and French, as a mode of intellectual release. These other languages have become a means for young Arabs to seek a new window on life and draw on energies of spirit that may one day afford an escape from their social and cultural prison. Only when that transformation has taken place will young Arabs begin to speak their own language with force and elegance and find that their culture will speak back in kind.

Only in Oral Arabic do ordinary Arabs feel at home. They use it to spin tales about their heritage, to compose the lyrics of their own songs, to celebrate the wonders of the land, to speak of the mysteries of God's creation, to remember their fallen patriots, to narrate the exploits of their ancestors, and to speak of their historic meaning. It is zestful and lively but in the end it is as helpless and mutilated as the people who speak it. It expresses the terrors of the individual and his inward flight from the make-believe world he inhabits.

The politics of terror in Arab society (and since the fourteenth century, Arab society has lived under the terror of Ottoman occupation, European colonialism, and indigenous overlords) press the individual to guard and stylize his words and to adopt the same convention of constraints in his speech as he does in his lifestyle. That is why the very hinge of Oral Arabic is evasion, conspiracy, ambiguity, and opacity. The Oral Arab has to take refuge in double-speak, for he knows that, in a coercive society, if he were to speak openly, he would stand in mortal peril. Hence, Oral Arabs have become skilled dissemblers. Language is no less a weapon of assault and vengeance in the hands of the Oral Arab than the state party and the government newspaper. And polysemy, the way words can be twisted around in a sentence to mean different, even opposite, things is no less a part of the semantic repertoire of the rebel than of the dictator. In discourse, dissembling and polysemy are worn by the Oral Arab like a coat of arms. In a social world where survival favors those who wear the mask, a world adamantly opposed to free utterance, a world where the individual is trained to place obedience above autonomy and orthodoxy above creativity, ambiguity is preferable, and spontaneous effusions are expressed only guardedly. In dealing with the world and all that is objective and factual in it, the Arab confronts revelation by concealment, information by misinformation, and sharing by withholding. Thus, what the Arab leader will say in what he does not mean, the Arab peasant will mean in what he does not say.

From all this flows the ceremonious nature of Arab daily life. The Oral Arab, over the past five centuries, has internalized his fear to the point where it now lies at the core of his being—fear not only of political authority but of divine authority as well. The relationship between the agents of state power and the individual, like that between God and the individual, is based so much on fear that the word and the adjectives that derive from it, *fearful* and *fearsome*, have come to attain a positive connotation in the semantic consciousness of Arabs. To instill fear is considered a positive attribute; while to describe someone as not "in fear" of God or King is to describe a misfit. In Jordan, for example, there was a time when one spoke of the upstart, the psychopath, the drifter, the nonconformist, the outcast, as he who "fears neither Allah nor King Abdullah." Unlike his Christian counterpart, the Arab Moslem would never conceive that his relationship with God is based on love. The idea that God "loves" you or that you "love" God is outside modern Islamic consciousness. You *fear* God, you don't love Him, just as you fear the king and other figures of secular authority. In Arab society, you may be expected to love your mother, but you must fear your father. He who exercises authority over you is not a sympathetic figure who suffers for you and needs your affection, as Christ does in Christian mythology; your relationship is based on the unilateral projection of fear, not the mutual exchange of respect. If you must love, you are told, love Creation, not the Creator.

For the Arab thus socialized to internalize fear and to hide, disguise, or stylize real emotion, a ceremoniousness has developed whose function is to dampen intimacy, individuality, and originality in daily life. The forced politesse, even theatricality, evident in Arab manners is in fact a calculated ruse by Oral Arabs who hope to survive by dissembling and masking their spiritual anxieties. As the idiomatic phraseology would have it, "Openly kiss the hand that oppresses you, but secretly struggle for its destruction."

Oral Arabs will say no when they mean yes; tell you that they have eaten enough when they are still hungry; explain how much they have missed your company when they mean the opposite; boast of their prowess when they are helpless; feel disgrace or shame for acts that warrant neither sentiment; value pomposity over modesty. They exaggerate and boast and lie as a matter of course, in a way that is commensurate with the counterfactual values of their society. Oral Arabs inhabit a world of secrets. Take these secrets away and the culture will stand empty, and utterance will be robbed of that balance needed, in a coercive system, between the said and the unsaid, the clear and the ambiguous.

The coexistence of these three languages in the Arab world is clearly a reflection of its social dichotomies. This linguistic polarization speaks more cogently than anything else about the anarchy of feeling that characterizes Arab culture. A society whose masses speak to each other in one language, whose social existence is defined in another, and whose mythology of hope is written in yet another is in severe peril of collapse. To ask how Arabs speak may well be one way of asking who they are. Language, of course, is more than simply a medium of exchange. It not only communicates experience but to a large extent determines it.

Palestinians are not only part of this Arab world but—because of their insecurity as a stateless, fragmented, and destitute community—they are a people who suffer more grievous forms of neobackwardness, who speak their language more ornately, and who are more subject to the tyranny of tradition than others around them.

7

Blue in Australia, High Times in India

I am standing at the end of the bar, in the Toowoomba Hotel, drinking a schooner of beer. It is Friday, payday at the sugarcane plantation where I work. The word *hotel* should be used with caution, since in Australia it has nothing to do with an establishment that offers lodgings to strangers. A hotel is a rough-and-ready bar where beer is poured out of a hose into your mug and where men— and only men—congregate in the "saloon." In the city, a hotel may have a lounge where women are allowed, but the Toowoomba Hotel is far from any city. The Toowoomba Hotel is there to serve beer and some food—English food, which is no food at all by anyone's standard—to the men who cut cane in the outlying sugar plantations.

It is the middle of December and the summer heat is endlessly tormenting. The bar has the look and smell of a lavatory. Because today is payday, it is crowded. The men, dressed in shorts, dirty T-shirts, and straw hats, stand in clusters sloshing beer out of middie and schooner glasses and talking loudly to each other as they get progressively drunker. Directly outside, a Salvation Army band is singing songs about Jesus and how we are all his sheep, songs that are taken up by some of the drunken patrons.

As I sip my beer, I notice a man who is drinking with two of his friends looking at me. It's a look of aggression he is giving me—a look almost of hatred. Moments later, the three of them stagger toward me.

"You shoutin' the bar, mate?" the man asks, as his friends watch, seemingly amused. That's Aussie talk for, "Would I buy drinks all around?" I can tell these men are smiling not because they are being friendly.

"I'll shout the bar if you will," I say.

"You're a wog, aintcha?" the man demands, catching my accent.

That is the first word a newly arrived immigrant hears in this country. I have been here for six months and have heard it countless times.

"Go on, thump him, Neil," one of the man's friends urges. The name comes out pronounced "nile."

"Ya, go on Neil," the other friend says, "thump the dago."

"You wanna blue, mate?" Neil persists, looking at me sidelong. By "blue" he means a fistfight.

I look back at him, uncertain what to do. Here we go again, I think, another fistfight. Neil is smiling, as if giving me time to ponder a decision that I obviously have no choice in making.

"I said you're looking for a fucking blue, matey?" Neil asks again, more forcefully. He brings his head forward, widening his eyes and pointing a finger at me, to show his distaste for all us wogs and dagos for the way we had invaded his life, for the way the Italian–Greek combine in this country had robbed Australians of their jobs and polluted their lily-white Anglo-Saxon way of life.

"Come on Neil, thump the dago," his friend demands.

Neil is really an anomaly in this part of the bush. To begin with, he is too old for the hardships one puts up with here. The man must be in his late forties. There aren't too many men that age around here. Maybe that's his problem. The older ones, the pathetic ones, the losers, the ones who are still cutting cane after all these years, the ones who are now feeling the terror of their dried-up pride, are shriveled-up creatures, living mournful lives. This Neil is a frightened, unhappy man who thinks he will get a cheap thrill out of terrorizing a docile immigrant.

But I am hating this man and what he and his friends represent. I am hating again. I am hating Australia. I am hating the Arab world. I am hating the hate that I feel. You are repudiated by one world and then by another. God and humanity owe me a debt, and here they are acting as if I was the one to pay up. Men chased me out of my country, robbed me of a childhood, killed my sister, and banished me to this whatnot land, and here they are claiming their rights for a wog bashing. There is not one spot in this world where one can find a little peace, a little freedom, a little time when one's intricate silence is not burned in effigy. You escape the rotting traditionalism of the Arab world and come face to face with the rotting racism of the Western world.

"So what do you reckon, mate?" Neil goes on. "What do you reckon, wog?" His eyes tear over me, head to toe, eyes enfolded in a mountain of wrinkles. He seems to be wondering if I will dare say anything back. Otherwise, he wants me to back away, to show the humble rectitude expected of the inferior species I belong to. I find myself involuntarily, and a trifle nervously, folding my pack of cigarettes into the short sleeve of my T-shirt, as if to display my muscles.

I can't keep fighting these bastards forever. But I have no choice.

I know these men. I know them well. They come at me straight out of the twilight zone of my parents' past, from my parents' tales about British soldiers in our homeland, about their racist pigheadedness, their imperial hauteur, and the way they pushed us around, hanged our patriots, incarcerated our intellectuals, and determined our political destiny because, they claimed, we were "not yet ready for independence" or "could not govern" ourselves. Even those semiliterate dregs among them, those who hailed from Manchester and the East End of London, felt privy to the rights of the white man's burden. They needed to despise us, and we had to hate them. And here's my mother, in one of my earliest memories of her, having finished her evening prayers, kneeling on a prayer rug, stringing her prayer beads, reading a *sura* from the Koran, her hands outstretched before her, pleading with Allah to aid the Korean people in their war against the *Engleez* (the English, the term her generation used to dismiss all Europeans). She didn't know anything about the Korean war, but she suspected the Koreans were a little people like us, and the *Engleez* were devils repudiated by God.

Outside, I hear the Salvation Army band singing about the flock of sheep that Jesus the shepherd was herding. Inside me, I hear the screams of the woman on the wayside, helpless in her labor pains, giving birth to yet another Palestinian child. And my fists, as fast as lightning, are raining down on Neil's face, chest, earholes, and head.

In me is the disdain, the rage, I feel for a man who has, for centuries, contested my name and my being.

I am punching and kicking and slapping with all my might. Then suddenly there were fists slamming into me from all directions as Neil's two friends entered the fray. Before I passed out, it felt like a ton of bricks had fallen on top of me.

When I came to, I was crumpled in a heap outside the bar. I stood up and walked, looking like a whipped dog, two blocks down the one and only street of this sleepy bush town, before I realized I could walk no more. My face was swollen, and I ached in every part of my body. So I sat under a tree, curling into myself, and waited for the pain to go away. And that's where my friend Peter came upon me. Everybody in the fields called him Peter because his real name was too long and too difficult to pronounce. He came from a village outside Dubrovnik and had been in Australia for five years. Peter was a hulking man of fifty and looked as if he had worked for most of them. When he saw me sitting on the road, his lips drew tight between his teeth and his voice boomed in his language, as he cursed those who had beaten me. And my voice boomed back in *my* language: "*Ana Abu* blues, *Ana Abu* blues!" I am the father of blues.

But that day, the day I stood my ground with Neil and his friends, was a victory for me, a kind of night journey in this promised land, this land behind the mountains where I have come to live and work.

On the plantation we started our day by punching those bundy clocks that record what time you come to work, how long you take for lunch, and when you leave to go home. The cane fields stretched to infinity. Behind us, the prefab houses where the workers lived— or rather slept—stretched, without a single tree, to another infinity.

By midday, the sun would be suspended motionless in the sky. A merciless sun beat down on us. After lunch, it formed itself into a dazzling, cruel flame. A sultry, misty haze would hang down over the fields from a cloudless sky that shimmered as if its surface was made of metal. At the end of the day, we would troop back the two hundred or so yards to our homes or to the air-conditioned interior of the cafeteria. On the way, some of the older men, like me from countries difficult to locate and with names too difficult to pronounce, would move slowly down the dirt track with their heads down, looking half-dead. Once I saw a man moving beside me with strings of spittle hanging from his mouth, his eyes closed, as if he walked in his sleep.

Yet I liked the work. My field was not far from the ocean, and on certain days, as I went whoosh, whoosh with my blade, I would feel the hot air saturated with the sweet smell of sugar and sea salt, and the long, monotonous hours wouldn't matter. There was something about the way the rays of the sun seemed, miraculously, to kindle the riches of the earth, something about the heady sweetness of the scent of freshly cut cane, something about the way it looked, springing erect into the sky, so sensual, as if it had blood in its veins. And every ten minutes or so, I would reach for my water bag and pour water into my mouth, rejoicing with every gulp, and letting it wash down my face, conscious that water was not only needed to sustain life but was life itself.

We had a fifteen-minute tea-break every two hours, and during it, if he was not working too far from me, Peter and I would get together, sit in the shade, light a little fire, and make tea, drinking it out of empty cans of baked beans. Peter had a bad habit of blowing his nose in his thumb and forefinger, throw the spittle on the ground, then wipe his hand on the side of his pants.

"Peter, you're disgusting," I would say.

"Please?"

"Damn it, use a handkerchief, man."

"Please?" he would ask again, looking at me askance, his eyes now vanishing under his hat.

"Never mind," I would say playfully and clink my can against his.

Peter had a family back in Yugoslavia to whom he sent all his money. His joy in life was to receive letters from home describing his three children and the news about the village. His ambition in life was to open what was known in Australia then as a milk bar, which is the old-fashioned American soda fountain.

Peter's room was directly adjacent to mine, and we often sat up talking, he communicating in his improbable English his love for his family and life back in the village. He would tell me how much he hated Australia but how he never regretted embarking on his journey to these shores because, above all, his "families" back home were now doing well. He always referred to his family, of whom he had innumerable pictures nailed to the walls, in the plural.

"Why you come here?" Peter would ask me. "Why you leave your place?" And I would tell him the simple truth: I left the place I grew up in because it was not really my place. Lebanon was not my country. The Lebanese had made it clear that I would never be at home there. I returned the favor by never feeling any loyalty to Lebanon. It was not I who rejected the Arab world and its culture. It was they who had rejected me. I was a person without a country, but not without a name. And as I grew up, I found that I was adding to my name and sensibility attributes beyond those my own culture was willing to allow. People who want to be free in the kind of world I come from are considered dangerous. They live like prisoners. It was the United Nations Relief and Works Agency, an agency of the United Nations—the very body that was responsible for our original displacement—that finally enabled me to seek another exile in Australia. The more Palestinians who emigrate out of the Arab world, never to be seen again, the fewer there are for UNRWA to feed, employ, educate, house, and care for. UNRWA is always happy to pay the airfare of a Palestinian refugee who wants to flee to Alberta, Canada; Queensland, Australia; Detroit, Michigan; and other far-away places. UNRWA not only provided me with a ticket and an additional five hundred dollars but wished me godspeed, which meant they did not want to see me again. I did not want to see them or the Arab world again either.

"Why you leave your place?" Peter wants to know.

"It's not my place."

"Where is your place?"

"Any place, Peter, any place."

"You piss on your place?"

"I don't like places."

Peter sits back on the edge of the bed, his hat pulled down to his eyebrows, puffing on his cigarette. The matter appeared to be settled. But it was not.

"Why you don't like places?"

"I was made that way."

"Please?"

"I had no control over it."

"Strange you are."

...

My neighbor on the other side was an Australian, a man in his early thirties, whose wife had died the year before in a car accident. He was a nice enough man (not all Australians were like Neil and his friends), but he was a terror to have next door. Night in, night out, he would drink heavily in his room and then start talking to himself, or carry on a long conversation with Emily, his dead wife. When he got tired of that, he would play one song on his record player over and over and over again. It was a silly song, something to do with "open up your heart and let the sun shine in." When he was finally drunk enough to sleep, I would lie on my bed reading a book, wondering why all these big bow flies and mosquitos had chosen my room to sing, dance, and mate in before they expired.

After I turned out the lights, I would feel this dull yearning for the streets of the Basta, but just for a moment, for soon I would sink into the comforting, dense darkness of sleep's oblivion.

I spent two seasons cutting sugarcane in Queensland. That was punishment enough. One day I picked up my duffle bag, along with my savings, and headed south.

Immigrants arrive in this country stamped, labeled, and defined. That did not bother me. Life came with a daily ration of torment but also, in equal measure, with a daily ration of joy. I drifted around the country, picking up odd jobs, mostly in the bush, not yet quite sounding or looking like anyone around me, like a soldier stranded behind enemy lines, except I was not waiting for a rescue party.

I am readjusting and rearranging my past to suit my sensibility in a shorter period of time than I expected. I can do that because my life is moving in a rush, like a river flooding its banks, dislodging the debris of the past.

I finally arrive in Sydney and decide to go to school. I have saved enough money to last for two full scholastic years. Moreover, college education in Australia is, or was then, virtually free.

Outside the campus of the University of New South Wales, students congregate at a little café called Gino's. I am there almost every day. I like the people here. They are a different breed from those I met in the bush. Everyone's parents are well-off. No one's father had worked as a bricklayer or waited on tables when he was a student. These kids, liberals all, would never let a single bigoted remark slip out of their mouths. It was there that I met Gillian, the first girl, outside the *souk*, I had shared my nakedness with—a bony girl with blond hair who always dressed in frumpy clothes, as if she was not conscious, or did not want anyone to know, of how beautiful her body was. What attracted me was the intensity in her eyes, the pure expression of a mind that had long since determined its own direction in life.

"I saw you at Professor Gillmante's class," she said and sat down at my table. "What's your major?"

"I don't know. I'm just doing a few courses here and there."

No one knew where Professor Gillmante, a man in his late fifties, came from. It is doubtful that he knew himself. Australia at the time, around the early 1960s, was full of people who had gone there after the Second World War. So many countries had been wrecked, so many documents destroyed, and so many people dislocated that it was difficult to know what place one was talking about since many no longer existed on the map.

Gillmante was so totally bald, and his eyelashes so totally blond, exactly matching the color of his skin, that he looked like that cartoon drawing of a smiling face telling you to have a nice day. But he was a brilliant anthropology professor whose unorthodox ideas never ceased to freeze us by their daring.

"It was Nietzsche," he would thunder, "who said that 'the lie, not the truth, is divine.'" Gillmante would never fail, in discussing even the most elementary question in anthropology, to draw on disciplines as far apart as economics and music, philosophy and physics, linguistics and architecture.

"All literature should be pulped," he would say, discussing cultural homeostasis. "All art should be burnt because it is worthless." After we all looked blankly at him, he would continue: "That is because not once in human history has any creative work acted as an impediment to human barbarism."

"Where you from?" Gillian wants to know.

"I'm Palestinian."

"Where is that?"

"It is difficult to say."

She just smiles at me, assuming a look of pensive tenderness.

"I will tell you some other time."

"I also saw you at the debating club," she offers. "You were crazy."

She is referring to the day when I had caused a minor scandal two weeks earlier. The committee had moved to put the silliest subject up for debate: whether women should wear the pants around the house. I was chosen as one of the panelists, but I thought the issue was so unworthy, so trivial, that I decided to show off my Basta ghetto cynicism. When it was my turn to speak, I satirized the whole subject by talking, instead, tongue in cheek, about how women should indeed wear pants around the house, since women always looked nice in pants. It took a while for the audience to realize what I was doing, but when I finally finished, ending my presentation on a somber note, suggesting that from here on we should address ourselves to more pressing social issues, I got a lot of applause.

"How old are you?" Gillian asks me.

"I'm twenty-two," I respond, amazed to think how old I had gotten.

Gillian is only nineteen but we begin to date.

By the end of the semester, we move in together, in an apartment on a street called Kissing Point Lane. That was the happiest time of my life. I don't know why the addition of another life to mine should have so transfigured me. It felt as if I was complemented as a human being.

One night after making love, she complains to me that I never, ever talk to her about my past. So I sit up in bed and for the rest of the evening tell her story after story about life in the Basta streets, and we laugh and laugh together until tears fall down our cheeks.

"You never tell me about your family," she says. "Do you have any brothers and sisters?"

I think about that for a minute.

"No," I respond.

"You're an only child?"

"Yes."

"Did you like being an only child?"

"No."

"Are your parents alive?"

"No."

"Both of them are dead?"

"Yes."

She can sense I am not telling her the truth. "Is anything wrong?"

"No," I say, jumping out of bed, away from her, away from her questions. I cannot let her enter the stillness of my past. It is against my will to pronounce the crazy fatigue of our exile and let her hands enter the brutalized body of my ruined world. Gillian could never possess enough frenzy to enter that world. It would be a violent blow to the triangle of freckles on her innocent, Anglo-Saxon face.

One day our dog Yallah, a name I gave it, which translates in Arabic as "let's go," is run over by a car and dies instantly. Gillian is so crushed she can't eat or sleep for days. I laugh at her sadness, and she is saddened by my laughter. What is the matter with me? she wants to know. To get her mind off Yallah, she decides to go visit her mother, and her mother's live-in boyfriend, in Melbourne. She insists on taking me with her.

Gillian's mother is in her early forties but looks twenty years older. She has been an alcoholic since her late teens. Her boyfriend, Phillip, a boorish Englishman dressed in blazers and cravats, is also an alcoholic, and a racist to boot. These two people are forever drunk, morning, afternoon, and night, and they do it in splendor. Gillian's father, who had died of a heart attack five years earlier, had been truly wealthy, and Phillip too had "made his money in the colonies."

When our cab stops outside the family house in Toorak, the most fashionable neighborhood in Melbourne, I am amazed at the spectacle of where my girlfriend had grown up. I may have seen a house that big before, but I had never been inside one. There are living rooms and lounges and family rooms and game rooms and sun-rooms and guest rooms and dining rooms. There is a room called a "study" and a room called a "library" and rooms called "servant quarters" and rooms that have not yet been named.

Gillian's mother, her eyes drooping, speech slurred, greets me effusively, telling me how happy she is that Gillian has finally brought me to visit. Phillip is aloof and cold. I have, after all, an accent—a slight one, to be sure, but an accent nevertheless. In the evening, on the way out to dinner at an expensive local restaurant, Gillian's mother stumbles all over the place as she walks down the path and has to be helped to the car. She is complaining loudly that she has left her purse behind.

"Where is my purse?" she demands. "Where is my purse?"

"Mom, you're carrying it," Gillian tells her. "You're holding it in your hand. Right there, see?"

At the restaurant, Phillip insults the waiter, who is Greek, because he brought him the wrong kind of soup.

"Why don't you people learn to speak English?" he asks haughtily. "If you want to live in this country, you have to learn to speak

English, do you hear?"

The whole four days I am in Melbourne, I remain a hair short of killing Phillip.

"Why do you allow your mother to hang out with a pompous fool like that?" I ask Gillian.

"He's good for her," she responds, "because he doesn't drink as much as she does."

On a later visit, soon after our final exams, the four of us are sitting in a living room (I don't recall which one) when Gillian's mother asks: "Gillian dear, why don't you bring that ever so polite boy, that ever so handsome boyfriend of yours you met in Sydney, to visit anymore?"

Gillian asks her mother if she means me.

"Yes, him, dear."

"But Mom, he's right here."

She looks up, opens her eyes with great effort, momentarily unsure what direction to focus in, and says: "Well, my goodness me. He is at that. He is at that. How are you dear?"

"I'm fine, thank you."

"You're the nicest boy my Gillian has ever dated, you know," she continues.

Phillip looks in my direction, then at the ceiling, as if to address it, not me. "I don't much care for dagos myself," he says.

I stand up. "Listen, shithead, you're too old to get into a punch-up with me, so shut the fuck up."

And pathetic, little Phillip; rich, English Phillip who made his money "in the colonies"; stupid, laughable Phillip who thinks that His Majesty is still running an empire inhabited by vermin who should know their place, actually says to me: "How dare you use that kind of language around here!"

"Your language is more obscene than mine, you stupid idiot."

I don't think a bigoted, ignorant man like Phillip understood that. Why should he? He comes from a depressing, little island nation off the coast of France somewhere that, in its heyday, believed openly, unabashedly, in the superiority of its race over those other races it ruled.

Phillip and Gillian's mother spend the rest of the evening in the living room, drinking themselves into a stupor. Gillian and I go to bed.

...

"I'm pregnant," Gillian says to me one day in Sydney. It is around the end of my second year at college.

"I'm not ready to be a father," I answer despondently. "I don't want to be a father."

"Well, I want to be a mother. I don't need you around for me to be a mother. I want a baby. I'll take care of it when it's born. I'll bring it up myself. I can afford to do that. I'll be the best mother in the world," she says.

"You just go on and be that then."

Gillian goes on to be a mother, and I go on to the bush.

...

I take a train to Melbourne and then another from there all the way to Perth in western Australia. As the train pulls out of Adelaide, the capital of South Australia, we begin our two-day journey across the Nullarbor Plain, the most forbidding outback in the country, what Australians call "the back of beyond" and the government calls Zone A. If you work in Zone A, exploring for oil, mining iron ore, shearing sheep at isolated stations, and putting up with the hardship there, you pay virtually no taxes. Compared to Zone A, cutting sugarcane in the Queensland bush is a boy scout outing.

Hour after hour, the train moved through the flat land of the Plain. The rocks glowed red and shone under the merciless sun, as if someone had smeared them with oil. There were anthills as big as houses, as hardy as stone, scattered for miles along the way. When every four or five hours the train stopped at a station, a mere shed with one attendant at the job, Aborigines would be waiting, some on horses, to ask passengers if they had newspapers to give away, which they would take back with them to the sheep stations where they worked. The men there, isolated from the outside world except for radio contact, would read them passionately. These native Australians, with beautiful black faces and white teeth, are the lucky ones, for they have remained in the bush. Their counterparts who have made it to the cities, crushed by culture shock and by racism, invariably end up becoming alcoholics, their will to live sucked out of them.

Life in the bush may be hard, especially in Zone A, but there is a clean authority about it, a kind of naked, simple truthfulness. I can hardly wait to live here.

When I finally get to Perth, I go to the office of a bush contractor, where I know they are hiring men, and ask for a job. The person who interviews me, a man in his late forties who never stopped biting his fingernails, is surprised that I want to work in the bush. He even picks up the phone and dials a colleague's number: "Hey, Riley," he says into the receiver, "got a bloke here who sounds like Perry Mason, uni student too. Wants to work in the mines at Tom Price. Pommy, he is." He thinks I'm from Britain. I let that pass. There is no point in telling him that I am not. Besides, when you're ready to go to the bush, you leave your nationality at the door.

After he hangs up, he looks at me for a long while. "Why do you want to work in the bush, matey? A bloke like you, with a uni education?" he asks, in a pleasant tone of voice. He looks like the kind of man who always asks questions with a smile on his face.

I tell him I just love the bush.

He signs me on and tells me to be ready to fly to Tom Price in three days.

I stay at a youth hostel close to the water. I want to be by the ocean for the next three days before I go to the back of beyond. The bush is the only place left in the world where truth is truth and facts are perfect. There no one has yet tampered with God's creation. But I want to see the sea before I leave.

Every day I sit by the water, stretching blissfully on the sand, my arms under my head. The sea gives off a stupefying pungent smell of salt, and the smell takes me back to the Mediterranean and my childhood years. Once when I was sitting there, I don't know how long, my face cupped in the palms of my hands watching the horizon as the sun began to set, I realized that tears were falling down my cheeks.

I am happy here, I tell myself. I am truly happy. I remember Gillmante introducing us in class to the writings of Theodor W. Adorno, the German émigré writer who escaped from his homeland in the 1930s and went to live in the United States. He explained to us what Adorno meant when he said: "Homeland is the state of having escaped." The escaping writer must be the architect of his own state, explained Gillmante, and that is always a state of awareness.

I feel comfortable in this land, far away though I may be from mine. I feel serene in the knowledge that I am made for my time. I am a Palestinian. A man without a country. I am free to make any and every country I live in my own. No man can claim a more exulted kind of freedom.

Someone may have swallowed up my name—stained as it is with my childhood memories—and the country I come from may now be paraded naked in the streets of Western history books, but I am still a native son. A kind of shadow. And you can't bind a shadow, like a horse tied to a tree. I am the shadow of everything that came before me. Today I have no liberated zones to fight anyone from, to live in, except here in outer space, in the Australian bush, where there are worlds enough.

I finally arrive there.

When you live in the Australian bush, you soon learn to be rugged, uncouth, tough. If you do not, the bush will devour you. You go from one mine to another. From Tom Price to Darwin to Mt. Isa. Then you go from one sheep station to another and shear sheep. You work with sheep. You smell of sheep. You dream of sheep.

But there is a region rougher still. It's deep in the heart of the bush, three, five, or ten hours away from the nearest town (population a hundred souls or thereabouts) where geophysical firms (as they call themselves) explore for oil. There you live in tents with a dozen or so other men who look and act like cavemen. Never mind the snakes, centipedes, and merciless flies. You grow used to them. It's the heat you can't take, which could be 110 degrees in the shade on a nice day. So you start work at 3:00 A.M. in order to beat it, and you're back in camp before noon. You drink yourself into a stupor and go to sleep. You do this for twenty-eight consecutive days; then you get a week off. You're flown by Cessna to Perth, Brisbane, or Melbourne, whichever happens to be nearest, and you touch base with civilization, get laid, and fly right back. There are times at camp when, because of weather conditions, you're idle. That's when we hop into jeeps and drive for four hours to get to the nearest town to get smashed. A bush town is a genuine replica of the American pioneer West. The one bar in it has swinging doors, as you would expect to see in some bad western movie, and recognizes no closing time. So you go there with your mates, the cavemen, and get drunk and get into fistfights—with them or with other drinkers in the bar who are bushmen from outlying stations. You get beaten up. You beat up someone else. You are thrown out through the dutch doors by the publican. Or you go crazy and walk outside, take your gun out of your holster, and shoot in the air just for the sheer delight of it. If you're a more sedentary party animal, you just pass out. And when it's all over, you drive back to camp. You get up again at 3:00 A.M., eat your breakfast of T-bone steak with four eggs, and head on to work.

If you get tired of all this, there are always the road gangs to join. They always want men to build roads all the way from Barkaldine in the west to the town of Banana in the south. That's hard work, but the money is good.

I love it here. I'm so far away from the Arab world. So far away from its tormenting demands, its bestial traditions. I've reached behind the mountains, and I'm finding out what there is in the land that lies there.

Jasmine. There is no poison here. No tradition here to punish you with death. I love it here. I'm beginning to live, look, and sound exactly like the people in the land behind the mountains.

I stay in the outback for two years and then decide to go to Melbourne, where Gillian is living with our son. When I saw her again, she looked more beautiful than any woman I had ever seen. She had acquired the beauty of emotional maturity and the self-assurance of a woman who was being precisely what she wanted to be at that time in her life and was confident she had the means to do so in the future. She exuded that beauty with her body and her gestures and her voice. When she saw me she said: "You sound . . . I mean you don't sound like you did when I first met you. You sound like an Aussie now. You even look like one. It is strange."

I stay with her and the boy in Melbourne and attend school again. One day, in 1966, the Australian prime minister, Harold Holt, goes for a swim and is swallowed up by the surf. His body is never recovered. The American president, Lyndon Johnson, flies to Melbourne to attend the memorial service. When his motorcade passes through downtown, we students are waiting for him, shouting the slogans of the day, including the query about how many children he'd killed that day. I'm standing next to my friend Karl Ostberg, who, like me, is holding a bucket of red paint. Karl throws his at LBJ's limo when it passes by. Before I can throw mine, Karl and I are picked up by the cops and carted off to jail. But they gave neither one of us poison to drink. Hey, you can do anything you want in the land behind the mountains. You can also smoke pot and listen to Bob Dylan.

So I smoke pot and listen to Bob Dylan. And I get bored with school and drop out. I can't abide city life. Family life. Student life. The bush is where I belong. I am restless and I want to return there. So when Gillian leaves me, taking our son, Malcolm, with her, I return to the back of beyond, with the wondrous stars, the rugged land, the uncouth men, the basic facts. I spend another year there, in Tom Price. I love it here, I tell myself. I want to live here forever. From time to time, when I'm drunk or stoned, I find myself making a rendezvous with one or another unsettling memory from my past, but I push it away. *Go away. Leave me alone.* I'm free from the madness of those who want to send you to their Glorious Maker. In the state of having escaped, which is now my homeland, everyone brings with him the conviction of his own free verse.

One day I fly down to Perth on my week off and see a travel agent. I tell her I'm thinking about taking a boat trip to Singapore. She asks, "What date?" and I say any date, I'm easy. She tells me about boats leaving in three months, boats leaving in five weeks, boats leaving in seventeen days, and so on.

"In fact, we even have one boat leaving this afternoon," she says, "but I shouldn't imagine you would want that?"

"Why not?"

"Okay, I'll book you on that if that's your plan."

"It is now."

I ask her what I need and she says, in addition to my ticket, a vaccination certificate and a passport.

"You work on the ticket," I find myself telling her. "I already have a passport, and I just need to know where the nearest clinic is to get my vaccination."

She tells me, and I run off to be vaccinated, go to the youth hostel to pick up my knapsack, and stop at the bank to withdraw all my money. My Australian passport is in my pocket already. I'm a citizen of this land behind the mountains.

When I return to see the travel agent, she hasn't gotten my ticket ready yet. "I forgot to ask you," she goes. "Is it one way or round trip?"

"One way."

She takes a long look at me. "You fellows from the bush are really strange," she says.

Yes, we fellows from the bush are strange. I've become a veritable denizen of the bush. I've lived it and loved it and become it. Now it's time to move on, to find out what there is in other lands behind those other mountains. I'm twenty-six years old. The new land I am going to is just about to gain its independence. It has no flag, no government, no army, no written constitution, no bureaucracy, no history, and no traditions. Just a name: the Woodstock Nation. Anyone, of any race, color, or creed, could become a citizen. Its only requirement for naturalization is love—love for drugs, music, and abandon. My kind of nation.

On the boat, I meet Jennifer. At twenty-two, she has a kind of fresh, zestful beauty not perverted by makeup or fancy clothes.

"Where you going?" she wants to know.

"I don't know. I'm just going. What about you?"

"I don't know either."

"Let's go together."

"Do let's."

"Great."

Before we land in Singapore, Jennifer confides in me: "You know, I've been wanting to do this for a while."

"Do what?"

"To freak out," she says, using the idiom of the day. "You know, for me, it all started at college. I'd do one outrageous thing after another, defying my middle-class traditions. I don't know why I did those things. I was just driven. And with every tradition I broke, provoking my parents' hysterics, the more ecstasy I felt."

I laugh approvingly.

She brushes her hair from the nape of her neck and holds it there, dangling over one side as she talks. "I was like Salome, you know," she says, her tone balancing mockery and self-confidence. "I was like Salome dancing before Herod, dropping one veil after another. Now I've dropped all my veils, and I'm free. I'm not fighting anyone or anything anymore."

I fell in love with her there and then.

Yes, Jennifer and I belong to the same nation, the same state of having escaped. She has passed through the Disneyland of her middle-class culture, just as I have passed through the torpor of our immobilized culture, and emerged with good cheer. We may not have known what we wanted or where we were going, but we certainly knew what we didn't want and would not go.

I am walking down the street in Kuala Lumpur with Jennifer, feeling good. We have just taken a few hits on our *chillom*, the hash pipe, in our hotel room. The strange sounds of this Third World, predominantly Moslem city are coming at me from every direction but I hear them as one coherent symphonic composition. The hash is so strong that I feel able to deconstruct these sounds and listen to them separately. As I do that, I hear one sound that is familiar to something raw and native in my consciousness, reaching me like light sent from an outermost galaxy. It is the *muazzen* calling the Moslem faithful to prayer.

Leave me alone alone alone.

This mindless ritual has turned Moslems into zombies. It has debased all that is beautiful in the Koran and cheapened the miracle of words in it. Islam never told men and women to submit to oppression when it is meted out to them—submission is only to the Word—and it never told them to acquiesce in the forfeiture of their human rights by a *zahem*, a tyrant. It told them the opposite. It told them—urged them—to seek *el ilm*, the knowledge of freedom, even though it may be "as far away as China." The fiercely independent desert tribes to whom the Prophet (a poet and a freedom lover if there ever was one) preached the Message would have responded to nothing less than a call for genuine freedom. By living the way I'm living today, I tell myself, I'm true to the authentic values of my culture, not the depraved ones that the age of neobackwardness has bequeathed us.

Jennifer and I finally reach Katmandu. We live there for five months. One beautiful, clear day I go to the Swayenbu Temple, on top of the Swayenbu Mountain, directly outside the city. Behind me is the exquisite Buddhist shrine. Below that is the beautiful Katmandu Valley. To my left I can see the awesome Himalayan Mountains. And closer on my left, at the foot of Swayenbu itself, is the village where Jennifer and I are now staying in a hippie commune. I couldn't have chosen a more beautiful day or a more beautiful place, or a more beautiful mood to be in, to take my first acid trip.

There is no other, more acquisitive trip of discovery than the one that you take on acid. On an acid trip you are not in any time or any place. You just are. You are at once translating and being translated by the being of things. You can enter the veins of a leaf, become part of the cloud you are watching, or exercise on your trip the most penetrative authority over the color, the shape, and the function of any object you wish to contemplate. Acid frees you from the constraints of time as we know it. On an acid trip, time just is not. (That's about as close to God as you can get.)

This hit me with blinding clarity one day when poor Jennifer dropped a trip (not her first), and it turned bad. Just as we can say a good acid trip is heaven, we can equally say that a bad acid trip is hell. When someone is having a bad trip, all you can do is sit next to that person and, as we used to say, just let out good vibes. Jennifer was sitting in our room at the commune having her bad trip, with me touching her lovingly from time to time. At one point I realized I had run out of cigarettes and asked her if she would be okay by herself while I went down to the tea shop in the village to get some. She said she would be fine. So I stood up, opened the door, and smiled at her. She smiled back at me as I closed it. I went all the way down the hill, bought some cigarettes, sat around for a short while taking hits on a *chillom* that the freaks, who always gathered there, were passing around, and walked back home. I was gone for about half an hour.

When I opened the door and walked in, Jennifer looked up and said: "Hey, what happened? Have you changed your mind about buying cigarettes?"

To her, I had just opened the door, closed it, and immediately walked back in again.

I had a bad trip myself once. I took it where I always took my trips, by the Swayenbu Temple. The mountaintop is thick with trees, and on these trees harmless little monkeys are always running around. My trip started great and proceeded to get greater. Then this damn monkey landed on my shoulder, just for a second, and jumped off again, just long enough for me to turn around and see it on my shoulder. What I saw was this *ugly* face staring at me. Then everything turned ugly. The Himalayas. The valley below. The trees. The temple itself. Everything was speaking to me in ugly sounds. Emitting ugly colors. Taking on ugly shapes. Threatening me with death and void. The monkeys looked as savage as tigers. A Buddhist monk, wandering around the courtyard of the temple in his pink garb, looked like my father, mumbling incoherently to himself about how soon, for surely it must be soon, he would be returning to Haifa. Dumb fuck. Leave me alone alone alone.

I walk down the mountain, heading home. In the courtyard of the commune, there are three girls bathing at the fountain. One of them is Jennifer. Three gorgeous girls, naked, free, beautiful. They all greet me and ask me to join them. But they look so ugly. So menacing. Their faces and bodies keep twisting and deforming right before me. Jennifer reaches out to touch me with her hand and I flinch. Her hand looks like an ape's—hairy, slimy, smelly. I feel a terror, a menace, the threat of death stalking me.

Jesus, this is hell. I want out. Jesus, I want out. Out out out.

...

There is nothing to do in Katmandu other than take drugs, listen to music, and make love. There is nothing more exquisite than this nothing. Night and day. Day in day out, night in night out. Drugs music love. At the commune, there is a room where, at all hours, at all times, there are people sitting around listening to sounds and taking hits. You walk to the village and sit in the tea shop, pass *chilloms* around and listen to the great music coming out of England and the States. Sometimes you walk to the city, twenty minutes away, and hang out with the other freaks at one of the joints there and again pass *chilloms* and listen to music. If you're in the mood, you can always go, on a Friday, to the marines' TGIF party at the American embassy. The marines are so lonely here they don't even mind the hippies coming to their parties. Between the Peace Corps and AID, there aren't more than a dozen resident (normal) Americans in town. There are ten times as many other resident (freaky) Americans though.

When it started getting cold in Katmandu around October, Jennifer and I, along with virtually the entire hippie community, evacuated, heading down to Kashmir or Benares or Goa. On the way, Jennifer and I stopped here and there, encountering fellow freaks, some of whom were joining ashrams and listening to swamis pontificate about the life of the spirit. But our final destination was Panjim Beach in Goa—a paradise on earth. A five-mile stretch of beach that was deserted except for a few fishermen and their families. In Benares, by the Ganges River, we rented a houseboat, and I proceeded to practice my tablas. I had one tabla master who was blind, then another who wasn't but spoke no English. To play an instrument you need neither eyes nor words. I learned a lot from both of them.

Nirvana. Sitting on the deck of our houseboat, watching the sun setting on the Ganges. And just before it sets, sinking behind the ancient river, as it has been doing ever since time became time, there is a bronze glow in the sky, deepening as it suffuses a tundra of clouds just before the sun vanishes. Smoking hash, playing tablas, making love. Jennifer is so beautiful, almost as beautiful as her voice. I love the sound of her voice. When she talks to me, I don't hear the words, just the arc of their melody that I want to replay on my tablas. Listen to this, I tell her, listen to this baby. Here is one *raga*, with its own precise melody form to match the way your voice sounds. *Ta ta tira kit, ta ta tira kit, ta ta tina.* And a *tala* with a rhythmic cycle of sixteen beats. *Tatatirakit, tatatirakit, tatatina.* Now with a different ascending and descending movement. *Dha dhin, dha dhin, dha dha, dhina.*

The freaks from the other houseboats join us often and we play together. Tablas, sitar, guitar, vina, along with spoons hitting a bottle, sticks hitting the deck, hands hitting each other. Only sounds matter now.

In Goa we rent a hut by Panjim Beach. There is no running water, no electricity, no bathroom. We get our water from a well, our light from candles. Panjim Beach is paradise, unviolated by people or things. It tapers off to the left and right to a blade point of rock, enclosing it, making it just the right size for the seventy or eighty of us freaks who live here. Jennifer and I get up in the morning and walk twenty yards to the beach.

We swim, walk around, make love. The freaks visit each other, parading their nudity. We smoke hash, listen to music, make love. And sometimes we talk.

Jennifer and I discover opium in Goa, which we start eating from time to time. You eat the stuff and go sit on the beach and scratch yourself, which is what you do when you're on O. Just gently, barely touching your skin. And you feel this great sensation. Sometimes we would just sit outside the hut in late afternoon, wait for the sun to set, and do a *chillom* or two. High. Watch the low rays of the sun slanting inch by inch, minute by minute, into the hut. The sky shows a warm fulvous hue. The palm trees rustle. The air is cool and fresh. And the sea, with the barest of waves reaching the shore, lies calm as glass, sparkling and lazy beneath the sun. That's the problem with Panjim. It is too perfect, a replica of paradise.

When the September harvest of hash from Nepal came in, I scored three keys and had them shipped in a variety of packages to Paul, an

English kid who is a dealer in Amsterdam. I'd met him in Katmandu earlier, and we'd made this arrangement. I send him hash, he sends me money via American Express in Bombay. Every two months or so, I send him a couple of keys, and he sends me the money without fail. Hash in Amsterdam is virtually legal. In India, it is neither legal nor illegal. No one has bothered to introduce legislation formalizing its status, just as they have never bothered to do with tea or bananas.

I always love going to Bombay to pick up my remittance from Paul. It's a two-day journey there and back by boat. Getting my hard-earned money via American Express, and meeting all the newly arrived freaks. *What's the latest on the Chicago Seven, man? Hey, man, did you go to Dylan's concert on the Isle of Wight?* I always loved returning home, after an absence of three or four days, taking the boat back from Bombay to Goa City, a canoe across the river, à la Graham Greene, a bus to Panjim village, and then walking home from there. I would go to the hut, take my clothes off, and run to the beach looking for Jennifer. There she is, galloping on the sand, sprinting toward me like a child, as beautiful in her nakedness as truth, her lips already forming my name, her hair blowing wildly about her face. After we kiss, she would jam her nose into mine and then climb on my back, jumping up and down like a monkey. Jennifer. My sweet little monkey.

One day a petite American girl, as slender as a wand, with long red-brown hair and eyes speaking of both innocence and inquisitiveness—she looks nineteen—walks into our hut. There are no locks, doors, or formalities in Goa.

"Hi there," she says.

"Hi," Jennifer and I respond in unison.

She sits down on the floor with us.

"Just arrived here?" I ask redundantly, since she is lugging a knapsack.

She nods. "Can I stay with you?" she asks, her expression arch and childlike.

"Sure," I respond. No one stands on ceremony here. "What's your name?"

"Jennifer."

Another Jennifer.

"Okay, I'm Jennifer I," my Jennifer offers, "and you're Jennifer II. Get your sleeping bag out and feel at home."

"What tapes do you guys have?" Jennifer II wants to know.

We show her our tapes and she shows us hers.

"Where did you come down from, Jennifer?" I ask.

"Kashmir. Before that I was in Katmandu and in Pondicherry. Stayed at the Shro Orobindo Ashram for three months."

I pack a *chillom* and pass it around. We go for a swim and a long walk on the beach. On the way we meet Betty and Mark from Rochester, New York, with their two kids, whom they now call Fields and Rivers, seven and eight. The kids are having their math class. Mark simply asks his kids to add, subtract, and divide pebbles. At home, they are taught reading and writing. We talk about the upcoming Christmas party we're all going to have on the beach Christmas night. But that's almost a month away.

After we sit and watch the sun set (a formidable sight in Goa), Jennifer I, Jennifer II, and I return home and cook dinner on our kerosene stove. While our vegetables are cooking (that's all we eat here), we sit on the floor, do another *chillom*, and listen to our tapes.

"I love you," Jennifer II says suddenly.

"I love you too," Jennifer I says.

"I love you," I say.

This is mighty good hash, man, this September harvest.

I play my tablas for a while.

It gets dark out. The darkness is soft and rich.

Jennifer II lights a couple of candles.

We eat our dinner, using palm leaves for plates.

We do another *chillom*, sitting outside the hut on a blanket. The music is not on, but I can hear all the sounds, and they are all native to nature: the sound of waves breaking, the wind, the palm trees swaying, the crickets, a dog barking, seagulls, the guffaw of a loon. The sound of the three of us breathing. I can hear it all as one composite. There are no artificial sounds here. No intrusive sounds. Just sounds native to nature.

Suddenly I start giggling uncontrollably and repeating the word *wild* over and over again in between giggles. And then Jennifer I and Jennifer II also start giggling uncontrollably, as if I have shared a great joke with them that they find immensely funny. We are falling all over the floor, and each other, with merriment.

"That is so wild," Jennifer II titters, a strand of her hair blowing directly across my face.

We get up in the morning and spend another day on the beach. We swim and make love and smoke hash and listen to music, and later hook up with other freaks from the other end of the beach and we swim and make love and smoke hash and listen to music some more.

There is Jennifer II on the beach dancing with slithery grace—water up to her ankles, her naked body shining in the sun, her tiny round breasts topped by brownish nipples—and raking red-brown hair before her face. How could such a petite body look so voluptuous?

"I want us to live together forever," Jennifer II says to me and Jennifer I.

"I love you," I say. And Jennifer II and I make love. And then we listen to music and smoke hash.

We are together for a month. So the calendar said. I know it was longer, much longer.

Jasmine, it's a wondrous land that lies behind the mountains.

On Christmas day, after the sun sets, the three of us drop acid in preparation for the party and wear our most colorful clothes, put on our beads and bracelets and anklets and earrings, and head on up the beach, taking with us, along with my tablas, the food that we had toiled all day to cook that was to be our contribution to the party. When we get there, someone has already started the bonfire. There were more people there than I had suspected the hippie colony in Panjim contained—well over a hundred. It was, by an incredibly happy coincidence, a full moon.

After everyone had eaten and it had gotten dark, the band started playing. This was a band like no other. No lead vocalist or guitarist. No backups. No keyboards. No bass. Anybody who wanted to could join or drop out of the band at any time. This band was comprised of a hundred or so freaks, together on the beach, under a full moon, playing the instruments of their choice. Making up the tunes of their choice. Following the rhythm that was in their heads. Playing a composition that had never been played before and would never be again.

Anyone who felt like dancing stood up and danced alone. The bonfire burned. Bodies swayed. Music was made. I heard it. I played my tablas to it, with it, from it. Jennifer I, tripping, kissed me. I love you. I, tripping, hit my drums *ta ta tira kit, tata tira kit, tata tira kit, tata tina.* Jennifer II, tripping, smiles at me. I love you. We are drugs and music.

Drugs are a thing that takes you on a free trip to find, actually find, that which is not there. And music is a thing, the only thing, that can make meaningful what our human meaning is. Without it life is empty. Life is cliché. Life is a presence without mystery and celebration.

Sometime in the night—no one here knows what time it is, or what time itself is—Jennifer I, Jennifer II, and I leave the party and walk along the beach on the way home. The three of us are coming down from our respective (great) trips. We take our clothes off and run up and down, back and forth, playfully throwing our shirts and pajama pants and other clothing at each other. Then we sit on the sand, by a fisherman's boat, naked, and hug each other and make love.

"The sun will rise soon," I say, sadly.

"Why do you say that?" asks Jennifer II. "The sun never rises. The sun never sets. The sun doesn't move in relation to us. We only think the sun rises and sets. It's a silly term. But in reality we're the ones, here on earth, who rise and set. Not the sun."

I love you. The three of us hug each other and kiss and make love.

We wake up in the hut, and Jennifer II tells us she has to go. We don't ask why. The last thing she says to us is, "Remember, the sun doesn't rise or set. We do. I love you."

I am distraught with sadness at seeing her go. Jennifer II remains frozen in my memory, to this day, like a statue that commemorates our season of love in the Indian subcontinent.

A week later, there is a man, an embassy type, dressed in a suit—a fucking suit—walking up and down the beach showing a photograph to all the freaks and asking them: "Have you seen this girl?"

Jennifer and I are lying naked on the sand when it's our turn to be shown the photo. He is embarrassed and hardly looks at Jennifer's naked body as he shows me the photo.

"Have you seen this girl?" he asks. "She's an American citizen. Her dad is a member of the U.S. Senate. He's anxious to know of her whereabouts and to have her return home."

He shows me the photo.

Jennifer II. I love you. I spent my season of love with you. Seasons of love come and go only once in a lifetime. And you're right. The sun doesn't set or rise. We're the ones who do.

"Have you seen this girl, sir?"

The man looks silly in his suit here on the beach. I look at the photo some more.

"No I haven't," I say. Then I add: "I can't say that I have."

I will not be party to allowing Jennifer's tradition to chase her down and tie her up. Our nation was created as an antidote to the poison of that tradition. The poison that blinds us to light. That banishes us to emptiness.

...

Everything loses its spell after awhile, even paradise. Panjim Beach remained our habitat for four months after Jennifer II had left, but already Jennifer I and I were thinking about leaving ourselves. Sometime before we did, a newly arrived couple came to live with us. Josh and Barbara, both Canadian, both twenty-four. Josh had read William Burroughs's *Naked Lunch* and wanted to be Burroughs and live his life—as in to hell and back with the heavy drugs. Let them eat away at your body and soul and then, at the last minute, just before they finish you off, you draw back. He got into heroin. The fool. He didn't even know how to shoot when he first arrived in Panjim. He had to bring this Swiss junkie, Marcel, over to the hut to show him how to look for a vein. Josh would sit there, looking intently, lips pursed, eyebrows arched with the anticipation of the prick from Marcel's needle, and wait for the heroin to send him on that trip to hell that he was so anxious to make. Soon he learned the tricks of the trade and didn't need any guidance. He himself became a guide—for Barbara. Barbara was a rabbi's daughter. Josh's father, whom Josh hated, was a corporate executive. His mother, whom he didn't hate, was dead. She had died of hepatitis just two years before, at forty-four. Less than six months after her death, his dad married a woman a year younger than Josh. It was awful being around these two strung-out junkies. They talked about junk all the time.

Who said the West does not have mad obsessions, different in kind but the same in degree, as the East? Who said neobackwardness does not afflict Europeans as much as Arabs? Surely the degradation that Josh and Barbara have stooped to is evidence of that.

Arab culture may have been sapped of élan, but Euro-American culture has been robbed of its sense of enchantment, its capacity to feel, by its commitment to the "conquest of space" and the "taming of nature" that finally extended to the conquest and dehumanization of human souls. The *procès de chosification* that Franz Fanon talked about in *Les Damnés de la terre*, where colonialism, in its heyday, often turned its victims into *choses*, caricatural clones of the colonizer, is active on another level in Western society. For there the process turns its victims into abject slaves of excess, waste, and pillage both of self and the environment.

Soon Jennifer and I took off, leaving Josh and Barbara with the hut. Rent seven dollars a month to be paid in dollars, not rupees, to the Indian fisherman who owned it. We roamed around India for a while and ended up in New Delhi. We invested most of our money (Paul had been ordering increasing amounts of hash) in a bunch of colorful Indian clothes and jewelry that we planned to sell in Europe (the stuff was still a novelty there) and then hopped on a bus that was to take us all the way from the Indian capital to Amsterdam. We had figured on a three- or four-week trip. The bus was owned by two asthmatic upper-class Englishmen, twin brothers, whose business was to run the bus from Delhi to Amsterdam and back again. Our trip, as it turned out, was destined to be their last. The bus broke down, and the twins ditched it, along with its passengers, somewhere in the middle of Afghanistan, absconding with our money. (They claimed they'd spent it all.) Before they did, I grabbed one of the twins by the throat and said, meaning every word, "I'm gonna break your fucking neck, you piece of shit!"

And he says: "Oh, I do *so* wish you wouldn't."

Hell, how could you hit someone who talks like that?

And to think that I had just saved their lives, and those of the other passengers, or at least their possessions!

We were driving through the Khyber Pass, a region inhabited by a tough group of tribes known as Pathans, with the Afridi tribe being dominant. The Pathans recognize the authority neither of Pakistan to the east, nor of Afghanistan to the west. And over the years, when the government of either country tried to subdue them, they failed. Invaders from Alexander to Queen Victoria had failed in the same endeavor, so why should the ragtag armies of Islamabad and Kabul have succeeded? These guys in the Khyber Pass don't let anyone toy with them. They run free. They are armed at all times (a man from the Khyber Pass would be as helpless without his weapon as a man in L.A. without his car). And if they feel like holding up a stranger, they do it, melting into the vastness of the Khyber Pass expanse. They've been doing it for two thousand years. You wanna chase them, go ahead.

So here we are, being driven over the Pass by these two upper-class Englishmen, with sickly blond skin and freckles, and the bus breaks down in the middle of nowhere (the first of many breakdowns). We discover it is overheating and simply needs water. Before we get moving again, one of the two brothers, who has a comical English name like Nigel, points to the hill on our right.

"Oh dear, oh dear, look who is here," he says in his wimpy, sonorous, upper-class accent.

We all look up, and there is this Khyber Pass dude, dressed in robes, his headgear covering most of his face, glaring at us. He is, of course, armed—not with a handgun, but a Kalshnikov, the weapon favored by Third World guerrillas, who call it *harek-kharek* ("to burn–to explode").

"Come on, man, let's get on the bus," I urge Nigel with desperation.

"Oh do let's stop and talk to the man," he suggests.

"Let's get on the fucking bus. Come on, move!"

There was no dissuading him.

Mr. Khyber Pass sprints down the hill and walks over to us. Gesturing with his hands, he tells us in Pashtun, his local tongue, that he wants a ride up the road. You can't say no to a guy who could easily make your brains burn and explode. He climbs on the bus. We drive on. Any minute now he's going to hold us up, demanding our money, passports, traveler's checks, and maybe our lives. The man sits in the front of the bus, looking furtively at the passengers from time to time. There are about twenty of us, all freaks with long hair. He takes his Kalshnikov off his shoulder. Jesus Christ, Jesus Christ. Here we go. I don't think too many of the people in the bus knew what the hell they had coming. Certainly not Nigel, who is happily driving and humming some moronic English tune about how he wants to "fuck them all, fuck them all, the young and the short and the tall."

I'm trembling with fear but I still have some presence of mind. I walk down and sit next to Mr. Khyber Pass.

"*Essalmu Aleikom*," I say with a confidence that I far from feel.

"*Wa Aleikom Essalam*," he responds, stunned.

I had greeted him with the Islamic salutation, universally recognized in the entire Islamic world, of "Peace be unto ye."

Where do I go from here? Maybe I should try to communicate with him in Classical Arabic, the language of the Koran. He might know a few words.

"Art thou an inhabitant of the lands of the Khyber Pass?" I ask. I have one hand in my pocket and the other gripping the back of the seat. I don't want him to see me trembling.

Not only does he readily respond but in fluent, impeccable Classical Arabic.

I ask him how come he speaks Arabic so well, and he tells me he is a reciter of the Koran at the mosque and has learned to read, write, and speak the language in order to pursue his career.

Okay, I'll try this one and see what happens: "Say He is Allah, the One and only, Allah the eternal, the absolute. He begetteth not, nor is He begotten. And there is none unto Him."

I've recited one of the first *suras* from the Koran, imprinted in a Moslem's memory since childhood, just as the Lord's prayer is imprinted in a Christian's.

"Thou art a Moslem?"

"We all are Moslems on this bus."

"Thou art afeared of the same Lord, the Lord Allah, as I am?"

You bet we are, if that is what we need to be afeared of in order to save our lives and possessions.

"We are afeared of the Lord Allah, His Messenger the Prophet, and the Angel Gabriel through whom He delivered the Message," I respond.

Tell me what else you want us to afear and we'll afear it.

"Thou art Moslems?"

"We are that. And we are journeying to the blessed city of Mecca to do the *omra*," I say. I knew enough to know it wasn't Hajj time yet. Just *omra*, a kind of unofficial, spiritual visit that Moslems make any time of the year they choose.

"Thou art fortunate," he says with a sly smile, putting his weapon back on his shoulder.

We drop Mr. Khyber Pass two miles up the road.

"Okay listen up everybody, thou art fortunate because I've just saved thine asses from being robbed," I stand up in the middle of the bus and declare.

Imagine, I was able to prevent a tough Pathan with a machine gun from robbing us but unable to prevent a couple of wimpy Englishmen with names like Ian and Nigel from doing the same.

And here we are, me and Jennifer, dumped in the medieval town of Kandahar, in southeast Afghanistan, with very little cash and a pile of Indian clothing and jewelry that would fetch a lot of money in Europe but are worth nothing here. Jennifer and I are in a hotel in the center of town, sitting in this room with lizards crawling up the wall, trying to figure out what to do. We can make it perhaps as far as Venice, the first affluent city in Western Europe, where we can unload our Indian goods. We should also have a key of hash that I had shipped to myself from Bombay waiting for us in Amsterdam—barring the possibility of our being kidnapped, robbed, or killed on the way.

Happily, none of that took place except in Turkey, where various "treacherous Turks," as Jennifer called them, harassed her relentlessly, blatantly pinching her bottom or fondling her breasts in the street.

We finally arrive in Venice by train, with barely enough money to store our goods in the station and none for a room in a hotel. We buy a slice of pizza that we share before going to sleep in our sleeping bags outside the station.

"Tomorrow, baby, tomorrow is the day we make the buckeroos," I tell Jennifer cheerfully, in the way of good night.

We get up in the morning and have another slice of pizza and a couple of hits on a joint. (Our *chillom* days are over. It's too risky around here.)

We take one of the four bags containing our Indian goodies from storage and head to the Piazza San Marco. We sit in the middle of the square, by the foot of a statue, take out our stuff, and spread it on a small sheet on the ground.

This stuff is so beautiful, so colorful. It is crafted, woven, designed in wildly exuberant styles. And it has not been seen in Europe yet. Within minutes, more than a dozen tourists are fighting to buy our goods. Minutes later, another group descends on us. Cops. They tell us to move on, that what we are doing is illegal. I ask them in my (very) bad Italian if we're allowed to peddle our stuff elsewhere in Venice.

One of them says: "*In nessuna parte di Venezia, in nessuna parte d'Italia.*"

We walk around dejected for half an hour, lugging our bag. We sit by the foot of the Academia Bridge, broke, hungry, and miserable.

"What now, my love," I sing in mock desperation.

"I know one thing," Jennifer says pensively, out of the blue, after more than five minutes of silence. "I'm not writing home for money. I'd sell my ass first."

"Come to think of it, I don't care to write home either," I say, still in mock desperation. Jennifer laughs and nudges me, knowing I have no home to write to.

We're sitting in a pretty, quiet neighborhood. Not too many tourists around. The Academia Bridge connects directly to the Academy of Arts, and there are a lot of students going up and down the bridge on their way from or to classes.

"Hey, I don't see any cops around," I say.

"You're right. Let's see if we can move some of this stuff here."

No sooner do we spread our goods on a sheet by the foot of the bridge than we are mobbed by students who not only want to buy them but are anxious to hear about India. Jennifer and I don't realize that we're a couple of wild-looking hippies and are as much an object of curiosity as the goods we're trying to unload.

By early afternoon, with still no cops in sight, we've sold everything in the bag, mostly to students but also, here and there, to tourists and regular residents of the city.

I run back to the station to get another of the bags. Jennifer holds the fort, and the attention of the students, while I'm gone.

We sell everything in the other bag before nightfall. We also find we've made a lot of friends, one of whom offers us hospitality in his digs, which he shares with his girlfriend. About ten of us go out and party that night. I turn them all on before we go out. I tell you, man, a good September harvest can take you far in the world.

Over the next three days, we go to our spot by the bridge. In addition to being the place where our goods sold readily, it was also a place where the kids would hang out to talk about politics, the war in Vietnam, rock music, Andy Warhol, the Common Market, Antonio Gramsci, the Black Panthers, jazz, the New Left, *L'Etranger*, and a host of other issues.

We sold everything we had, except for a few things that we gave away to friends, especially Roberto and his girlfriend, Ondine, the couple who had put us up, and decided to stay a few extra days to see Venice. Before we left, I gave away my last ten grams of hash. I had a whole key waiting at various postal offices in Holland. And here we are on our way by train, to the Dutch capital, loaded. (Well, it always sounds like you have a lot a money when you talk liras.)

We live in a commune in Leiden, half an hour away by train from Amsterdam, for six months. We go to the city every day and sit at the Daam with the other freaks and pass *chilloms* around. There are cops all over the place, but they don't care. The stuff is virtually legal here. At night we go to Fantasia or Paradiso, where I finally unload my key. At the commune we smoke hash, listen to music, make love. I want to live here forever.

One day Jennifer and I are walking down the street around the Daam, and we see Josh.

"Hey, Josh, how you doing, man?" I say, genuinely pleased to see him.

"Josh, Josh, good to see you," Jennifer adds, equally pleased to see our old friend from Goa. "Is Barbara with you?"

Josh looks awful. Strung out. Sickly white complexion. Sunken eyes. The works. He and Barbara have been in town for three weeks. Barbara is walking the streets, doing tricks, to keep them in junk. The first time she tried plying her trade in the famed red-light district, she got beaten up by three Dutch prostitutes—not their pimps, mind you—for invading their turf. Now she hangs out by the main railway station selling her body to migrant workers from North Africa and Turkey.

"Man, like, you know," Josh gushes his junkie incoherencies. "I mean, like, man, we're just trying to make enough money, like, you know, to blow this place and go back to Toronto. I mean, like this scene here man is like heavy duty and my girl and I, like, we just want out. I wanna go clean. Barbara too, man. Honest."

After he sponges twenty dollars off us, promising that "me and my girl" will get together with us soon, he walks away, looking like a sad and obedient dog to his merciless master.

There is a contagion of anarchy spreading across the heartlands of our nation, enfeebling and brutalizing its denizens.

Around that time, Bob Dylan came out with his *Nashville Skyline* album. When I heard it, I said, that's it, I'm not going to listen to any more Dylan music. What's all this nonsense about "throw my ticket out the window, throw my suitcase out there too"? I hated it. For me Dylan was dead. Soon after that, Jim Morrison died. Jimi Hendrix died. Janis Joplin died. The Black Panthers were dying. The antiwar movement was dying. The New Left was dying. The Beatles, as a band, were dying. In short, the Old Order was dying. The *ancien regime* was going bad in the teeth. The Woodstock Nation was losing its grip. The drugs, the music, and the sense of abandon that had helped it to perceive its own new consciousness were going haywire. The drugs were now hideous. The music was speaking in a benign, pedestrian voice. The sense of abandon had been supplanted by a sense of paranoia. The denizens of Woodstock were doing heroin, blowing up the physics department at Madison and trashing downtown Chicago, and saying throw my ticket out the window, throw my suitcase out there too.

This is the end, my friend.

What Morrison didn't realize when he sang that was that every end is also a beginning.

I have peaked as a freak. It's time to move on. There is always another land to see behind the mountains. My hair is now almost down to my waist (it's been growing for the last three years since I got on that boat in Perth, leaving the outback behind, and a child in Melbourne whose mother did not want me near him because I was, in her eyes, "a no-hoper") and I'm wearing crazy biblical clothes and a wild beard and earrings and bracelets and beads and anklets and paint on my face. I'm so freaked out that the newcomers at the commune (latecomers to the scene, from Kansas and Missouri) cannot resist taking pictures of me and Jennifer, who is always wearing that Indian coat of hers, with its wildly exuberant colors, that she'd stitched patches on when she was tripping one day, to make it project a psychedelic aura of flaming red, blue, aqua, yellow, gold, lime, and vivid crimson. A coat so huge that when we walked down the street on a winter night in Amsterdam, I thought she would be blown away.

This is the end.

It is time to move on. Those years I spent in the bush and on the road showed me how wondrous freedom and personal discovery were and how, without them, life is meaningless and hollow. If everything in the universe is in constant motion, then freedom is the poetry of motion. And I, a Palestinian from the refugee camps and the ghettos of Beirut, took to that life-style because it seemed like a natural evolution of my rebellious instincts as a street kid who rebelled against tradition and mocked its repressive social norms. I have not really changed over the years in my "state of having escaped." I have simply honed an already existing call for meaning within me that transcended narrow national culture. I was a Palestinian when I left Beirut to go to Australia, and I am still a Palestinian today, only more so. I am more so because I sought my Palestinian identity, and found it, in the place where it was not. I have carried it on my back all these years the way I have carried the memories of our flight from Haifa along the coast road. Whatever I was being and becoming in the land of others was the shadow of that name and of that exodus. A man can no more escape his identity and his memories than he can jump over his own shadow, as Goethe put it. So it was in the land of others, in the place where it was not, that Palestinians found their peoplehood. For the Palestinians did not truly become Palestinian until their country was dismembered and its population scattered to that state of having escaped. Our name was born in exile, not the homeground.

So here I am in Amsterdam, walking down the street one day tripping on mescaline. And I'm standing there staring at a hairdresser's salon. Finally I walk in and sit in the hairdresser's chair. I tell the man to cut my hair.

"How much do you want me to cut? An inch? Maybe two?" he wants to know.

"No, cut it all, real short," I hear myself saying, knowing all the while that I'm not in conscious control of my words. "And trim my beard too."

"Okay, if that's your plan."

"It is now."

I go home and Jennifer wants to scream with fright. All she can say is: "My God, my God, my God!"

This is the end.

I gather my things.

"Where you going?" she asks.

"I don't know. Where *you* going?"

"I don't know."

We sit and hug each other, engulfed by an immense silence that is filled with something equally immense, something clawing its way into me. Something that would take tenure there forever. Her hand grabs my wrist: "I don't know where I'm going. It's great we met. We'll always be together in a way. Just around the corner from each other. Even if we never meet again."

Whenever I think of Jennifer—and I still think of her today—I think of the way she said that. I knew that her meaning, like some happy verse, was not in the words she uttered but in something else, something behind the words. When we attempt to speak our selves, truly speak our selves, words fall short. Besides, having lived in Woodstock for so long, you hold words in derision. Discourse is found only in music. It is in song that you celebrate and realize your self. In Eden you don't read books. You don't write books. There is nothing there to verify, or know.

This is the end, my sweet friend.

I walk out of the commune and shut the door behind me. Another door shutting on everything I had been. But every end is also a beginning.

8

Immortal Longings, Mortal Wounds

I leave Ramallah and check back into the American Colony Hotel in Jerusalem. Leila comes to see me from time to time. It's been determined by her parents that I am "honorable company" and that she can visit me at the hotel, though not in my room. Just in the lobby and preferably with someone else present.

One afternoon, sitting alone with her there, drinking copious cups of coffee, I tell her bluntly: "My trip is not panning out right. I want to meet some leaders of the underground. Can you swing it?"

She hedges.

"Is that a tall order?" I ask.

She says that it is. Leaders of the *Intifada's* unified command are a rotating group. No one knows who they are. Former leaders don't know the identity of those currently in leadership, and these have no inkling who will follow them.

"I know that," I say patiently. "But I want to meet some of them. It's important to me. I want to get a feel for what's going on, to learn whether there is really a new political consciousness here. I want to know, very simply, whether we're dealing with a new generation, or just *another* generation, of Palestinians."

"These leaders," she says, "come from every segment of society, every political faction, every intellectual persuasion. And our society, obviously, like any other society in the world, is imbued with a great many ideological currents and political sensibilities. Hundreds of us have already served in the underground. You've probably met some UC leaders already without knowing it."

"Have you been one of them?" I ask with genuine amazement, though heaven knows there is no reason I should doubt it. Leila has been an activist intellectual ever since I've known her, a Gramsci intellectual as she calls herself, and a highly respected scholar in her discipline as a psychologist.

"Listen," she says, ignoring my question. "Why don't you meet instead with Faisal Husseini and the others operating above-ground?"

"I've got better things to do than hang out with those jerks. What can they tell me that I don't already know? Come on, Leila, what am I, some foreign journalist after a quotable quote from a family boy?"

"Why don't you go talk to them anyhow? They might have some information to give you. And you might have some information to give them."

"Believe me, Leila, we have nothing to say to each other. We come from different worlds. I'm from the refugee camps. That's where my head is at when it comes to seeing Palestine."

"I understand your anger at the Palestinian establishment," she says wearily. "We too are angry."

I like that "we too" bit.

"Have you been part of that rotating leadership?" I ask again.

"You're beginning to sound like a broken record," she says with a discomfited look, and sits back in her chair, hooking her fingers in her belt loops.

"Can you swing it then?"

"I'll see what I can do."

From the way she says that, I know she can. You don't live with a woman for a whole year, as I did with Leila in Buffalo, without eventually learning to hear what she does not say. We shake hands, and then she's off.

I sit in my room, put on my Walkman, and read *el Kods*, the local Arabic newspaper. Today is the ninth of January, and Tarek Aziz and Jim Baker, I read, are meeting in Geneva. Six days to go before the deadline expires, allowing the allied forces, by authority of the U.N. Security Council, to attack the Iraqi forces in Kuwait. Baghdad seems adamant about its intention to stay put. The Iraqi leaders are talking tough, promising to wreak havoc on all and sundry. The reports emanating from Radio Baghdad, read in Formal Arabic, sound out of this world. The satanic forces of the infidel will be crushed. Allah is on the side of the righteous. The heroic people of Iraq will die for the cause, the cause of good against evil. Moslems of the world, rally against the New Crusade. The Arab masses love this kind of bombast—identical to the drivel that emanated from Voice of the Arabs Radio in Cairo on the eve of the Six Day War. *Plus ça change.*

Baker has already arrived in Geneva. He is staying at the Intercontinental Hotel, where the meeting will take place. The Intercontinental used to be a hangout for the oil sheiks who held their semiannual OPEC meetings there. The irony deepens when it is revealed that Baker has booked the very suite formerly occupied by Sheik Zaki Yamani, the deposed Saudi oil minister. Yamani, in an ostentatious display of Saudi petrowealth, used to lease the suite all year round and leave it vacant most of the time.

I turn to the back page to read the obituaries. There are boxed announcements with black borderlines, chronicling the death of Palestinian youngsters killed in clashes with Israeli soldiers. *From Him we come, to Him we return. We mourn the death of our fallen patriot Ali Adwan, aged 17, who died and was buried in his land in the town of Khan Younis, Gaza.* Another one goes: *Ramzi Sansour, aged 16, from Nablus. Bless his soul and may our Lord open to him the length and breadth of His Paradise where he shall reside forevermore with all our other fallen patriots.* And yet another: *Members of Abu and Um Taha Rashidi, in Palestine and in the Exile, mourn the death of their son Taha, 21, who fell a patriot in defense of his nation, his land and his cause in the arena of struggle. Return, Oh thou spirit, reassured of Allah's blessing and of thine entry into Paradise.*

On my Walkman, Bob Seger is singing:

Some men go just where they want

some men never go

blame it on midnight. . . .

They've only got one thing in common

they got the fire down below.

There is a knock on the door and I ask who it is. Um Ali, my chambermaid, identifies herself. I let her in.

"May your day be blessed," she says, by way of a greeting. "Brother, I'm here to ask you to do me a favor, and those who do the poor favors are in turn favored by God."

Um Ali is a middle-aged woman who lives in a refugee camp on the outskirts of Ramallah. She has lived there since the exodus of 1948 when she fled her native Acre as a child. She is married with three kids.

"I have two sons in prison, and my husband is an invalid," she tells me. "I'm the only bread earner, and it has been difficult for us to survive. My nine-year-old boy, Jamal, has dropped out of school and now works in a grocery store in Ramallah, where the owner treats him like a slave. I don't mind any of that, my brother, except, as you know, I'm entitled to my stipend from Faisal Husseini's office of eighty shekels a month [$40] on account of my two sons being political prisoners. But I have not been paid a single piaster for the last five months. Every time I go there, I stand in line for hours, but Husseini's people just send me away. Well, my brother, I saw you with brother Salem a few times recently, talking to him in the lobby, and I know Salem works at Husseini's office. I just thought you might help me by perhaps talking to Salem and seeing if he could get me the four hundred shekels already owed me. Will you please do that for me?"

I tell her that I would most decidedly do that. The woman looks broken, tired, emptied. Her face seems to hold a permanent shape of hurt. All the Um Alis of Palestine still believe in the struggle; but there is no reason to think that the struggle has ever believed in them.

"They are rich, and we are poor," she says, tugging at the white scarf covering her head, sounding at once accusatory and plaintive. "They have everything, and we have nothing."

I assume she means the family boys. I consider all sorts of comments but choose none. "I am from the refugee camps myself, Um Ali, and I understand your difficulties. I understand your sentiments."

Her face lights up with surprise, as if I had said something profound. "Are you really a son of the camps?"

"I am indeed."

"Oh, the Lord blesses whomever He pleases, for look at you now brother, you have moved, with His guidance and His will, far in the world."

"With His guidance and His will, I have moved far in the world, but not far from the camps. My heart and soul, not to mention my politics, are still there."

Um Ali falls silent for a moment, focuses on her hands, and then looks at me in total repose: "In that case, it is not presumptuous of me to invite one like you, son of the camps, to share what modest *nimeh* we can feed you at our house this evening."

I tell her I would be most happy to come. Palestinians from the refugee camps, including those like myself who left when they were children, feel a deep affinity. To begin with, we were the poorest Palestinians and thus the ones hit hardest by the loss of home and homeland in 1948. We were forever singled out for the harshest treatment by our host states, ostensibly because of our radicalism. We were also brought closer together because, living as we did in the encapsulated locale of the camps—some of them larger than many towns in the West Bank and in pre-1948 Palestine—we turned our world into a homeland in exile where we perpetuated and reinforced the customs and the idiom of the old country. While other Palestinians got lost in or melted into their host states, we continued to believe in *el awda*, the Return, and to mourn our fate in *el ghourba*, the land of others. When our generation rose in revolt in 1968, the overwhelming majority who took up arms came from the camps. Inevitably, the greatest number of *shahids*, fallen patriots, and political prisoners also came from there.

While middle-class Palestinians outside the camps enjoyed privileges similar to those accorded the citizens of their host states, we were denied even the right to travel, since we were considered stateless. There was nothing more terrifying for a Palestinian from the camps in those days than to be caught at an airport, clutching his useless travel document, and then be turned back, harassed, or detained—for next to the word *nationality* in his papers there would always be an *X*. Perhaps that is why these Palestinians chose to terrorize airports in the early Seventies. In the end, Palestinians from the refugee camps bonded in a way that other Palestinians did not. For while they were losing many attributes of their national identity, we remained, we felt, more genuinely Palestinian, more true to the dream. Not only did we keep the notion of *el awda* alive and endure the harsh existence that *el ghourba* imposed on us, but we had the numbers—we comprised well over half the Palestinian population.

I happily make arrangements to meet Um Ali at the hotel later. I also tell her that, come what may, she'll be getting her money then, intending as I did to go to the desk in the lobby, change $200 into shekels, and give it to her.

I leave the hotel and go wandering around the city. It is the ninth of January, and every month on this day the whole West Bank, including East Jerusalem, goes on strike. I'm not sure what the strike is supposed to commemorate. There are so many strikes that even the people here have stopped bothering to ask what they are about. I was shocked one day when I asked Salem to tell me what the people were protesting, supporting, or stating, and he said he didn't know.

"I'll find out for you, though, if you want to know," he kindly offered.

People have become like sheep. They go along with whatever the Unified Command tells them. Strikes are part of the routine. And this routine represents a constant, repetitive pitch of daily life. The rhythm of people's material existence is no longer punctuated by the lyric, exhilarating power of the unpredictable, as you might expect in the lives of a people in struggle, but by monotony, repetition, dullness.

I'm wandering down Saladin Street, because of the strike not so busy now, with little traffic passing through. I am wearing a *hatta*, the Palestinian checkered scarf, around my neck (thus advertising my identity) and holding my backpack loosely over my shoulder. In it I have all my notes, on over a hundred sheets of white paper. Unbeknown to me, my backpack is not fully zipped, and now these sheets of paper go flying all over the place as I'm hurriedly crossing the street in front of a passing car. Before I know what's going on, half a dozen fellows materialize out of nowhere, some frantically helping me pick up my notes and others standing in the street authoritatively stopping traffic from passing on either side until I'd put all the sheets back in my bag.

"You'd better be on your way now, brother," one of them tells me solemnly, almost reverently, patting me on the back.

Oh, heavens, these guys think I'm an underground runner distributing leaflets of the Unified Command, a Palestinian patriot risking his life for the cause. I don't want to deceive them, so I tell the truth.

"We thought, brother, you had leaflets in there," one of them tells me with visible disappointment.

I wander around some more and find myself lost and late for an appointment at the National Palace Hotel with Salem and Mohammed Shadid, a Palestinian sociologist whom I knew in the United States when he was working on his Ph.D. So I hail a cab, and who should the driver be but Ahmad, a man to whom Salem had introduced me when I first arrived and who had solemnly promised "to turn his soul's concern in my direction" whenever I needed him.

"How's our boy doing?" Ahmad wants to know after I hop in his cab. He means Saddam Hussein.

I tell him I don't know. I don't want to shock him by telling him that, unlike most other Palestinians, I despise Saddam.

"He's going to put them all, all these American sons of whores, in a barrel of shit. Just wait and see. And that Thatcher woman. I tell you, she's *shaybee wa aiybee*, gray haired and still slutting around. The daughter of a whore thinks the British are still running an empire. Brother Saddam has raised our heads high, no doubt about it. And he's linking Palestine to the whole issue of the Gulf. *That* shows honor. What Arab leader has had the courage to do that, I ask you?"

When he drops me off at the National Palace, I ask him how much I owe him and he says: "Whatever you want. I shouldn't even take money from you because you're a guest here."

I insist that I pay what I owe him.

I am a fool. I should have gone along with his offer because he ended up ripping me off mercilessly. But hey, he was just being a regular, down-to-earth, honest-to-goodness taxi driver like any other anywhere in the world. These guys belong to a transnational freemasonry of crooks who probably meet once a year in a secret convention for workshops on how to rip people off.

At the National Palace, I tell Salem and Shadid, who are waiting for me in the coffee shop, that I am deliberately late in order to show respect for our culture. That immediately starts a discussion about our exaggerated preoccupation with respect, shame, honor, boastfulness, dissembling, flowery speech, and above all, secrecy, that form the basis of the oral world of fantasy that Palestinians inhabit.

"A great many of these facets of our national character have unquestionably hampered our social progress," Shadid says, and adds with a smile, "but our preoccupation with secrecy, an art we have almost perfected because of our historical experience with foreign occupiers, has been an asset to us in conducting our *Intifada*."

Then he turns to Salem, and they get into "in" talk about the Palestinian uprising, referring to it in the third-person feminine, as if it were a woman. It was the talk of people who have worked together for so long on an issue so exclusive to them that they have dispensed with the need for parenthetical explanations.

"Hey, do you remember when they picked up Majid?" Salem asks.

Shadid laughs like a hyena. "I sure do! And how he actually pissed in his pants when they suddenly burst in on him."

"The dumb fool." Shadid turns to me to explain. "I mean they caught him there and then, red-handed, with a rough copy of the Unified Command leaflet in front of him, along with his press and ink and paper. He had been entrusted that month with printing it and putting it out."

"So what happened?" I ask.

"Two hours later the leaflet was out. No one knew how, from where and by whom. The Israelis were going crazy. Another time they caught four of them, representatives of Fatah, the Popular Front for the Liberation of Palestine, the Popular Democratic Front for the Liberation of Palestine, and someone from the Communist Party. Boy, did the Israelis gloat. Finally, they claimed, they'd caught the top leadership of the Unified Command! Before the day was out, so was the leaflet. The Israelis are pathetic. They've arrested well over a thousand fellows already whom they've identified, after each arrest, as the 'top leaders' of the *Intifada*. There have been dozens of times when high Israeli officials, including Rabin in the early days of our uprising, would smugly proclaim that they've finally smashed, crushed, wiped out, eradicated, destroyed the *Intifada*, only to be proved wrong. Israeli judges, after trying over a thousand cases in military courts, were exceedingly embarrassed by the comic assertions of the prosecution that this or that defendant was 'a top leader of the *Intifada*.' And Palestinians would just laugh and love it when they'd hear that so-and-so had been picked up and accused of being a leader in the underground. Hell, he was their neighbor, a fellow student in their class at college, their teacher whom they had thought all along was apolitical, their apathetic uncle, their service cab driver, their dentist, and so on. And that's why the underground leadership has acquired this mystique, this larger-than-life attribute of heroism—an attribute, I may add, that the *fedayeen* acquired for themselves after the battle of Karameh in 1968, began to lose after their expulsion from Jordan following the war of Black September, and which finally deserted them after their excesses in Lebanon and the siege of Beirut in 1982. Already the excesses of the Strike Forces are doing the same thing to the *Intifada* here."

Shadid looks somber. He tells me that the *Quoate Darebeh*, or Strike Forces, were essentially youngsters who, in the absence of local police and traffic cops—who had been called upon by the *Intifada* to resign their jobs—had taken on the admirable task of regulating traffic, settling disputes, picking up garbage, and so on. Initially, they did a great job. But they progressively turned into thugs. Now it was doubtful that they could be controlled. They had become undisputed enforcers and hit men.

Palestinians fear cadres of the Strike Forces, all of whom are school-age kids, more than the soldiers of the occupation forces. In the street, their word is law. The kids who represent Hamas are notoriously vicious. They rule through intimidation, brutality, and murder. Like their fanatic leaders, they disdain the PLO and secular nationalists, whom they identify as "decadent homosexuals." Palestinians who have died for the cause of Palestine are "dead, rotting meat" because they did not die for "the cause of Allah." Symbols of the nationalist struggle, such as the Palestinian flag and the *hatta*, are "dirty cloth" that "debase the word of God."

"I should say they have turned into enforcers of disorder," Salem offers. I had begun to like Salem ever since that night at his house when he told me, in his moment of drunken candor, about his experiences in Lebanon. "They're turning into thugs. They kill fellow Palestinians on the pretext that they are collaborators. Unquestionably, collaborators are among them, but the overwhelming majority are simply victims of interfactional or even personal feuding. The Strike Forces are getting so out of control it is doubtful that the leaders of the various political factions, by whose authority they were formed, could rein them in. They are turning our *Intifada* into a long day's journey into chaos. Mind you, there's a reason for the transformation of these youngsters from the idealist, well-behaved, politicized boys they were at the outset to the degenerates they have now become. They are alienated from the leadership of the movement, both in the West Bank and Gaza and in exile, whom they see as having failed them, perhaps even betrayed them. They have taken matters into their own hands, but they are too young, too unsophisticated, too alienated to deal with the real world. Most of them have brothers and sisters, friends and relatives in jail. They themselves have been imprisoned, beaten up, had their bones broken, or seen their friends killed before their own eyes. They want out. Nobody is getting them out of the daily grind that is life under occupation. They can't take it out on the Israelis—except you hear from time to time about some youngster who picks up a knife, goes to West Jerusalem, and stabs Jews at random—so they take it out on their own people."

Salem is puffing mightily on a cigarette. "This is scary, you know," he says. "In the 1930s, during the revolt, Palestinians were killing each other as well on the flimsiest of evidence that the victims were traitors or collaborators or accommodationists. In the 1970s, we did the same thing, chasing after each other in European capitals and accusing each other of being stooges of Israeli Zionism, American imperialism, and Arab reactionism! And we're doing the same thing here. The chaos, the hooliganism, the nonsense I witnessed in Beirut myself when I was there." Salem looks at me, and I catch the disillusionment, the cynicism in his voice, as he knew I would.

But as I listened, I was thinking that there might be other reasons, beyond the failure of the leadership, for the fact that Palestinians have continually turned on each other. Palestinians inhabit a repressed society that does not give its members an outlet for their libidinal impulses. When the national struggle is going well, young rebels find that outlet in their political activism. When the struggle ebbs, leaderless activists delight in orgies of bullying, terrorizing, dominating, and killing other, weaker Palestinians. The Strike Forces have become, literally, a mob, just like those small factions that were spawned following the devastating defeat of Black September in Jordan in 1970–1971, and, operating in the vacuum that followed, proceeded to do the same thing. A mob rarely has leaders, and its tactics rarely have a design. Like the mob they have become, the Strike Forces feed on a massive dose of masculinity, exaggerated professions of patriotism, and an affected sense of mission.

But there is yet another, and probably more important, reason for this ongoing tragedy in Palestinian history. The Palestinian struggle—a very costly one indeed—has been going on for the last sixty years, without letup and without results; as each phase ended, the Palestinian people were left with their dream betrayed, their goal unrealized, and their society drained. In this vacuum the bully-boy code of maleness is the outcry of a choked psyche, a desperate summons to sane leadership.

As we continue talking in the coffee shop, we are joined by a woman named Salwa, who lives in New York and works for the PLO mission there. Salwa is a Palestinian whose family stayed behind in 1948 in what later became Israel, and she grew up there as an "Israeli Arab." She emigrated to the States in 1970 and has since returned every two or three years to visit her family in Haifa. She is just back from such a visit and will be staying at the National Palace before she flies back to New York.

In addition to her suitcase, Salwa is carrying two huge peasant baskets that she sets down beside her. "My sister gave me these," she says. "She knows I'm going to be in Gaza for a day this week."

Her sister had filled the two baskets with secondhand clothes, jars of marmalade, home-pressed olives, dried yogurt, a dozen loaves of pita bread, and so on.

"My sister insisted I take these with me. She said, 'Please give these to our people in Gaza.' It's not charity, you know; it's just that she wants to feel connected to them. And you fellows know us and food. People in our part of the world, that's all we have to exchange, to show our love for each other. I remember when I accompanied the PLO delegation to Tehran in 1979. The Iranian officials were so excited about our arrival, about taking us here and there, from the Martyrs' Cemetery to the Foreign Ministry, from the Palestine embassy (which had been the Israeli embassy under the shah) back to our residence, that they forgot to feed us. Well, word went out to the crowds outside that we hadn't had dinner yet, and within less than an hour there were thousands, I mean thousands, of Iranians with pots of hot food that they were fighting the guards outside to bring to us. It was touching, their wanting to share their *nimeh* with us. We all had tears in our eyes."

All around us in the coffee shop, people are talking about whether there is, or is not, going to be war in the Gulf. Everybody is railing against America's arrogance and the UN's hypocrisy in rushing in to end Iraqi occupation in Kuwait but doing nothing about Israeli occupation in Palestine. And everybody is supportive of "brother Saddam" who, according to one fellow with a loud voice sitting behind us, "has raised our heads high."

"All the patrons here appear to be Palestinian," I tell my friends.

Shadid tells me: "In the old days before the *Intifada*, there would be Israelis all over Jerusalem, all over the West Bank, all over this very hotel. Now you don't see them anymore. Today there is not just a psychological barrier but also a physical barrier between us as occupiers and occupied. In effect, Israelis are saying we have nothing to do with East Jerusalem or the West Bank. That's an achievement of the *Intifada*, because by saying that, regular Israelis are in effect saying this part of Palestine is not theirs."

Just then, a group of men walk into the coffee shop. One of them, clearly the star, is Karim, a Fatah boy who belongs to the powerful landowning Abdel Hadi family. Karim works with Husseini aboveground. I'd heard of him but had never met him. He is said to wield a great deal of influence in the West Bank because of his family and PLO connections. He controls and dispenses millions of dollars to the "brother strugglers."

He swaggers into the coffee shop accompanied by his two *morafekeen* (literally, "companions") who act as his guards, assistants, and runners. He is in his mid-forties and is bald. His swagger is slow, impeded, most probably, by his awesome gut. The man has an air of self-importance, almost impatience, that he carries on a fleshy face advertising its intention to turn sullen any moment—as in the moment you displease him by disagreeing with his views.

He waves at Salem, Mohammed Shadid, and Salwa and comes over, with his *morafekeen*, to join us at our table.

I am introduced to him, and he pumps my hand repeatedly. "I've heard that you were in the homeland. Welcome, welcome. Thank the Lord for your safe arrival. Welcome, welcome. Palestine shines by your presence and you honor us all by . . ."

His *morafekeen* don't say a word. They sit there like obedient dogs on either side of him.

We talk for a short while about this and that, and then he turns to me and proceeds to tell me how evil America is. In a display of his total ignorance of the dynamic of the Palestinian struggle, he wants to convince me that "Israel is nothing" because decisions are "always made in Washington, not in Tel Aviv." The man sounds as if he is giving a lecture, and not just because he is speaking in Formal Arabic.

Then he tells me he wants to write a book about his "life in the struggle." In English. But he hastens to add that it would be written "with assistance from a brother who is competent in the language."

I ask him bluntly why he wants to write his book in English and not in his native tongue.

"Oh, it is pointless to write this book in Arabic. We want Americans to know us. Not Arabs. Arabs know us already. The whole point is to convince Americans of the justice of our cause. That is what is important, brother, that is what is important."

The man's Formal Arabic is beginning to get to me. And his calling me "brother" and all. When I'm addressed in that lingo, it always feels as if someone I don't like is hugging me too hard. And to communicate in Formal Arabic is a chore, like trying to stimulate a sluggish dinner party.

"And how much would it cost me to have this book published in the United States?" he wants to know. The man is ignorant not only about politics but also about publishing.

He persists. "I'm determined to have this book about my life in the Palestinian struggle published. Our people need justice."

This brings to my mind Um Ali, the chambermaid at my hotel, and I get testy as I tell him about her case. I explain that we cannot expect justice from the world if we ourselves are loathe to dispense it.

"Oh, I swear to you by the Prophet," he offers, "these sisters exaggerate. You're not familiar with them or their subterfuge."

I give him a murderous glare that I hope will put him in his place. It does.

Now I'm on my high horse. "Listen to me," I say aggressively, with a calculated lack of tact. "You fellows are not doing your job right, here. You're ignoring the people. The poor people. The families of the foot soldiers who are dying or going to prison every day to keep the struggle going. Without them you fellows would be selling falafel off a cart to make a living."

The man's Formal Arabic becomes more formal. "I will not permit you to address me thus!"

Permit? Did he say *permit?*

"I don't need nobody's fucking permission to say what's on my mind," I retort.

Salem is wiggling in his chair as if hoping it will swallow him up; Salwa cups her face in the palm of her hand; and Mohammed Shadid suddenly becomes preoccupied with folding his newspaper, all the while crossing and uncrossing his legs. The *morafekeen* narrow their eyes unpleasantly and stare at me.

"Thine words are inappropriate, brother," he says, shifting now from Formal Arabic, the language of political authority, to Koranic Arabic, the language of divine command. "I demand that you desist at once."

"And I'm telling you something else, buddy, I ain't letting thine ass fuck with mine head either, dig?" I retort.

"Art thou not in respect of the company of brothers?" he wants to know.

He doesn't get my answer to that one because by that time I'm on mine feet walking out on mine way to the lobby.

Stupid family boy!

When I get back to the hotel Um Ali is waiting for me. I give her her money, and she doesn't say much beyond thanking me profusely: "May the honor of your womenfolk remain unviolated, and the soul of your dead relatives remain blessed." I was thoughtless enough to hand it to her still in the envelope, with the hotel logo on it, that the cashier had given me. She knew what I had done.

When we get to her home at the refugee camp, I discover that she, her invalid husband, her mother-in-law, and her nine-year-old son live in one room on the ground floor of a two-story ramshackle house, with no windows except for a hole in the wall where a brick had been scraped out for ventilation. Clothes hang on a dozen nails hammered into the walls. There is a straw mat on the floor and practically no furniture to speak of. In one corner are stacked the family's thin mattresses and blankets. In another, the kitchen, stands a table holding various pots and pans and utensils, plus a kerosene stove. Another corner, where there is a thick mattress with cushions laid out on it, serves as the living room area. (There is an outdoor communal toilet, which, later in the evening, I had the misfortune to inspect. Inspect, I say, not use.) And in that corner, when we walked in, sat Um Ali's husband, motionless. He is paralyzed from the waist down, hard of hearing, and suspected of being senile. He looks twice his wife's age, with deep wrinkles covering his face and forehead. But he has sharp black eyes that, from time to time, tell you there is still a spark or two leaping in that dying fire. His mother is smoking a water pipe, apparently as contentedly ignorant of the world's existence as the world is of hers. Jamal, the nine-year-old son, is a bright boy with blondish hair and intelligent, inquisitive eyes.

We eat dinner on the floor off a round tray made of straw. Dinner is dried yogurt, black olives, thyme dipped in oil, one thinly sliced tomato, goat cheese, and pita bread, washed down with syrupy sweet tea. That is all. These people eat like this most of the time. They haven't had a hot meal in ages.

Over dinner, I tell Um Ali about my encounter with Karim Abdel Hadi.

"That dog! But beware. Beware these dogs, my brother. They can hurt you. Remember, when the axe comes to the forest, the trees say the handle is one of us," she says in a voice that seems to come from somewhere deep in her throat.

I tell her I will, wondering at her wisdom.

"My two sons. My two sons in prison. Those dogs don't care about them. Omar, the oldest, he's twenty-three, has been behind bars for three years for belonging to what the cursed Israelis, and may the Lord have no mercy on their dead ancestors, call a political organization. When I go to prison to see him and wait outside the gate for six hours before they let me in, I go through four sections, and with each section, it's clang, clang, clang, behind me. Why? Are they caging a dangerous animal there? It's only my beloved, obedient son Omar." Her anger darkens her face as she talks.

After taking a mouthful or two of food in silence, she says: "My other boy, Lutof, well, he's only fifteen. Why do they want to imprison a youngster like that?"

"Why did they imprison him?"

"The boy is too young to be in politics and in factions and in organizing and in resistance and so on. It's just that after his brother was arrested and tortured, he went crazy. He went out and painted a slogan on the wall, and they caught him doing it."

I ask her what the slogan was. She answers sheepishly: "It said, *man darabni, sa yantakni.*"

Fuck with us, pay the cost. In Arabic it rhymes.

Actually, Um Ali herself was pretty adept at summation. When, after dinner, I asked if she followed the news and was aware of developments in the national struggle, she did something quite dramatic. She stood up, went to the wall, and hit it twice with the palm of her hand. "Do you see this wall, brother?" she asked, in a voice full of pathos, speaking barely above a whisper. "This wall gives me my awareness every day. It tells me all about our struggle and how our struggle is developing. When it rains. When it gets cold. When it gets hot. I don't need these people from the PLO, cursed be they by both parents, to tell us how our struggle is going. We struggle just to eat. I struggle to visit my two sons in jail. I struggle when the hooligans from Kach come here. I struggle when the soldiers come. I struggle when this nine-year-old boy, who is being denied a childhood, comes home from work every afternoon tired and miserable and bent," she says, then walks over to Jamal and lovingly wraps her arms around him as an athlete does his trophy.

"Sometimes," she continues, "I tell myself we have died and are living in hell. But I tell you we are strong. We will survive. Believe me, we are strong. And if you want to know how strong we are, just ask yourself how many enemies we have. I just know that we are strong and we will make it. God is on our side. Unlike the Franks, including the Jews, we fear and respect God. We follow his rules. We allow these rules to govern our lives. We do not spit on His blessings. Look at the Franks at the hotel. They throw food away, God's *nimeh*; they put out their cigarettes in it. I know God cannot be on their side. I just know."

Palestinians like Um Ali, the mass of Palestinians, "just know." Unlike their Westernized, intellectual elite, they know. That is the frame of reference, the paradigm, through which they filter objective events. They "just know" what is right and what is wrong. To them "the objective" is not an arbiter of reality. As teleological creatures, Palestinians somehow feel, they sense, that reality submits to rules outside the domain of the objective. Intuition, the free impulse, is the guide to how life should be lived. The formidable, coherent energies of this intuitive mind, such as those exhibited in Oral poetry, song, and narrative (the only authentic expression of Palestinian literature), have always ripened into being apart from the rational.

Sometime before I leave, Um Ali is called by a neighbor, and she excuses herself. Jamal picks up a broom made of twigs and starts sweeping the area where we'd eaten dinner.

"Have you read about Mohammed el Deen el Kassam?" I ask him, referring to Izz el Deen el Kassam, the most famous peasant revolutionary from the Great Revolt of 1936–1939.

He turns around. "Brother, you mean *Izz* el Deen el Kassam, don't you?"

"His first name is Mohammed, not Izz," I persist.

"But brother, I swear to you by the Prophet," he responds, his eyes awash with innocence, "the name is Izz."

"I bet you six hundred shekels [about five hundred dollars] his first name is Mohammed."

"I'm sure it is Izz, because Daddy is always talking about him. He was one of his followers."

"Well, ask your father. The bet is on between us."

Jamal turns to his dad and says passionately: "Daddy, Daddy, tell the brother what Izz el Deen el Kassam's name was."

Abu Ali comes to.

"Tell the brother," Jamal continues, "tell the brother what Izz el Deen el Kassam's first name was."

Abu Ali turns his head a half-circle to see where I was. When he locates me, he thunders: "Praises be to Allah, what foolish question is that? The man's first name, of course, was Izz."

"Oh damn," I say, affecting disappointment. "I guess you win the bet, Jamal."

I give him six hundred shekels.

"You'll give that to your mom *after* I leave?"

He nods.

Before it gets dark, I say good-bye to the Alis and walk down to the main road to hail a service cab back to Jerusalem. Um Ali insists that she accompany me down the dirt track to the road. I try to explain that it isn't necessary, but there is no dissuading her. There are stray dogs all over the camp—no one has pets around here—and some of them run in packs, especially at night. I can hear them in the distance. In fact, I can see three or four of them, scrappy little creatures of skin and bones, at the foot of the hill, and I'm scared they might be rabid. So I pick up some stones, one in each hand, to throw when I get to the bottom.

And that's when Um Ali flips out. "Oh no, don't, please don't hold rocks in your hand," she pleads. "In the name of Allah, don't be seen with a rock in your hand."

You forget about these things. In the States, when you say "rock," you're talking either about a geological phenomenon or a typology of music. Here it is a weapon, one for which, if you get caught, you go to jail.

The money Jamal "won" off me is worth a lot to the Alis, I tell myself on the way back; to me it's worth nothing. In my room at the hotel I tell myself, no, it's the other way around. The money is worth nothing to them and a lot to me. Money is not what the Abu Alis and Um Alis in Palestine need. They need something more precious than that. And I guess you can't buy freedom. What I need is a kick out of knowing I have done good in Palestine, connected with my people. Well, a mere five hundred dollars, what I gave the Alis altogether, will buy that.

It's already dark. It's too late to go wandering around the streets of East Jerusalem but it's too early to go to sleep.

•••

I feel the urge to go to the other side of Jerusalem, to see how people in the other half of this tormented city live at night. I can't take it here anymore. Whichever way you turn is pain. It clings to the trees. You can smell it in the air. Pain is everywhere. *Intifada* or no, the people here have truly been cowed into submission. The suffering they endure is pervasive. And it is also democratic; it touches everyone. There is not a single Palestinian who has not been arrested, tortured, beaten up, humiliated, or been otherwise made miserable by the occupation. There is not a single Palestinian who does not know someone who has been imprisoned, deported, shot, or had his land expropriated, his village placed under collective punishment, his freedom to travel, study, build a house, denied. Pain has become so pervasive here that it has turned into political banality. I have been witness to this for only four weeks, and I'm already choking for breath.

Who put forth the proposition that human beings are hallowed by the evil of their enemies, ennobled by the oppression of their history? That is not happening here. Instead, Palestinians are devouring each other. Their political outlook has become archaic, their institutions unruly, their worldview distorted.

...

I need relief from all this pain. I'm outta here. On to West Jerusalem for the night, hitting the bars. Incognito. Hair in a ponytail. Leather jacket. Black pants. Earring. And my American passport in my breast pocket, as blue as the ocean, with the great seal of the United States embossed on it.

To hell with my weeks at NA, rehab, detox, AA. And the fact that I've been clean and sober all this time. Yo, bartender, keep 'em coming.

Ahmad, the taxi driver, who *loves* to turn his soul's concern in my direction, is parked outside, and I hop in his cab and tell him to take me to an interesting bar in West Jerusalem.

"Are you a Moslem, brother?" he wants to know as he drives on.

I tell him I am and that I have even gone to Mecca.

"Blessed is your soul. Then why would you want to block your entry into paradise by drinking alcohol?"

"Being here is enough to drive any man to drink," I say, which comes out gibberish in Arabic.

Ahmad drops me outside a dingy-looking place in a busy, well-lit downtown street that looks more like a restaurant than a bar. It'll do for starters.

"How much do I owe you, brother Ahmad?"

"Oh, whatever you want. Maybe I shouldn't take money from you because you're our guest here."

Come on, rip me off. I know you will.

He does.

I walk in and sit at the bar close to the door to watch the street. There is a constant stream of traffic and pedestrians. Couples holding hands. People coming in and out of restaurants and theaters and shops. Neon signs blinking advertisements for cigarettes and toothpaste and soft drinks and appliances.

The bartender, who is also the owner, cook, waiter, and cleaner, turns out to be a North African Jew. He gives me a friendly smile when he serves my drink, but he doesn't say much to me. Loquacity is an art invented by American bartenders, and their counterparts here haven't learned it. There are a few young Ethiopian Falashas drinking beer at a table nearby, and when our eyes meet, they grin. I grin back. A young, fashionably dressed couple are sitting across from each other at a table down the end of the bar, deep in conversation, sipping their drinks. It's a wonder, I say to myself, that this highly diversified people have reassembled themselves here after such a long dispersal. How deep must be the echo of their selfhood!

Damn it, two scotches washed down with a bottle of beer and I'm already halfway there. That's what Chuck, my AA sponsor, told me: After you're off it for a long time, it only takes a couple of drinks to get you there.

But I feel benign and good. I leave the bar and walk down the street. I find a more stylish bar and walk in. The bartender here, also North African, is more loquacious than the other one. We exchange as many as a dozen words. He asks me, in French, where I'm from, and I tell him I'm American. After the first drink, I ask him, in French, where he was born, and he tells me he's from Algeria. And after the second drink I tell him I'm outta here and would he know of a club with live music I could go to.

When I get there, I discover that the place could be a duplicate of a fashionable club anywhere in the District of Columbia, with a fashionable crowd in hip outfits and in a clearly partying mood. Great. When I walked in, I was still feeling benign and good, but now I'm copping attitude and feeling snobbish. For there is an Israeli band covering B52's "Love Shack," and it is pathetic. And when they finish their set, another band comes on to cover "Crosstown Traffic." I'm sure Jimi Hendrix was turning in his grave.

When these guys finally shut up, I find myself talking to an Israeli couple in their mid-twenties standing just behind me at the crowded bar. The man, whose name was Shlomo, was a casual sort of fellow with an easy manner, the kind who would readily enter into bar banter. His girl, who he later told me was his fiancé, introduced herself as Habiba. She too was a casual sort of person. Well, I should say everything about her was casual, except for her eyes. At first you think she's looking at you flirtatiously. But no, you realize later, they're monitoring eyes.

When people introduce themselves, you tell them what *your* name is. I reach for it, almost find it, and then lose it again.

Who am I? I'm Martin, from Washington.

Why can't I bring myself to tell these good people who I am? Perhaps I thought it would prove too intrusive, too jolting. After all, I'm a Palestinian, and they're Israelis, and we are communicating in a place and time that almost bar a rational exchange, that blunt our capacity to share our humanity.

We talk about the band and how popular this club is. After I buy them drinks, Shlomo tells me where he's going to live when they get married, how he once visited the United States when he was around six and doesn't remember much about it, and about his job at an export-import firm. Habiba tells me she was born in Argentina and came here with her parents when she was nine.

"I always wanted to come here, long before we finally arrived, ever since I heard about Israel," she narrates to me, throwing up an arm and leaning on Shlomo with the other. "I remember once when I was six or seven, I cut myself and was bleeding. As my mom bandaged the wound, I told her that it wouldn't have happened to me in Israel. Children don't cut themselves in Israel. That's the image I had of this country."

I smile at her.

"Do you like Israel, Martin?" she asks. Again the monitoring eyes.

I lean my back against the bar, facing them, hands pocketed.

"Well, you know, I haven't been here long enough to sort of, you know, form any definite impressions."

I know I am, in a way, having fun with these people. Toying with them. But I like them. Their humanity is real. I am communicating warmth to them. I find the moment interesting. Wondrous. Sort of surprising. And yet I still can't tell them who I am. Whenever I met Israelis in the past, as a Palestinian, we danced around each other, invoked the echoes of our long struggle. In this Holy Land, we are forever advancing and retreating from, advancing and retreating from each other like the holy sword dancers that we are. We hear the voices of each other's pain but can't make out its desperate integrity.

Why can't people in this land, holy or not, just be jolly and funny and playful and nutty and shallow and innocent and apathetic, like people in the States, and go out looking for their connection, or divorce their spouses and get into a custody brawl, or buy a new car, or go to a health spa or a bar to pick up someone, or read *Rolling Stone* in the bathtub, or rent a couple of movies at their video club, or call the president an asshole in a fit of pique and wish the Grateful Dead were really dead, or buy *Playboy* and check out the scene with a magazine, or *something*, for heaven's sake. This is too somber, too humorless, a way to live.

It's the end of the evening.

"I'm afraid, you know," Shlomo says to me, referring to the imminence of war and the threat of missiles raining down on Israel. I find what he is saying, and especially the way he says it, quite moving.

After last call, around one o'clock, the band came back on to do something that an American band would have done only as a spoof: it played the national anthem. And here I am standing stiffly, with a straight back (well, not too stiffly or too straight, considering how much booze I've consumed), next to Shlomo and Habiba while the Israeli national anthem is being played. For me the moment had the quality of fable. I mean, you play, you pay. If you want to go around incognito, you pay a price at the end of the evening. The trickster will be tricked.

Only the third cab I manage to hail to a stop agrees to take me back to my hotel in East Jerusalem. And this driver is a mean-looking son of a bitch, fat and ugly and loud. The moment I get in, he starts railing against "the dirty Arabs" and "Americans like yourself" who would stay at hotels in their towns.

"I say the best Arabs are those who are ten feet underground," he thunders.

Jesus Christ.

"And what do *you* think?" he wants to know, giving me a dead stare through the rearview mirror.

"Just some of them," I offer tentatively.

"All of them," he insists.

Jesus Christ, I've got a Travis Bickle on my hands.

That was the longest cab ride in my life.

I stagger to my room, lie on the bed with my clothes on, and wonder about Travis and Shlomo. Old Travis is no riddle. He will be forever locked with his Palestinian counterparts in an embrace of mutual loathing and rage. Send him to the West Bank as a settler, a soldier, an interrogator, or a prison guard, and he will, respectively, play the bully, shoot to kill, torture for pleasure, and humiliate on whim—without the slightest remorse. It is Shlomo that I wonder about. What does someone like him do when he's sent to the West Bank and told to break children's bones? What kind of metamorphosis does his psyche undergo there? Is there something about occupation that always creates in the occupier, regardless of his abundant resources of humanness, a bias toward the caprice of the inhuman, a drift toward the awry in the workings of the soul?

If so, then the more Israelis dominate Palestinians, the more they will submit to them. For in their struggle to subjugate, Israelis will succeed only in expending their own humanity.

9

PLO Blues

I get to Paris from Amsterdam with sixty dollars in my pocket and part with ten to rent a manual typewriter. I move into a small room with a hot stove in a *hotel-residence* and proceed to write my first book about growing up in the refugee camps. All of a sudden I want to be a Palestinian again. A Palestinian activist. I don't know why. There is a drive in me, an animate will independent of self-consciousness, demanding deliberate focus and free utterance of my identity. I suppose that when one's consciousness is shaped by an environment of rootlessness, as mine has been, sooner or later it begins to seek its opposite.

As a child, I had felt a certain apartness as a Palestinian. As an Australian, I had felt—despite my at-homeness there—a sense of conscious acquisition of the cultural idiom. As a citizen of the Wood-stock Nation, I had always felt the stress of extraterritoriality that the nation's members claimed for themselves. In each of these worlds, my identity was provisional, a partial construct. Wanting to be Palestinian now must mean, I suppose, that all the facets of my identity could be defined at once by Palestine's "national" struggle. What better place for a flower child, fleeing the ruined Eden of Woodstock, to seek a pivot for his identity?

I was now, in a manner, *plus royale que le roi*, more Palestinian than

185

any of the activists I came to know in Paris. Not only was I organizing demonstrations and solidarity conferences at La Mutualité in the Latin Quarter, but I was working on my book and publishing op-ed pieces about "the struggle" every other week in the *International Herald Tribune*.

While still writing my book, I moved in for a few months with a Palestinian activist friend, Izz el Deen Kalak. Izzy was one of the first Palestinians I met when I arrived in Paris, and he had addressed me in Arabic. I hadn't uttered a word of Arabic since my late teens, when I landed in Australia. Izzy's words seemed to hiss and slip from his mouth in a kind of chalky, gritty prattle. I understood what he said, of course, and managed to respond, but the language merely spoke to me; it no longer spoke from me.

When I moved in with Izzy, I brought along all my possessions: my manuscript, my rented typewriter, some clothes, and my sleeping bag.

Izzy works on his *Magistaire* at the University of Paris. I work on my book. In between, you could see us outside the Cité Universitaire or down at the Boulevard St. Michel in the Latin Quarter shouting and screaming: "*Soutenez la révolution Palestinienne contre la regime fantoche du roi Hussein.*" This was September 1970, known as Black September, when the Palestinian movement was being crushed in Jordan and thousands of civilians were massacred by King Hussein's army.

Always with us would be Wael Zuaiter and Mahmoud Hamshari, both from the West Bank. When I first met Wael, he was with a group of other Palestinians, mostly students, in a café in Rue Moufetard, the main drag in the old quarter where turn-of-the-century anarchists used to live. Passed out from too many drinks, resting his head on the table, he was jolted awake long enough to shake hands with me and then went back to sleep. Mahmoud was the least interesting of my three friends. Whereas Izzy was a brilliant intellectual and a cultured man with many interests and Wael a fun-loving, poetry-reciting, joke-telling, back-slapping, uninhibited Oral Palestinian, Mahmoud was dour, intellectually limited, and one-dimensional.

All three were young men in their late twenties with promising roles to play in the struggle and, as they put it, in building "a reconstituted Palestinian state."

All three were murdered within a short time of each other.

Mahmoud became the first PLO representative in Paris in 1973 and was the first to be shot and killed by Israeli agents. Wael became the first PLO representative in Rome; he too was killed by Israeli agents, outside his residence in the Italian capital. Izzy followed Mahmoud as PLO representative in Paris, and he was shot and killed, soon after I left, by fellow Palestinians—Abu Nidal's terrorist group—who accused him of being "an accommodationist."

After Mahmoud's murder in 1973, French leftists, many of them French Jews, organized a march in commemoration of Mahmoud and in support of the Palestinian cause, which I joined with Caron, a nice Jewish girl from upstate New York who had already been living with me for almost two years. Caron had been in the Peace Corps in Thailand and later traveled the same route I had taken through the Far East and the Indian subcontinent. She had been away from home for five years and now was pregnant with our child—homesick and ready, as they say in certain quarters, to settle down. And would I consider moving to the States . . . and you know, like, getting married?

I would.

My book has already been published in the U.S., and the fact that *Newsweek* has done a profile identifying me as "one of the best known of Palestinian writers and intellectuals" wasn't going to hurt my reputation.

What neither of us really understood is that a relationship is anchored not only in the sum of its own empathies but also in a setting. The relationship that Caron and I had was housed in the emotional terrain that circled it in Paris. Severed from there, it got off-tilt.

By the time we arrive in Cambridge, Massachusetts, and set up house there, the sensual magic in our relationship was lost. The erotic fury that had possessed our lovemaking took a leave of absence. The romantic texture of even our most ordinary days in Paris, characterized by the excitement of café life, was now replaced by the frugal tastes of Hicksville.

Soon after our baby was born, we knew one of us would have to lift anchor and put out to sea. The hostility between us was something that the birth of our child was not going to stifle. And this hostility had nothing to do with our different faiths and visceral ethnic loyalties. It was born not out of rival ideologies but from rival sensibilities.

One day I return home from giving a lecture in California to find all my worldly possessions, which still fit into a backpack, ready for me to pick them up and be on my way.

Caron went on to Harvard to become a lawyer; Lisa, whom her mother decided to bring up in her faith, went on to become my little princess whom I would see once or twice a year; and I went on, with steady tread, to become Palestinian again.

If only I had known of the fantasy world that awaited me, the world of Palestinian politics, a world that I was to plunge into now with a frenzy, I would have stayed put in the real world and saved myself a lot of heartache.

...

The problem with most people, not least of all Palestinians, is that they take the PLO seriously, as if it were a sophisticated, worldly organization run by an elite cadre of dedicated revolutionaries, ideologues, theoreticians, and diplomats. It is not that. PLO leaders are essentially simpleminded folk who are dominated by the neobackwardness that enslaves their whole people. To be sure, the Palestinians themselves, given their social formation, could hardly have been expected to produce a more inspired leadership. There is nothing in their political, cultural, and social tradition to make probable the emergence of a revolutionary vanguard with the same grasp of world events as those produced by Russia, China, Cuba, Nicaragua, Algeria, and other countries with a tradition of national or class struggle.

The Palestinians (who picked up their name recently in history, like the Jordanians, Lebanese, Israelis, Kuwaitis, and others in the region) have always been a marginal group in Arab history, and Palestine, a backwater province of what was known until the First World War as Greater Syria. During the *nahda*, when Damascus, Beirut, and Cairo became the hub of the literary, political, and activist establishment, Palestinians in Jerusalem, Haifa, and Nablus wallowed in their dull, stagnant provincialism, cut off from all that was vibrant and alive in the world around them. Until the advent of Zionism to Palestine, which galvanized the Palestinians into some action by its threats of land alienation, economic pauperization, and stateless destitution, the Palestinian community was drifting into the twentieth century trapped in a fourteenth-century time warp.

How, then, does one explain the paradox of Palestinian exceptionalism, and the fervency of this exceptionalism, in Arab affairs? More than that, how is one to explain the inflated status accorded the PLO and the image of Palestinians as tragic heroes living at a higher pitch of self-awareness and intellectual intensity than other mortals?

There were many reasons to account for that—reasons derived more from the broad design of the Palestine conflict than from its details. The first was that the Arabs saw Palestine as an integral part of the "Arab Nation" and Zionism as a latter-day colonial movement implanting itself in their midst at a time when the rest of the Third World was being decolonized. They may have cared about the fate of their Arab brethren (who were now calling themselves Palestinians) in the refugee exodus of 1948, but their preoccupation was Palestine, not Palestinians. Their struggle became sacred to the Arabs because the loss of Palestine represented a loss of Arab patrimony. The Syrians felt the loss more strongly than the Palestinians themselves. Thus when Arabs pursued the question of Palestine with unflagging intensity between 1948 and 1967, the Palestinians were a marginal consideration: their right to repatriation, statehood, and independence was hardly seen as the major foundation of the conflict.

But Palestinians and Palestine finally meshed in 1967, following the vacuum and disarray that occurred following the collapse of the Arab armies in the June War of that year. The fate of one defined the other.

The Palestinians claimed to be "wresting control" of their cause from the Arabs, forming their own liberation organization, and becoming *azhab el kadiya*, literally, the owners of the problem. Suddenly Palestine became the Palestinians, the Palestinians became the PLO, and the PLO became, in an age that looked romantically at such things, a national liberation movement.

The PLO, however, was too ill equipped to solve any problem, let alone a problem with the regional, national, and international complications that, by the late 1960s, the Palestine conflict had acquired.

If Arab society in general is neobackward, manifesting the trappings of modernity but governed by fear and impotence, then Palestinian society is the most neobackward in the Arab world.

Palestinians feel more insecure, more lost, more adrift, more alone, more cast aside, more unwanted, than other Arabs. There is more havoc, more randomness, more uncertainty, more terror in their lives than in the lives of other Arabs. And there is less relevance, less anchor, less reason, less justice, less joy, and above all, less hope for the future in their condition than in that of other Arabs.

An Arab traveling abroad will, in a crisis, go with his own passport to his own embassy and ask that his own government assist him. During times of hardship, this Arab still has his village, his family, his clan to go to for help. When deported from Saudi Arabia, or laid off a job in Qatar, he can always return home. When at home, he has his church or mosque nearby, his neighborhood where he, his parents, and grandparents were born and grew up, his own friends and relatives, and above all his own roots.

The Palestinians have none of that. They are enmeshed in a world of disorder of which they, a simple people, have no grasp, a world whose workings they can neither comprehend nor master. Thus, the ills that afflict the average Arab who lives in his neobackward society, a society that discourages spontaneity and innovation, are more explicit in the constitution of the Palestinian personality. To compensate, they boast more than other Arabs. Their world of fantasy is more erratic and unstable than that of other Arabs. Their sensibility is more ornate. Their understanding of the world is more limited. Their politics, their social interaction, their work ethic, their cultural obsessions are more archaic. And their leadership distills less from the lessons of history. In short, Palestinians suffer more grievous forms of neobackwardness than other Arabs. And the fact that Palestinians, through their uninspired leadership, had failed to attain a single goal in the twenty-five years since they embraced the PLO as their "sole, legitimate representative" was the ultimate proof.

...

And here I was, a prodigal son, wanting to be Palestinian all over again, striving to be part of what I thought was a ripening national collectivity.

...

November 1974. A PLO delegation, headed by Yasser Arafat, has just arrived in New York. The Palestinian leader is to address the

UN General Assembly on the question of Palestine and "the legitimate rights of the Palestinian people." The PLO is flush with victory over a resolution passed earlier by the Arab League declaring it "the sole legitimate representative of the Palestinian people," and reveling in the press coverage it is getting in the American, European, Arab, and Third World media. The PLO is taking itself seriously.

I too am taking the PLO seriously. So when Nabil Shaath, the number two man in the UN delegation and the main theoretician of the Palestinian movement, called me at home in Washington (where I was now living) and asked me to join the delegation "to help out a bit," I was most responsive.

Nabil was a decent man. But despite his Ph.D., his international connections, his many travels abroad, and his status as a decision maker in Fatah's Central Committee, he was still a naif. Being an intellectual, he didn't have the primitive ferocity of a Palestinian fighter from the camps, but he did have a smug sense of the righteousness of "the cause" and the validity of the Fatah line—essentially the old wine of pan-Arabism poured into the new bottle of Marxist rhetoric and Che Guevara imagery.

Arafat will be flying into New York tomorrow. Nabil asks me if I want to go through the speech that Arafat would be delivering the following day and to suggest last-minute changes.

I read the speech and find that it is all about "the Zionist entity" and calls for "a secular, democratic state in Palestine" for all Palestinians—Moslems, Christians, and Jews—a solution predicated on the dissolution of Israel.

It was absurd. The Israelis were not going to consider that, nor were the United States, Europe, or the socialist world, the entities that mattered most in global politics.

I tell him that. He nods, because he knows my position. I was probably the only Palestinian around in those early days calling for a two-state solution, with the establishment of a Palestinian State in the West Bank and Gaza alongside Israel with its 1948 borders. This was the proposal that I expounded two years earlier in my first book. Though it has since become a near-reality, calling for a two-state solution then was regarded by the great majority of Palestinians as an act of treason.

"How about some changes instead in the style, context, syntax, whatever," Nabil asks.

I suggest some changes, but he's too wary to make them "until I consult with Abu Lutuf." Abu Lutuf is the nom de guerre of Farouk Kadoumi, the PLO's foreign minister, who was part of the UN delegation. Kadoumi is also a simple man who comes from a background of activism in the Baath party, the pan-Arabist group that Michel Aflak, a *nahda* intellectual, founded early in the century.

There was one change in Arafat's speech that Nabil went along with. "I'm having one problem with this 'legitimate rights of the Palestinian people' phrase, which by the way is repeated here to the point of litany," I tell him after reading the speech a dozen times. "I mean I don't think we can speak of 'the legitimate rights of the Palestinian people.'"

"Oh, why not?" he asks in honest puzzlement.

"Because, very simply, rights are by definition legitimate," I put in. "We can speak of 'inalienable rights' or 'fundamental rights' or 'basic rights' and so on, but not legitimate ones. I mean, there is no such thing as *illegitimate* rights."

That was the extent of my contribution.

In the late afternoon of the next day, the Man, whom everybody has been waiting for, arrives. To Palestinians he's known by many names. *El Khityar*, the Old Man. *El Rais*, the Chairman. *El Kaed el Aam*, the Commander-in-Chief. *El Waled*, Dad. And *Abu Ammar*, the Building Father. To the rest of the world he's known as Yasser Arafat.

That first night at the UN, the man is mobbed by well-wishers, supporters, diplomats from Third World and socialist nations, Arab ambassadors, journalists, and others who want to shake the hand that leads "the Palestinian Revolution."

I get to meet Mr. Arafat for the first time at the UN, though, of course, with little opportunity to talk or interact. Who was I when the ambassadors of Rumania, Cuba, and India, not to mention Gabon and Chad, were falling all over themselves to have an audience with him? In later years, and more relaxed surroundings, I had occasion to meet and get to know him—most notably when I spent a week with him, day in and day out, trying to get enough material for a book called *A Week in the Life of Yasser Arafat*. I also came to like him, which is not to say that I admired or agreed with him. I found the man to be simple, pleasant, friendly, and hospitable with not much depth, a man who was not too different in temperament or

outlook from the people he led and among whom he was unquestionably popular. He was popular precisely because he mirrored and
evoked the very contradictions of Palestinian culture: he was ornate,
aggrandizing, crafty, a consummate manipulator, not too informed
but with an aboriginal sense about survival, and utterly convincing
even in his ambiguities. He was the Old Man. Dad. The Building
Father. Head of the Palestinian family. Whatever he says goes. As
simple as that. You don't agree with him, or other PLO authorities,
fine. Just keep your disagreement to yourself. Go about your work
as you're expected to. Be a mediocrity. Regardless of how dedicated
and ardent a revolutionary you are when you join the corps, you have
to go along to get along; otherwise, you join instead the cynical mal-
contents who dwell in that forgotten wasteland reserved for Palestinians with talent.

Three days after Arafat left New York and flew to Cuba to meet
with Castro, Nabil asked me to go over the speech by Kadoumi that
was to be the PLO's intervention at the General Assembly and its
response to the speech of Yosef Tekoah, Israel's UN ambassador. I
tell Nabil it is beyond redemption.

I spend hours poring over Tekoah's text and more hours compos-
ing a response. Nabil likes it. That's it! He assures me that that is
what Kadoumi would read.

I go to the General Assembly and sit with the PLO delegation,
close—because of our alphabetical order—to the podium, and wait
with pounding heart to hear my own words read to representatives
of the entire planet by the foreign minister of the Palestinian Revolution.

What I hear is Kadoumi's original speech about the "usurped
homeland" and "the Zionist entity" and "the Arab nation" and the
honor and glory and heroism and steadfastness of "the brother
strugglers."

•••

What am I to make of my first encounter with these people? Nothing. I'm a Palestinian activist now. So regardless of all the manifes-
tations of neobackwardness, corruption, and opportunism I am to
see from here on, I'll turn a blind eye and a deaf ear. It's good for me
to do that and to go on believing in "the people." Or so I believed.

In Washington I'm able to pay the rent because I'm editing *Arab*

Report, the Arab League's four-page, biweekly newsletter whose lofty goal is "to educate the American public about the Arab cause" and "to counter Jewish influence in the United States." The director of the league, who had the title of ambassador of the Arab League of States in Washington, is Yasser Askari, a Palestinian Baathist from Damascus who was offered his post as a political appointment, for he was a Hafez Assad man. Askari spoke hardly any English, knew nothing about Washington, and cared less about what happened on the Hill. Arab diplomats, being the product of their political culture, forever extrapolate: in Washington there is one leader, the president, and he makes all the decisions; the legislative branch is just a rubber stamp. That's the way it is in their capitals. One man makes decisions. His word is law, and he is not answerable to anyone. Indeed, there was a little old Iraqi man by the name of Mohammed Mahdi, an activist with a group of his own based in New York, agitating on behalf of the Palestinians, who came to the office one day and tried to convince Ambassador Askari that "with a mere three or four million dollars" he, Mahdi, "could buy off all the anti-Arab senators on the Hill." Askari, I'm sure, was convinced of the argument, but Mahdi didn't get his money because the ambassador did not believe that Congress mattered. In any case, he could not have cared less about the Arab cause. His passion was soap operas. Every morning he would sit in his large office in the Universal Building, overlooking Connecticut Avenue, glued to his TV set. For lunch, he would meet his fellow Arab diplomats at the Hilton across the street and then come back to watch more soaps, read the Arab press (he didn't read English), and browbeat his staff about their dress code.

The newsletter, which I typed at home a couple of hours before I was to turn it in, kept coming out as long as it dealt with issues in a way not contradictory, or offensive, to the views or policies of any of the twenty-one regimes that made up the membership of the Arab League. The trick was to steer clear of issues on which disagreement existed among Arabs. Since Arabs disagreed on virtually everything there was not much I could write about that any nine-year-old would find interesting or that any adult would read. When the civil war broke out in Lebanon in 1976, pitting Arab against Arab, Syria against the PLO, and the Lebanese National Movement against the Phalangists—an event that was headline news in the

American press—I couldn't touch the subject in *Arab Report*. Instead the issue had to be filled with saccharine stories about "the Arab contribution to Western medicine" or "science."

The Palestinian community throughout the world was owned, controlled, and directed by the PLO and its functionaries. This community was divided into *igleems*, or community zones. Thus, the Palestinian communities in Lebanon, Jordan, Kuwait, the United States, and Europe, as well as in the West Bank and in Gaza, were assigned separate full-time functionaries whose job was to organize, recruit, solicit funds, marshal support, stage demonstrations, and the like. Those in each community who were already members of Fatah, the PFLP, the PDFLP, or other factions were the foot soldiers who would go from door to door distributing leaflets, doing the legwork for *hafles*—community dinners where speakers, sometimes from outside the zone, would give lectures, where a fundraising drive would be mounted, and where a local troupe might perform—and recruiting students for the General Union of Palestinian Students.

By the late 1970s, with PLO coffers stuffed full of petrodollars and the Arab world taking the line that the PLO was "the only official, legitimate representative of the Palestinian people," Palestinians everywhere were being consumed by their own glorified self-image. Their cause was not only an important factor in the Middle East or even the most important cause there but the only important cause. As for Palestinians themselves, they were the most cultured, the most educated, the most informed, the most tragic, the most lovable, the most heroic, and altogether the most worthy figures who had ever appeared on the scene.

We *must* be important. The socialist world and the nonaligned world and the Islamic world and the Arab world are all supporting us. What's more, they esteem and look up to us.

Money poured in from the bulging PLO coffers to the "American Zone." Much of it was spent to open what were known, among the few odd cynics who floated around in those days, as "PLO shops." These innocent-looking organizations, disguised as selfless groupings of activists working on behalf of the Palestinian cause, were in fact established to employ and lavish rewards on the *massouleen*, the top guys and their hangers-on who represented the various PLO factions. (The extent of these operations was not revealed until after the Gulf War, when most of the shops were closed and the *massouleen* retreated to their mansions in suburban Washington, San Francisco, Detroit, and Chicago with the money they'd stashed in Swiss banks.)

One of the biggest such shops in the American Zone was the Palestine Congress of North America, an umbrella organization that brought together the regional, state, and national groups already in existence in the U.S., along with representatives of the various PLO factions. It was intended to be the ultimate authoritative voice of Palestinian-Americans, with an executive committee, a board of directors, and fifteen full-time officers. Their aim was to represent the Palestinian community in America, to disseminate information about the cause, and to help Palestinians here become acquainted with their constitutional rights. But the officers who were hired to run the operation knew very little about how to organize a community, less about disseminating information, and virtually nothing about the U.S. Constitution. Almost without exception, these fellows were PLO stalwarts, factional cadres, or known supporters who were being rewarded with jobs.

I saw it all unfold before my eyes, for I was recruited to work for PCNA with the high-sounding title of Director of Writing and Research.

The Palestinian workplace is merely an extension of the relations that exist in the rest of their society. It is enveloped not only in fear of authority and its omnipotent representatives but also in an atmosphere of trivia, competition, intrigue, recrimination, and incompetence—all displayed in a high-tech office by men in fashionable clothes, with college degrees, who speak several languages and have traveled extensively.

At the PCNA, as in the PLO itself, an individual acquired his position not by merit but by closeness to the system of rewards, privileges, and sanctions in his political milieu. His workplace—where little work was done—was an extension of his living room, where friends, associates, and relatives dropped by at all hours to *yedardesh*, or chew the fat. Tea would be served, pleasantries exchanged, and personal matters discussed.

The work done by the staff at PCNA was worthless. Everyone knew that his job had been granted, not earned. Hence, no necessity existed for exertion or sacrifice. So long as his personal alliances, connections, and patronage were firm, his job was assured. No one at PCNA thought for one moment that he was there for any purpose other than to enjoy the privileges that the title conferred.

In addition to everything else, I was to see how these ostensibly politicized, sophisticated men who were supposed to represent the revolution never cooperated as colleagues but rather competed as rivals. And since personal interest took precedence over public service, the competition was rancorous and infantile—a truly neobackward competition that obeyed a tribal logic, since the officers were visibly attached to different patrons.

The man who directed PCNA, like Yasser Askari, didn't speak much English and knew little about either American or Palestinian history. His preoccupation was not soap operas but intrigue. He and his colleagues on the board of directors devoted the best part of their time to conspiracy and feuding and trying to pocket as much of the PLO funds and contributions as possible.

In no time, they were living in million-dollar homes and taking the Concorde to Europe. It's bad enough for a Saudi prince, but when "a Palestinian revolutionary" who represents a mass of disinherited, impoverished people does that, it becomes the most brazen hypocrisy. But these fellows were not answerable to anyone. On those rare occasions when a member of the community, in a fit of pique, raised the point at a *hafle*, that PLO officials in the U.S. and Canada lived too lavishly, he was told that these homes belonged to "the organization," not the officials, and to shut up about it. No one within the organization would dare risk loss of privileges, or worse, by making an effort to call for reform.

The fact of the matter is that the PLO had the Palestinians by the short hairs and wouldn't let go. Nevertheless, the Palestinians themselves, though they could see how they were being led from one political and military disaster to another, just as they could see their leaders' unbridled pursuit of self-interest, continued to support it.

Within the PCNA, as at other Palestinian shops in the U.S., things went along smoothly, in their own Palestinian way. Every *massoul* was out to eat the *massoul* next to him, for otherwise he too would be eaten. He ripped off as much money as he could. He sent reports to Beirut (where the PLO was still headquartered) about how well his group was doing and how badly the other guy's was doing. A *massoul* was a tyrant with his subordinates, who were as subservient to him as he was to his own *massoul*.

If you played the game, the rewards were abundant. The more rungs you climbed on the ladder in your shop or faction, the fancier home, car, and vacation you got.

These practices would not have been unseemly or unusual at a Wall Street firm or in Hollywood, but the PLO presented itself as a national liberation movement made up of dedicated idealists who toiled for the cause of Palestinian independence.

In 1980, a delegation led by the head of the PLO's Foreign Affairs Department came to New York to attend the UN General Assembly's fall session. I went with the director of the PCNA and two of his senior staff to visit them at the UN Plaza Hotel. The head of the delegation greeted us in his suite. After the interminable hugs, greetings, and best wishes for our families, he began to talk bitterly about the American hostage crisis in Iran.

At that time, the hostages were finally going to be released and handed over to the Algerians. He, however, wanted them handed over to the PLO. In that way it could have curried favor with the White House, and gained concessions, and enhanced its global stature.

"Those bastards," he thundered, referring to the Iranians, "should've given us the hostages. Why didn't they?"

Mercifully the question was not directed at me, because I would have told him the truth: misguided or not, the Iranians were true revolutionaries and felt nothing but contempt for the PLO.

Later in the evening, I told our distinguished guest that I wanted to interview him for a PCNA pamphlet about the Palestinian struggle for independence in 1936, and would he have an hour or so? I had planned to distribute this pamphlet, a ten-page affair, to Palestinian kids born in America and not familiar with their people's history.

Less than ten minutes into the interview, I realized that he knew nothing about the details of the Great Revolt and less about what Palestinians should have learned from it. I was embarrassed by his ignorance. Yet the other men in the room, who sat quietly through the interview, fell all over themselves to congratulate him afterward on his cogency and acumen.

The delegation stayed in New York for a week. There were approximately eleven members, including journalists from *Wafa*, the official PLO news agency, hangers-on, and aides. The emirates' mission at the UN, in a typical gesture of Arab hospitality, had at first offered to pick up their tab at the hotel. But the PLO delegates, who had spent their nights partying, playing poker, and ordering lavishly from room service, had run up such an enormous bill that the mission refused to pay it. Their objection, it turned out, was not to the amount of money involved but to the amount specifically charged for booze. The emirates' officials, as Moslems—at least publicly—were scandalized and wanted to make a statement.

One day the PLO sent one of its highest functionaries to run the whole U.S. organization—the zone, the factions, and the shops. He was to be their *mogharbel*—the *capo de tutti capi*.

Lebanon had just been invaded by the Israeli army, and PLO forces had been crushed. The organization's political cadres, fighters, bureaucrats, and leaders had been scattered like chaff in a storm, ending up in places as far apart as Tunisia, Yemen, Algeria, and the Sudan. During the battle, many top commanders in the South had deserted their positions, leaving their people to fend for themselves. Abu Zaim, the best-known among them, had, in true *opéra bouffe* fashion, fled the battle in an ambulance, taking with him his gold, cash, and family members.

From the day of their defeat and their expulsion from Beirut, PLO leaders, resorting to Formal Arabic, proclaimed that "our heroes," who had "confronted the Israeli army" longer than any Arab force had ever done, had "taught the Arab world a lesson in courage, commitment and endurance."

A short while later, the camps of Sabra and Shatila, shorn of PLO protection, were invaded by gangs of the Lebanese Forces who, with the Israeli army looking on, or looking the other way, massacred hundreds of unarmed civilians.

The massacre shocked the world by its brutality and silenced any further declarations by the PLO about its "heroes." But the organization's officials would not admit defeat. What mattered above all was that the PLO not be delegitimized in the eyes of the people— and that its officials not lose their livelihood and privileges.

In the middle of the war, I was heading the Palestinian delegation at the UNESCO Conference on World Culture in Mexico City. The official with me, Omar Masarweh, who headed the PLO's UNESCO office in Paris, said to me one day, during one of the most merciless and costly raids by Israeli jets on Beirut, resulting in the death of hundreds when a building in the Masane district received a direct hit: "Well, brother, we hope when this carnage is all over, our leadership will emerge safe and sound."

Meanwhile, back in Washington, the *mogharbel* was busy pursuing his three lusts: power, money, and sex. Everybody was scared of him and secretly despised his excesses, but no one would stand up to him. He consolidated his power by terrorizing his shopkeepers, including the director of the PLO office in the capital, and cowed his colleagues by threatening *tajmeed*, or suspension of their pay. Half the money he received from the PLO, now in Tunis, went for expenses; the other half was divided equally between himself and "the brother strugglers." He was a crude womanizer as well as being a spineless and cowardly man who cared little about the Palestinian cause.

He was also ignorant of the ways of the world. Once when he and I were in Los Angeles, we were invited to attend a private fund-raising dinner for the actress Vanessa Redgrave at the home of the Sabri Farra, a rich Palestinian-American family with connections to the Cause.

Redgrave had been having problems because of her political views. In 1978, during her Oscar acceptance speech for best supporting actress in *Julia*, she denounced the "Zionist hoodlums" who were outside the Dorothy Chandler Pavilion protesting her presence. Subsequently she was branded by some as an anti-Semite. Two years later, after her electrifying performance as Holocaust survivor Fania Fenelon, both Fenelon herself and screenwriter Arthur Miller denounced the casting. Two years after that, she was blocked by the Shubert Organization from playing in David Hare's Broadway hit *Plenty* and was rejected by the same organization for a starring role in *Scruples*.

In 1982, Redgrave was supposed to narrate Stravinsky's *Oedipus Rex* for the Boston Symphony Orchestra, but the BSO canceled, claiming threats had been received. The actress sued for breach of contract and violation of her civil rights; her legal costs amounted to half a million dollars.

And that's where the *mogharbel* came in. He, along with the two dozen or so rich Palestinian guests invited to the Farra's, were supposed to pick up the slack in Redgrave's debts.

After dinner, the actress spoke for ten minutes about her case in court and attendant financial problems.

Our *mogharbel* stood up and took it from there. He spoke glowingly, mostly in flowery, syrupy-sweet English, about what an accomplished actress and implacable supporter of the Palestinians Redgrave was. He ended with this appeal: "So I urge you, brothers, to take your checkbooks out now and write out checks for twenty-five, fifty, even a hundred dollars each."

Everyone got busy writing as instructed. Redgrave turned crimson. And I cringed at seeing one of the most riveting actresses in the world being humiliated. It was too painful to watch, so I left.

• • •

Our *mogharbel* was now busy addressing the Palestinian community, not only in the capital but all over the country. I accompanied him to one such affair in Brooklyn soon after the Sabra/Shatila massacres, while nerves were still raw. This was a dinner and fund-raiser whose highlight was the *mogharbel*'s speech. He spoke about the miracle of the siege of Beirut, the heroism of the fighters, and the commitment of the PLO, and he poured scorn on the whole Arab world for not coming to their aid.

"Where wert thou, oh Arab brothers?" he shouted, gesticulating at the heavens, "Where wert thou, oh Soviet comrades? Where wert thou, oh Moslem believers?"

He ended with the resounding outcry: "Palestine lives."

His speech drew thunderous applause and a standing ovation. "Palestine lives, Palestine lives," they were shouting lustily.

• • •

It was simply too much to endure. But endure it I did, for another month or two.

During that time, PLO officials—those to whom the State Department did not object—came and went in Washington soon after President Reagan, in a half-hour televised presentation in September, offered his proposals for the Palestinian-Israeli problem, essentially a resurrection of the Camp David Accords.

The PLO liked the plan but couldn't bring themselves to say so. Instead, they hedged, preferring ambiguity. They were, they said, going to hold a Palestine National Council session, their first since the expulsion from Beirut, to declare their official position. The *mogharbel* liked the plan too, and Nabil Shaath kept repeating:

"That is it. That is the peace plan that will get us our rights." Hani el Hassan, a top Fatah man with great influence in the PLO's executive committee, also liked the proposal.

I did not, and in my regular three-minute evening commentary—which Palestinians all over the country could listen to by calling a number in Washington—I said so in no uncertain terms. And when the other *mogharbels* heard it, they got in touch with my *mogharbel*, and I got called into his office.

"Now you will forgive me, my dear brother," he begins. There was a rebuke in *forgive* and an ugly twist in *dear*. "But I have to ask you to stop reading your commentaries from now on."

"Fine by me."

He stands up stiffly, at an angle, with his right arm lifted slightly like a boxer about to launch an upper cut. So I stand too, and stiffen.

"Don't think for one moment we don't value your contribution to the Palestinian revolution. You are a poet. And poets are the apple of our eye," he tells me with a robust laugh.

"You mean you're not asking for my resignation?" I ask.

This startles him, and he hastens to add: "Oh my dear brother, you are too valuable to us. You are too popular with the community and with the kids from the General Union of Palestinian Students. You know how when you give a lecture somewhere, anywhere in the country, Palestinians drive a hundred miles from every direction to hear you speak."

"I'm glad to hear I'm so popular, but I'm leaving anyhow. As of today I'm no longer employed by the Palestine Congress of North America," I tell him smugly.

When I first met this *mogharbel*, he was surprised that I did not, like him, live in a million-dollar home and enjoy all the privileges he had been taking for granted as a PLO official. He pitied me and looked at me as if I had taken an absurd vow of poverty. But he loved my bohemian bachelor life-style, and always wanted to attach himself to me when I went out. He wanted desperately to meet women. There was nothing wrong with that really—married though he was. But he would follow me to bars and think that every female friend who walked up and hugged me was a hooker. "Bring her home, bring her home," he would urge me. "And I'll bed her."

At times he would call me up at home in the middle of the night.

"Are you alone?"

"No, I'm here with my girlfriend," I would say. And a short while later he would show up at my apartment to ogle the girl.

Other times he would see me with a date walking down the street (he lived in a townhouse in my neighborhood) and ask where we were going. For the rest of the evening he would follow us from bar to bar and badger my date with questions about whether she had "a friend as pretty as you."

The PLO had become so infected by the poison of neobackwardness that I couldn't see an antidote. The damage that this organization has caused to Palestinians is awesome, but the center will hold. No people, Palestinians included, can remain forever immobilized. A new generation will come, bearing a new vision, and break on through to the other side of traditionalism.

Time to look for another country behind the mountains.

...

I travel to Mecca with my friend Hassan Abdel Hadi. Hassan is an African American who converted to Islam soon after he broke up with his wife, the soul singer Aretha Franklin. He was still new to Islam and wanted to discover it in its birthplace, Mecca, during Hajj. I guess I wanted to rediscover it. I wanted to believe in something. I needed a new tense in the grammar of my existence; otherwise I felt that I would choke on my own helplessness.

When we arrive, there are already well over a million pilgrims from all over the world in Mecca, and they have pitched tents that stretch to infinity in every direction around the Main Mosque. All are wrapped in white robes and have already, as Islamic tradition calls for—but does not dictate—shaved their heads, underarms, and pubic hair. There are tens of thousands inside the mosque, praying, reading the Koran, marching around the *kaabi*—a draped shrine majestically positioned in the middle of the mosque's open court— or simply sitting on the carpeted floors staring contentedly into the distance, as if convinced that their entry into Paradise is now guaranteed. For most of these pilgrims, the journey to Mecca represents the crowning achievement of a lifetime. They have saved for years to come here. It is a dream come true. They are, at last, *hajjis*. They have come from the Chinese mainland and the Indian subcontinent; from the *mashrek* (the land where the sun rises) and the *maghreb* (the land where the sun sets); from Africa and Europe; from North America and South America. They are black and white, brown and yellow, rich and poor. Yet they all look alike, almost interchangeable.

I am wearing a white terrycloth wrapped around my middle and slung over my shoulder to connote the purity of my soul—though I have balked at shaving my hair—and bumping into pilgrims as Hassan and I perform *tawaf*, marching counterclockwise seven times around the *kaabi*. And these pilgrims, smiling the smile of a fellow believer, would say: "God is great! Oh, God is great!" And I would respond in kind. These people are all brothers and sisters in Islam. They are united in the same faith here on earth and will be reunited in it when they go to the hereafter. As we go round and round the *kaabi*, chanting, "Oh Lord, grant those who venerate this house and make pilgrimage to it peace and forgiveness," I feel I am no longer alone. I am enmeshed in the poetics of group ecstasy. I belong to an immeasurable Presence—the same Presence, embodied in the *kaabi*, that has hammered at the psyche of Moslems for the last fourteen hundred years.

The *kaabi*, actually a meteorite that Moslems believe was an altar built by Abraham and Ishmael for the worship of God, bespeaks a world older than the Prophet. It was around this very stone that Arabs, before Muhammad's time, used to gather from all over the Arabian peninsula for three months each year—leaving their tribal enmities behind—to worship their gods and goddesses, to trade, to sign agreements, and above all, to attend the poetry forums held at Souk Okaz. If, to Classical Arabs, language was the crown of their civilization, then poetry was the jewel in the crown. A nomadic people forever on the move, who lacked the wherewithal to paint or sculpt, they expressed themselves in poetry. Next to God, they believed, the poet is most holy, and poets are therefore "entitled to rights denied other mortals."

Poets from the various tribes would meet at Souk Okaz and recite their verses to the throngs. Judges would choose the ten best poems and hang them on the *kaabi*, where they would remain until the following year. These poems were known as *moalakat*, literally, "hanging poems," and were revered as sacred documents.

Muhammad must have been the greatest of them all. When he came with his great Message, all in verse—verse as beautiful as the mind of God, as touching as the music of the spheres—the Arabs of the peninsula embraced it. How many individuals in history, save the Prophets, have been able to draw a new map of the human soul—one that would continue to enthrall for over fourteen hundred years?

On our second day in Mecca, Hassan and I joined a stream of pilgrims going to the Plain of Arafat, where, as per tradition, we drank from the *zamzam* well and threw stones at the devil. After that we went back to the Main Mosque for afternoon prayers. There, together with thousands of pilgrims inside and another half million outside, we followed the direction of the imam in kneeling before the *kaabi*, entreating Allah, blessing Muhammad, and repeating yet again that God is great.

I am loving every minute of it, not because of any serious belief in Paradise but because, very simply, I feel great, this happening is great, and God is great. I happen to believe in God—not necessarily a Koranic God, or a biblical God, or a Talmudic God; just God, the one and only, since there is surely only one, though we may call Him by different names. But I will have no truck with organized religion, which I abhor as deeply as I abhor nationalism. I have come here not in order to be one with my religion but with my true, authentic, and original Arab culture.

In the late afternoon, I am sitting with Hassan outside our tent making a pot of tea on our little kerosene stove. Pilgrims are passing by our tent, nodding their heads in greeting and saying, "Peace be unto you." One of them is a man my age, blond, with blue eyes, who, like me, does not appear to have bothered to shave any of his hair. As he passes our tent he greets us with the mandatory, "Peace be unto you," and I, distracted, respond absentmindedly in kind. Then he stops in his tracks, looks back, and walks toward me. As I look up he erupts in a shriek: "My God, is that you?"

I shriek back, as I stand up to hug him: "My God, Suleiman, is that you?"

I knew Suleiman from my teenage years in Beirut. His folks, a middle-class Palestinian family, lived on the edge of the Basta. We never really socialized much, though I liked him. Suleiman went to school, and people like me and Adnan thought schoolboys were sissies. They never went to the *souk*, drank alcohol, or hustled like we did. I met Suleiman again when I visited Beirut in 1979, and we had a long lunch during which he told me that he was then a PLO military commander based in the South. He had gone on several training missions to Russia and other socialist countries. He had even gone to North Vietnam as part of a PLO delegation in 1968, soon after the Tet Offensive, and there had met both Ho Chi Minh and General Giap. I was impressed, but he and I led different lives and lived in different worlds, and after we shook hands good-bye, I thought I would never see him again.

"What are you doing here?" Suleiman asks.

"What are *you* doing here?"

"I have just been released from Ansar," he says. This was a huge prison compound that the Israeli army had set up in the south of Lebanon soon after the 1982 invasion. Ansar held, at all times, around 10,000 Lebanese and Palestinian prisoners. Between June 1982 and November 1983, when the prison was finally dismantled, 30,000 prisoners had passed through its gates, half of them PLO and Lebanese national movement activists; the rest were lawyers, journalists, judges, doctors, politicians, shopkeepers, laborers, and others whom the Israelis had found in their way.

I cooked dinner for the three of us—mostly out of our supply of canned food—and we stayed up talking until all hours outside the tent, stretched on our prayer rugs. Hassan finally decided to retire and retreated inside, to his side of the tent, where he sat up for another hour reciting the Koran, reading from his English version. Hassan had been in something of a trance since we arrived and I felt that he was taking it all much too seriously.

"So why *are* you here, Suleiman?" I ask. "You haven't found religion, have you?"

"I suspect I'm here for the same reason you are," my friend responds. "Our world got screwed up, our movement enervated and our idealism, well, there is no place to go with *that* anymore. Our strategy never really measured up to the grandeur of our dream. It left us all with a vacuum. I'm here to reassess my life. To reflect a bit."

Suleiman tells me stories about the South that are almost identical to those that Salem, back in Ramallah, had told me in his drunken candor. One in particular stuck in my mind.

"I remember when we took over the town of Damour from the Maronites in early 1976," he said, grabbing sand in both hands and sifting it through his fingers. "Oh Lord God, I remember we rounded up a group of about seventy townspeople—mind you, there may have been some fighters among them, but they were mostly civilians—and detained them. Abu Musa and I led the takeover of the town and set up headquarters in a house by the coastal road. Early the next morning, one of my men, a boy called Walid, bursts into my office and tells me our fighters are getting fidgety. I said, 'What do you mean fidgety?' and Walid said simply, 'They want to kill the people detained from last night.' I went out and told the men in no uncertain terms that anyone who hurts one single civilian will be shot dead, by me, there and then. I meant it, and they knew I did. Then I told Walid to get on the phone and call Sidon to send two buses to Damour right away so the prisoners could be sent there safely and released upon arrival. Now these Maronites were just standing around guarded by a few of our men, and one of them broke away from the group and came to me. He was a priest or a monk or something, still dressed in his garb. And he started begging me to let him go back up the hill to his partially burned house to retrieve a manuscript on Sufism he had apparently been working on for a decade. He kept saying: 'I beg of you dear sir, I beg of you, dear brother, my manuscript, my manuscript, please!' It was so sad, the way he grabbed my legs and kept repeating 'my manuscript, my manuscript,' and sobbing uncontrollably. By that time, Abu Musa had come up and started telling me to 'kill the son of a whore.' I told him there will be no killing done here; we're not animals. I told the priest to get his manuscript, which he happily retrieved, and, upon his return, clutched it with both arms, as if he held on to a sick baby. Abu Musa kept saying he wanted to kill the man. That's when I raised my voice and told him he was second in command and if he killed the priest, I would kill him, because he was behaving like a jungle animal. And I left to go back to the office. Abu Musa was *damawi*, I tell you, a vicious *damawi* [a man inbred with blood lust]. In the meantime, a Maronite kid also broke away from the group of prisoners—he was probably about eleven or twelve—and approached Abu Musa. This kid wanted to retrieve a dog, only he wasn't as penitent about it as the priest had been.

"What happened afterward, well, I heard about it from my men. The kid, it seems, in addition to asking to retrieve his dog, told Abu Musa: 'You bastards, you killed my mother and father!' Abu Musa didn't like that. In addition to having been reprimanded by me in front of his men, he was now being called a bastard by an eleven-year-old kid. What do you think Abu Musa did?"

"He killed the boy," I guessed.

"He shot him in the back," Suleiman said, still sifting sand. "He told him to go get his dog, and when the boy started running he shot him dead."

"God! What did you do to Abu Musa?"

"I put him under arrest pending his trial by a revolutionary court of Fatah's Central Council."

"And . . ."

"And nothing. Nothing happened."

That August, the Maronites attacked the Palestinian refugee camp of Tel Zaatar in northern Beirut. During the siege, three months long, old men, women, and children starved to death, died of dehydration or unattended wounds, or were buried alive under the rubble caused by the heavy shelling.

Abu Musa was not among those fighting to lift the siege in order to rescue his people. (A few months after the *hajj*, the same Abu Musa, encouraged by the Syrian regime, was to start a secessionist movement within Fatah that would escalate in November 1983 into a mini-civil war outside Tripoli, a coastal town north of Beirut, pitting his Syrian-supported troops against Arafat's loyalist ones. The two-week-long confrontations were to result in hundreds killed on both sides.)

"We had quite a few *damawis* like Abu Musa in our ranks, brother," Suleiman continued, "and over the years—between Damour and the invasion when I was thinking seriously about quitting—they were responsible for much of the chaos, for turning many of our young men into animals like themselves."

It was almost dawn by now, and we decided to stay up for early prayers.

"Look, brother, I'm telling you the truth. I saw it all unfold before my eyes when we were rounded up by the Israelis and dumped in Ansar. Now I don't want to tell you the Israelis were nice to us there. We were treated horribly and denied access to the most basic needs, from food to hygiene, adequate housing, contact with the outside world—until the Red Cross was able to intervene seven months later. Our men were just not ready for it—civilians and fighters—and degenerated finally into something subhuman. By that time, I and two thousand other prisoners were taken to a prison compound, also part of Ansar, down into a valley called Wadi Jahan-nam, or Hell Valley, where they put us in three sections separated by barbed wire. The harsh conditions took their toll. One day a man started swearing, over the barbed wire, at another man in the adjacent section. One of them was a Lebanese Sidonite Sunni Moslem, and suddenly everybody from Sidon, who was Sunni, and that included Palestinians, along with prisoners who had a grudge against the man from the other section, who was from Beirut, began to arm themselves for attack. The Beiruti too had *his* men. You should have seen these people! None of them had shaved for the duration of their captivity; they had long, matted, filthy hair down to their shoulders; they were armed with tent poles, barbed wire knotted to a ball on the top, wooden sticks, metal pipes, shields of tent canvas strapped to their chests with wooden boards hidden underneath. Their clothes were tattered and dirty. Many were barefooted. And they stood there, two or three hundred of them, shouting at each other across the barbed wire, which some of them were already working to remove to launch their attack. I have never seen anything like it. They were cavemen. Our people had degenerated into cavemen. I have never seen anything like it, not even in the movies. They were a true reincarnation of prehistoric warriors."

Suleiman is laughing, and I'm laughing with him, urging him to tell me what finally happened.

"I said to myself, well, this is it; any minute now these people are going to make contact, and there will surely be a massacre. So I approached the warriors in my section and hollered for them to desist. I called upon the blood of our fallen patriots, the memory of our dead parents, the mercy of the Prophet—to no avail. I don't think they even heard me. Then I thought of something that always worked in the past: whenever there was a confrontation in my section between two men, I always told the other prisoners—my orders were followed in Ansar even among those who were not PLO combatants—to start throwing stones at the Israeli soldiers standing guard outside. The Israelis always responded by shooting in the air, which would act as a distraction and stop the fight. So that day I did the same thing, and when our prehistoric warriors saw that everybody was throwing stones at the soldiers, they too started doing the same. And by the time the stone throwing and the firing were all over, so was the impending confrontation."

I was laughing, as was Suleiman, the whole time he told his story, but deep in my heart I felt profound despair.

And we are both here, in Mecca, representatives of a generation that squandered, rather than seized, the crucial moment in its history. Our sense of disarray has driven us here to recover our past—in the place where it all began—to reconstruct ourselves, so that in the future, when a turning point comes again, we will turn with it.

After dawn prayers at the mosque, I slept for a few hours and headed on alone to the northern sector of the mosque, where five Koranic readers were chanting *suras*. They were blind Yemenis who each did a couple of sets a day. One would recite a *sura*, which he knew by heart, and when he finished, the fellow next to him would chant another, and so on until the whole book had been recited. Pilgrims would sit in front of them and listen, and before they left, drop a few coins in their cups. That's where I spent most of my time. My God, I would say to myself, I still know many of these *suras* by heart. I was a reader too when I was a kid in Beirut, earning a few liras here and there by reciting at cemeteries for families visiting their dead.

One day I noticed one of the readers reach in his pocket from time to time for a few green leaves that he would put in his mouth and chew. He was chewing *gaat*, the narcotic plant that is so popular (and legal) in Yemen. I waited until the man stood up, after he finished his recital, and accosted him on his way to the bathroom.

"Your reading was beautiful, brother," I offer.

"It is the words of God that are beautiful."

"How art thou, brother?"

"Thanks be to Him, everything is as everything should be."

"Art thou able to share thine *gaat* with a brother believer from the land of Palestine?"

He immediately digs into his pocket and hands me, in what he thought was a surreptitious manner, a bunch. "Of course I shall share," he says readily. "Property belongs to God, not man. He who hoards property is a robber."

So I sit in the northern sector of the mosque, chew *gaat*, and listen to the blind men reciting *suras* and sounding as if they loved it. I too love the Koran. Ever since my early teens, I have loved its historical atmosphere, its insights into the psychology of the human spirit, its notions about the dialectic of human life, its exhaustive definition of moral codes, and its erotic portrait of the hereafter.

Doing that is enough for me. I came here, much as Suleiman had, to find meaning of some kind. A passionate heart, lamenting a lost cause and a dream betrayed, cannot find meaning in religion—solace, maybe, but not meaning. Islam was a social ideology that was singularly suited to the temper of a tough, independent desert people. Today's Arabs, neither tough nor independent, have turned Islam into mere ritual, reproduced but never re-created, its inner form subverted by their neobackwardness. In the Middle East today, Islam is a monstrous imposture, with its original vision of freedom ("if ye wish to pursue freedom beyond the confines of Heaven and earth, Allah is with you") reduced to pitiless repression. When Moslem fascists, like their counterparts in Europe, burn books or pass the death sentence on a British Moslem writer for freely stringing words together, they are telling us, in their own invidious way, that they understand the power of the Word. But they are also revealing how little they know of its meaning.

...

On my way back to Washington, I stopped in Algiers to attend the first Palestine National Council session after the expulsion from Beirut in August 1982. The system had totally broken down. Between members, observers, journalists, bureaucrats, visiting dignitaries, and sundry supporters and hangers-on, there were five thousand people attending. No one knew where at least three thousand of them were staying. It wasn't until the third day that everyone was finally given rooms and name tags.

Few of the PLO officials, hugging and kissing each other and buzzing around looking busy and important, seemed aware that their movement was having its last hurrah. The old order was dying, and none of them entertained the possibility of a rival order getting ready to supplant them. Everyone was acting as if business would go on as usual, as if the drama of the siege of Beirut and the dispersal of the movement's fighting forces would not finally catch up with them.

Few even knew how to respond to the Reagan proposals. They wanted to appear, in their resolutions, to be saying no when in fact they meant yes. That is why the 1983 PNC session came to be known by Palestinian cynics as the *la'am* session. The word is a contraction of *la* (no) and *na'am* (yes).

Ahmad Abdel Rahman, the official PLO spokesman, came to my room at the Orasi Hotel, where he usually held his press briefings, and asked me to translate the clause in the resolution relating to the Reagan proposals into English. I read the Arabic version, which was handwritten on official PNC letterhead, no fewer than a dozen times. It made no sense.

"What are you trying to say?" I asked.

He tried to explain it, in Arabic, but he still made no sense.

I look at the man level-eyed: "I'll translate this for you, brother Ahmad, but I can't go along with this text."

He says only, "Why?"

"Because it makes no sense."

"Well, that's what the Executive Committee has decided."

"I can't accept it."

"You just have to accept it. You're a Palestinian. You're one of us."

"Leave it with me, and I'll have it translated for you in due course."

He never came back for it, but I did finally translate the resolution. It said that "the PNC refuses to consider the Reagan proposals, in text and substance, as an adequate basis for a just and lasting solution to the Palestine question." They refused to consider, but did not refuse, the proposals.

I go to the General Assembly at the Palais de Nations to listen to the PNC members give their speeches. Mercifully, each is assigned ten minutes. There are members who represent the various PLO factions as well as the unions of teachers, engineers, carpenters, nurses, and the like. And there are members, elected on an independent ticket, who represent refugee camps, academic institutions, overseas communities (five from the States), women's associations, and so on. From time to time there is an overlap, as when a member representing a labor union is also associated with a political faction. I can tell from their fiery language that all these buffoons have somehow convinced themselves that the 1982 debacle in Lebanon was a major victory for the Palestinians, not a defeat. Not one admits failure. Not one expresses remorse.

The fascinating thing about these speeches was their language. The speakers were using, in Formal Arabic, the beautiful vocabulary of Classical Arabic, and yet they managed to sound comical. The reason was obvious. Words are embodied in temporal context, not in a static, immutable lexical system. The vocabulary of Classical Arabic defined a thought world entirely different from that of the modern Arab. Words like *war, beauty, love, victory, labor, citizenship, justice, authority*, and *empire* came down from Classical Arabic as quanta of linguistic energy evoking a special context, rooted to a specific historical moment.

When a speaker of Formal Arabic employs these words today, his usage is anchored in his own modern mentality. Transplanted to a cultural moment when feeling is no longer energized by social experience but eroded by it, these words are rendered sterile. In the whorehouse of Formal Arabic—a language unsuited to logical thinking—words that once described rich twists of emotion that widened the Classical Arabs' existential repertoire, are now being put to prostitution.

Hardly anyone was listening to the speeches. People were talking and greeting each other across the rows of seats and down the aisles and paying little attention to what their fellow members were saying. There is no tradition in Arab culture where the speaker in a lecture hall is shown the respect of uninterrupted attention. The only place where that occurs is in a mosque, when a Moslem clergyman is delivering his Friday sermon. There no one dares to whisper to his neighbor, let alone interrupt the speaker. A lecture hall, on the other hand, is a free-for-all.

I walk out and go for coffee. I spot May Sayegh sitting at a table with two men and go over to join them. May is the president of the General Union of Palestinian Women, a powerful group indeed. Originally from Gaza, May, who is in her early forties, has been with the PLO since 1972. She had been based in Beirut, where the GUPW was headquartered, until her expulsion with the rest of the PLO cadres in 1982. Her husband, Abu Hatem, is also a PLO official, but he has slowed down because of a heart condition. I first met May in Beirut in 1979, but we later met repeatedly in the States where she used to visit, ostensibly to organize Palestinian women but actually to have a good time. I really would have liked her if she had not been a PLO official who like the rest was being progressively corrupted by the lavish life that she could now afford.

May is devastated by her expulsion from Beirut, a city that she loved. Originally a country bumpkin from Gaza, May had been suddenly thrust into the whirlwind of cosmopolitan Beirut as a high official in the PLO, which from the mid-1970s until August 1982 had virtually ruled the city.

"Where are you going to be living now, sister May?" I ask her.

"I don't know," she responds dejectedly.

"I guess you must miss Gaza?"

"To hell with Gaza," comes her retort. "I miss Beirut."

In the evening, at the General Assembly, Yasser Arafat repeats the ritual that he has gone through at every previous PNC session: he resigns his position as chairman of the executive committee. Immediately, the speaker of the Palestine National Council puts it to the vote, and the members reelect him. The process takes about an hour, during which the PLO is technically leaderless.

After his reelection, Arafat stood at the podium and gave a short speech. The members, along with the invited observers and delegates, not to mention sundry PLO officials, functionaries, bureaucrats, advisers and shopkeepers from the four corners of the world, were in awe of the man and listened attentively to his every word. He could have praised the weather in Algeria, or complained about the color of the sky, and they would have agreed with every word. What mattered was his presence—he was Dad, the founding father, a symbol of their transition from "Arab refugees" or citizens of Jordan, to Palestinians. He was a promise that, no matter how remote it seemed, salvation was imminent. Above all, he was their employer, who dispensed to every one of them generous rations of money, power and prestige.

Once, when I visited Beirut in 1979, I was invited to attend a lecture by Arafat at a refugee camp. Only this was not a lecture, it was a *happening*. With the exception of a few visiting local and foreign dignitaries, the audience was mostly made up of Palestinian refugees. These people were not listening to Arafat's words so much as imbibing his presence. On the balcony, on the second floor of the lecture hall, old women dressed in embroidered Palestinian garb, were ululating to heaven every two or three minutes, drowning out Arafat's speech. He kept giving them dirty looks, but there was no dissuading them.

Palestinians have lived through a thousand private hells since the PLO took on the task of representing them a quarter-century ago, yet they continue to accept it as their only official representative. Like other Arabs, inhabiting societies broken in body and spirit,

Palestinians simply believe that one's lot in life is given, not chosen. That's the way it has been for centuries. At the core of the Arab historical archetype lies the remembrance of that frightful cataclysm that befell them during the Mongolian invasions, which pulverized their civilization. The invasions rapidly reduced the Arabs from world leaders to destitutes, and much of that terror was deeply ingrained in the Arab psyche. Today they continue to live in dread of anything new and innovative that departs from tradition. Not even periods of profound crisis, when social life and political thought are disrupted, trigger revision or reform. Their cultural condition is an established fact, their value system an eternal verity, expressing the way the world is, so willed by both authority and divinity. In this make-believe world, a leadership need be neither skillful nor inspired to succeed in producing the submissive individual it needs—an individual whose personality is built on dependency, immaturity, neurosis, compulsive behavior, and inadequacy and who is capable of coping only with the most basic chores of daily existence.

For the next three days—the PNC meeting is usually a ten-day affair—I wandered around the Palais de Nations and my hotel and met with all sorts of Palestinians. They were the crème de la crème of Palestinian society: the intellectuals, the activists, the organizers, the theoreticians, the writers and the poets, or, as Palestinian idiom would have it, "the roses" of their culture.

Ideologically, these people could be divided into three groupings: Moslem fundamentalists, ardent communists, and Westernized liberals.

The Moslems were openly avowed fascists. Ironically, many of them were born-again Moslems, originally secular ideologues who had fled to Islam after their secular ideologies had begun to appear impotent and irrelevant. To them, Islam was the last great hope, a source of both identity and power that left no question unanswered, no issue in doubt. The solutions it offered were ones that secular ideologues had lacked imagination to invent.

Transform a corrupt, or in this case crippled, society into an Islamic one, and you tap into the mainspring of divine truth— except that in this society there is no room for anyone who does not believe in this truth. You live like a Moslem, or else!

Among the "roses" of Palestinian society, the communists are the most comically harmless. Palestinian communists, whose ideology, though it comes from the West, is inherently anti-Western, remain mimetic in their importation of Marxist ideas and policies. Lacking the ruthlessness of the Bolsheviks or the dash of the Maoists, who adapted communist dogma to their own needs, Palestinian communists (whose concern is not just Palestine but the entire Arab world) merely parrot, in their long tracts, the virtues of the "class struggle" and the "solidarity of the working classes"—even in agrarian societies where there is hardly any industry and hence no proletariat. It is not surprising that these Westernized elite are often dismissed as self-loathing *franjis*, or Franks, by folk culture. Palestinian communists constantly denounced Europe, but in effect also idealized it via Marxism—the false imperialist West versus the true communist West.

The Westernized liberals, mostly family boys, are graduates of American and European universities to whom the West is God. They believe that to compete with the West, or simply effect a leap in modernity, Arabs must take Europe as a model. They must not only learn from the West but in effect become Western. To them, modernity wears one face, progress is propelled by one model, and culture speaks in one tongue. These people, Ph.D. holders all, and caricatural Arabs, have gorged so voraciously—and, finally, so senselessly—on Western ideas, that now they suffer from indigestion. Surely you cannot be defined as a genuine Lockeian liberal if you import the ideas of capitalist enterprise but do not tolerate ideas of democracy. Liberalism, along with other ideas derived from the Western intellectual tradition, is shared by all but lived by none.

Deep down, despite their education, these Palestinians are mired in neobackwardness, their consciousness pulverized by the dictates of tradition, and their thoughts constrained by the obscurities of Formal Arabic.

On the last day of the conference, I drove in the same car with Nabil Shaath from the Palais de Nations to the Orasi Hotel. Shaath was addressing me in English. He spoke faultless textbook English, but his archaic imagery was quintessentially Arabic. Like other Westernized Palestinian intellectuals, especially those who now embrace Islam and reject the West as the Great Satan, Shaath is tormented by the dilemma of a man who has gone far—but not deep—into an alien culture to which he suddenly realizes he can never belong, and is now drawn back to an Arab culture to which he can never return.

On my last night in Algiers I sat up with my friend Uri Davis, who fancied himself an anti-Zionist Israeli, complaining to him about how the Palestinians, as a people and a movement, have been reduced to a point where they could not even give a straight answer to something as simple as the Reagan proposals.

"All this would not have happened," he said, "if the Palestinians had not made that error in 1947 by rejecting the UN resolution that called for a two-state solution."

I laughed. "Look, this error that you speak of reminds me of what Talleyrand once said to a European king who made an error of judgment that resulted in a war that killed thousands of people: '*Sire, c'est pire qu'une crime, c'est une erreur.*'"

"I don't care," he said, "but I, as a Palestinian Jew, still believe in the secular, democratic state that the Palestinians proposed back in 1968."

"You're not a Palestinian Jew; you're a Messianic Jew. Why should you believe that Palestinian claptrap? We've never been secular, we've never been democratic, and we've never been a state. There is nothing even in our language to correspond to any of these terms."

"You're a self-hating Palestinian," Uri said to me mock-seriously.

Self-hatred has its own nihilistic logic. It helps you relinquish those lunacies that cling to your history and soul and language and integrity. A self-hater has autonomous problems. There is no spuriousness about the idea of self-hate. It's a problem you have to deal with, but it's not your problem. You've got nothing to do with it. Like otherness, self-hate is something visited upon you by others. It is the poison they give you because you've challenged their tradition. And if it doesn't kill you, you emerge from it transformed, since it can trigger fundamental energies of adjustment that will take you beyond your fixed meaning.

10

Disorderly Conduct in Washington, D.C.

I am back in Washington wondering to myself why my trip to Mecca has left me emptied and not the less uncomfortable about my name. I am wondering why those who come from my part of the world have so reduced the meaning of their names as Moslems, Palestinians, Arabs, that now its echo comes back to them as unintelligible babble.

There is nothing to believe in anymore. Where does one go after being betrayed by one's own name? Where does one start?

Well, if you're a Palestinian writer without visible means of support, a man who has never held a regular job in his life, you can do one of three things. You can apply for food stamps, emigrate to the Gulf to hustle a fortune, or hit the lecture circuit. Since the Welfare Department is weary of people who live in apartments full of Persian rugs, artworks, and expensive hardbacks, food stamps were out. The Gulf was also out because I am a blabbermouth; had I gone there, I would have said what I thought of the clans that run these ridiculous emirates, principalities, sultanates, and sheikdoms. And you don't do that in the Gulf—or anywhere else in the Arab world—unless you crave leisure to write your autobiography in the reflective atmosphere of a prison cell. So I hit the lecture circuit to promote the Palestinian cause. All you do is grab the microphone, pontificate for half an hour, get wined and dined, and in the morning pick up your honorarium and go home. Nothing could be simpler. It's easy, hip, and profitable. And if anyone asks what you do for a living, you say, "I'm between books."

I sailed along like this for a year or so, and then in appreciation of my efforts and, above all, anticipation of my "next book," the Palestine National Fund gave me a grant. Great news—but it also had its downside. Before the grant, I could criticize our officials as mediocrities, our movement as a mom-and-pop organization, and our political strategy as worthless. And the audience loved it, I guess because they needed at least one enfant terrible to lighten the stodgy, somber atmosphere created by the effusions of serious Palestinian intellectuals. Now, however, the Fund would return me to the ranks of the homeless if they so much as heard me intimate something negative about the movement.

Once I was invited to participate in a panel discussion on some inter-Arab accord the PLO had signed. I ask the guy who is sponsoring the lecture if criticism of the Palestinian leadership is allowed.

He says: "Yes, definitely."

I say: "Well, then, I can't attend."

I wasn't going to throw away my meal ticket. If the price was to stop criticizing the Old Man and ridiculing PLO officialdom, then hell, I'll pay it. Besides, I've talked so much and answered the same old questions about "the Palestine question" that I got sick of hearing my own voice. There is no need or reason I can think of to be serious or controversial anymore. I'd been through that in the old days, when I was an idealist, a dreamer, an earnest revolutionary who felt grief at every defeat and joy at every victory. That was then. This is now. And, in addition to my grant, I enjoy all the fringe benefits that come my way. As a favored son of the Palestine National Fund, I get to see the world: I travel back and forth from Washington to Tunis (stopping in Paris and London on the way back) whenever I can think of an excuse to see some PLO official. Most of all, I get to pay my rent and all my bills at the end of the month.

I thought it would last forever, but all good things come to an end, and this one ended in less than a year. I lost my grant and my audiences around the country. I guess the Fund figured out that I wasn't working on the great Palestinian novel, and the audience knew I wasn't really being straight.

Besides, I was already becoming a cokehead and a drunk. I started avoiding other Palestinians. I didn't want to think about their cause. I didn't even want to think about myself. Dream engenders antidream. Betrayal breeds betrayal. Rage begets more rage. And then the self stands mute, devoured by its own exactions.

My straight friends—the few I still saw—were worried about me. They invited me to their suburban homes and did their best to set me up with nice women who were consultants at the World Bank or interpreters at the Organization of American States. Rog and Michelle, whom I'd known since I came to D.C., had me over for dinner at their house in Arlington. It was a sit-down dinner for eight; an unescorted woman who worked at the State Department's section for Near Eastern Affairs was seated next to me.

After dinner we retired to the living room for cognac. Most of the guests, like Rog and Michelle, were professors of English and creative writing and romance languages, all talking nonsense.

"I say it was Proust who expanded the frontier of our perception of adolescent and gay sexuality, in metaphor, in idiom, more than any other writer, French or otherwise," one of the guests was saying.

"I don't agree," Michelle said heatedly, stretching the word *agree* and showing genuine concern. "I think the *Alexandria Quartet* is more perceptive on the erotic forces in social life than *A la recherche de temps perdu*. Lawrence Durrell saw the *spiritual*, not, as Proust did, the *neurotic*, in the sexual act."

I go to the bathroom and do a line. When I come back someone asks me, "as a writer," what I think.

"There are nuances of emotion in *Perdu*," I offer, "that negate the very universe that Proust had chosen for his characters to perceive." I thought it was the most significant and eloquent set of words that anyone had ever been able to string together since hieroglyphics.

I don't remember what they thought of that pearl, but they continued with their discussion. Someone quoted William Blake that "the road of excess leads to the palace of wisdom."

Out of the narcotized fog in my brain came the retort: "I think it makes more sense in reverse: The road of wisdom leads to the palace of excess."

"And what does that mean?" someone wants to know.

"It means," I said vehemently, "an uncompromising negation of the conventional wisdom."

···

One night I went to a Moody Blues concert with Scarlet, the woman I was living with, and our friends, Clay, Lulu, and Mark.

Clay is the drummer for the Rhomboids, a local heavy-metal band; he came along because Lulu liked the Moody Blues. Mark just thinks a rock concert is a great place to be—to dig the sounds, get high and drunk—and he's right. When the band started doing their old songs, the crowd went wild. There were tens of thousands of bodies on the lawn of the Merriweather Pavilion, outside Baltimore, swaying to the music like some ancient tribe performing its religious rites.

After the concert, Mark, Scarlet, and I went over to Mark's houseboat. We dropped off Scarlet, who was too drunk to go anywhere. Mark's wife Trudy was at her desk at the *Washington Post*, working the night shift. Before Mark and I left, I tucked Scarlet in and kissed her goodnight.

I got so drunk that night I didn't even know my own name.

I woke up at my apartment with Diane, who used to date Andrew and now worked as an artist's model. We are naked on the floor with a blanket over us.

Diane wakes up first. "Hey, wake up, come on."

"Hi," I say groggily.

"Hi," she says. "You do blow?"

"I sure do."

"I got some. Let's go down on it together."

"I like you, babe," I say, and fetch the mirror.

No sooner do I sit down again than Scarlet walks in, using her key. She takes one look and hollers: "What the fuck do you think you're doing, you son of a bitch?"

Before I could stammer, "It's not what you think," Scarlet had turned to the mirror with Diane's half-gram of coke already on it.

"Hey, what do you know!" she exclaims. The look of outrage turned to one of ecstacy. Her face lights up all of a sudden, and she sits right down on the floor with us.

By four in the afternoon we are wired up like demons, so we get dressed and walk down to the Four Provinces, a local Irish pub, to drink Guinness and eat fish and chips.

"You wanna call Roger?" Scarlet asks me, with a knowing smile. Roger is our dealer. I call him—he and Sally lived just down the street—and he says they'll be right over to have a couple of beers with us at the Four P's.

Scarlet and Diane meanwhile have hit it off famously, and when Roger and Sally arrive, they score half a gram each and leave together. Roger and Sally offer me a ride to Eastern Market, in Southeast, where I was going to pick up a chapter that my typist had been working on.

"Hi, Barb," I say when she opens the door to her apartment. "You got my chapter?"

"What chapter?"

"The chapter I gave you last week."

"You haven't given me anything to type for five weeks."

On the way back, they drop me at Columbia Road in Adams Morgan. I go looking for Scarlet. At Dan's Cafe I see Randy sitting by himself at the bar. Randy had stayed at my place for a couple of weeks when his girlfriend kicked him out.

We drink a beer together. Randy looks depressed. So I decide to pass my half to him and have him do a line. He's all over me with gratitude before he goes to the bathroom.

"You bring the rest back now, do you hear?" I warn him. Even your best buddies can screw you sometimes when it comes to blow.

Next, I hop in a cab and go down to the Childe Harold in Dupont Circle. The place is full of people waiting for their coke connections.

"Hey, Rodney," I say to the bartender. "Seen Scarlet tonight?"

"Yeah, man, she just left. Said she was going home," he says, putting a napkin on the bar in front of me. "So what you having?"

I tell him I'm having nothing.

Archie comes over, but before he can engage me in conversation, I slip away. Archie's a lawyer and straight as an arrow. But he likes to hang out with us in the bar. When a bunch of us are standing in a huddle, he comes over, trying to affect our shorthand talk. But coke fiends are a tribe, and they won't let you join unless you've been tested and proved self-destructive. I guess Archie can sense how paranoid we get when he's around.

It's way past midnight, and I'm so tired—having long ago come down—that I can hardly stand, so I grab a cab to take me eight blocks home. The cabbie is an Iranian who wants to talk politics. Mercifully, it's a short trip, barely long enough for me to mutter,

"Long live Khomeini" and for him to answer earnestly, "Long live Arafat."

Scarlet is not home. I go to the bedroom and crash, mumbling, "bitch, bitch."

···

One day the phone rings in my bedroom, and I pick up the receiver. I look at the time. It's eleven o'clock in the morning. If it's a friend, it must be an emergency. Otherwise it's a wrong number.

"Hi, there."

I recognize the voice but can't place it.

"Hi there yourself," I say gruffly. "Who is this?"

"Roy Barber." Roy is the director of *Children with Stones*—a *musical* about the struggle between Palestinians and Israelis. The Palestinian part is a liberal adaptation I made of my first book, and the songs are based on some of my poems.

Roy reminds me that he's invited me repeatedly to attend the rehearsals, but I never show up. I tell him I'm sorry, but I've been snowed under. Happily, he misses the pun. He says there is a reading tomorrow to which a paying public will be invited. There will be a panel discussion afterward in which I and two Israelis, along with an American discussant, Milton Viorst, will participate.

He expects me there, he says.

I get to the Source Theater the following day all coked up. During intermission, everybody goes to the bar for refreshments. I go to the bathroom for mine, where I do a line. When it's time for the panel discussion, I'm flying.

After it's over, all these Palestinians and members of the Arab-American community are crowding around me, like old times. *Get away from me.* A few guys whom I knew from the old days introduce me to a visiting PLO official who had come with them, and he's all over me explaining how he loves my work. He insists I come to dinner that night at the house of "father of all youth," Mr. Hamdan, a rich Palestinian businessman.

I haven't had dinner yet and someone will give me a lift later, right outside the door of the Tucson Cantina where I intend to hang out tonight. So I accept.

When we get to Mr. Hamdan's house in Georgetown, I find myself sitting next to Mr. PLO. He is such a boring bureaucrat that

I have nothing to say to him. But I couldn't ignore him either because he kept telling me how delighted he was to read my work and how "truly frightening it is." At first I thought he had me confused with some other writer, a Palestinian counterpart to Stephen King, but I remembered that in our argot, *frightening* means "good." Anything that frightens you warrants respect.

The dinner was *mansaf*: a mountain of greasy rice on a large tray, topped with a sheep's head, eyes and all, staring dolefully into the distance. Chunks of lamb, dripping with fat, lay all around the tray. You are supposed to eat off the tray with your hand, communally.

The worst thing were the sheep's intestines. They were not there for decoration; filled with ground meat and rice, they were meant to be eaten. It was mandatory. And Mr. PLO, faithful to Palestinian traditions of hospitality, kept shoving gristly morsels into my hand, which I then had to put in my mouth.

At the door, when the evening was over, our host said that he hoped I had enjoyed myself. By way of an appropriate compliment, I said: "It was truly frightening."

...

Children with Stones had its opening night at the Source Theater three weeks later. The *Washington Times* gave it four stars and compared it to *West Side Story*. I went with a bunch of my friends who had come to my apartment in the early afternoon to party beforehand. Scarlet and I had by then broken up, and I was hanging out with Sandy, a florist. Wisely, she had kept her own apartment, though she often stayed over at mine.

By the time we got to the play, the small theater was packed. Roy took us all backstage to meet the cast, and said to them, "Hey, you guys, this is the real Fawaz." They broke into applause. We all got a kick out of that.

I got another kick watching an actor play me and enact my private anguish on the stage. *Children with Stones* so accurately dramatized my grief as a disillusioned activist who no longer believes in anything that I flinched. The thwarted energies of the Palestinian dream and the decline of our hope in the struggle, my character was saying to another actor—a Palestinian revolutionary set in his ways—are leading to a terminus of madness and death. But since the Palestinian struggle has universal attributes that concern all of us—including the audience, since the impulse to freedom lies at the root of our common humanity—then the pain of Palestinians is pain we all suffer. Then I railed, with the confident malice that only a cokehead can muster, against the sweetness of Israeli liberals who, in recent years, have only succeeded in robbing us of our right to be totally angry. I railed with equal malice against young Palestinians for not developing a counterculture that would break with traditional values and the fraudulent conventions of their parents.

To hell with your university degrees and fancy ideals, I was saying. What good were they against our barbarous tradition? What use are they if they have not yet elevated you above being mere intruders in the land of others? What is the point of having them if they do not make you hunger for a new awareness? If you must throw stones, then throw them not only at the enemy who occupies your homeland but at the enemy who occupies your home.

To see these private thoughts of mine—originally written for the solitary reader—displayed on the stage was disquieting.

In my present state of mind, driven headlong on that journey into madness and death, I saw my words as an exhausted rhetoric ransacked from the attic of my idealistic youth. I recognized myself in this actor, but only faintly, as though I were a star receding at incredible speed into a bend in the cosmos beyond visibility.

Roy Barber, the director—he played keyboard as well—had turned the warring tribes in the play into a reincarnation of the two street gangs in *West Side Story*. My poems, along with the translated Israeli poems, became the lyrics of the songs about two peoples who had each invaded the inner history of the other, in a struggle with each other and themselves.

After the play, my friends and I headed to Casey's in Georgetown to celebrate by having a fancy dinner and later to the Guards up the street for last call. Liz and Edward were themselves celebrating that night because Edward had just returned from the mountains of Afghanistan and from Peshawar in Pakistan, where he had spent two months collecting material for a book on the *Mojahedeen*. They invited everybody to their place to sample some Afghani hash that Edward had brought home. Everybody is ready to go. Sandy balks because she has to get up early. She has a business to run, and it's her busy season, she tells me. I end up at Liz and Edward's. When given the choice between hash from Afghanistan and Sandy from Pittsburgh, I opt for the former.

Yet Sandy and I got along fine over the next few months before she slipped out of my life. She had a way of moderating my excesses, having gone clean just before we met. It was good that she had because the woman used to free-base. But she still drank and smoked pot like a demon. Often, on her days off, which she had the luxury to designate herself, we would go to Thai Town or Petito's or the Lebanese Taverna in the neighborhood and sit in the terrace café all afternoon, stoned out of our heads, going through two or three bottles of wine with half a dozen appetizers, and giggle madly about nothing in particular. Sometimes we went on picnics. And every time she came over to my place, she brought flowers and more flowers until it started to look like a funeral parlor.

Once we went to see her dad, who lived in Prince George's County in Virginia, about an hour away from Washington. The man had dropped out of high school in his teens and drove a truck until retiring on a pension.

When Sandy called to say that she was coming with her boyfriend, he asked this boyfriend's name. When she told him he asked what kind of name *that* was.

"It's Palestinian," I could hear Sandy hollering into the phone. The man was hard of hearing.

"Your boyfriend is Palestinian?"

"Yes, Daddy, he is."

"Does he speak English?"

She tells him I do, and he's reassured.

When we arrive I'm introduced and we exchange polite greetings and a few words about the weather.

Then he turns to Sandy and says: "I thought you were bringing your Palestinian boyfriend over. Where is he?"

"That's him, Daddy."

Now he turns to *me*. "You don't look like no goddamn Ay-rab. You don't sound like no Ay-rab either. You're American, ain't you? Why did Sandy tell me you were an Ay-rab?"

"I don't know, sir," I reply. "I'll have to speak to her about that."

•••

As for Palestinians, I pointedly avoid them. When they leave messages on my machine, I ignore them. From time to time, I still get speaking invitations from community leaders who are not yet wise to me. I don't return these calls either. I've got nothing to do with them, they've got nothing to do with me, and I want to keep it that way.

Still, there is one I see occasionally when I'm up early—around one or two o'clock in the afternoon—and we meet at a place like La Rondo to drink coffee and "talk Palestine." His name is Marbout, which in Arabic means "all tied up." Since he hasn't changed his name, he must be happy with it, I guess. In any case, it suits him. Marbout has been in the States for years and hasn't once been to a movie, worn a pair of jeans, had a drink in a bar, dated a woman, or learned how to take money out of an automatic teller machine. He is brilliant intellectually. He's read everything there is about Hegelian phenomenology and can rattle on about Marxist praxis, the Leninist concept of imperialism, and the social formation of peripheral capitalism. But he knows absolutely nothing about his own social environment.

Marbout is thirty-nine years old and has lived here for well over twelve of them. But in a sense he still lives in Abu Diss, the West Bank village he was born in. One day Janice drops by to see me at home while Marbout was there. Janice lives in Chevy Chase, but on her way home from work every evening she drives down Columbia Road, where I live, and occasionally comes up to smoke a joint and gossip a bit. Janice is a lobbyist for a nonprofit conservationist organization and, with her dad a well-known former senator, a few more doors open for her on the Hill than they do for other lobbyists. We've been the greatest of friends for years.

When Janice drops by, I introduce her to Marbout, and she and I smoke a joint—he moves away to the other end of the living room so as not to inhale any stray smoke—and then she's gone.

"How old is she?" Marbout asks.

"Thirty-three."

"Is she married?"

"No, she's not."

"Poor girl! Thirty-three and not married!"

I guess you can take the man out of the village, but you can't take the village out of the man.

Marbout himself is not married. One day his mom called from Florida and said that she'd "arranged someone" for him, a nice Palestinian girl in Detroit. Would he fly up there to meet her at her older brother's place where she lived? So Marbout flew to Detroit, where the brother made a big fuss of the *khateb*—literally, demander of patrimony—and introduced his sister, a graduate of SUNY-Buffalo who worked in marketing somewhere in the city.

Marbout didn't like her and flew back to Washington.

"What happened?" I asked him.

"Brother, they want to unload her on me," he said indignantly. "She's thirty-four."

Marbout is not exactly a bargain himself. He's almost forty, bald and overweight. You can tell immediately that the man needs a new coat of paint. All he does is bury himself in esoteric books. On those rare occasions when I invited him to a party or a social gathering, he would just stand there tongue-tied the whole night, not saying a word to anyone. Not that Marbout was inarticulate, but who wants to hear about the fundamental laws of the capitalist mode of production or the contemporary social formation of the periphery?

I really liked him, though. He was genuine and decent. To be sure, he wasn't much fun, but there was something about the man, most notably his raw Palestinian quality, that I did not want to hide from completely. So from time to time we would meet at La Rondo, drink coffee, and "talk Palestine."

One day Marbout called up breathless with excitement. A well-known Palestinian was in town and wanted to meet me.

"So what's the big deal?" I asked.

"Well, you don't know this guy," he said, and told me his name, which meant nothing to me. "He's one of the richest Palestinians around. Made millions in the Gulf. He wants to meet you. He has read your work. He thinks you're a great writer."

"I am not a writer," I say to him. "I *was* a writer."

"Come on, he wants to meet you. He's staying at the Washington Hilton. He'll be in town for a week."

To get Marbout off my back, I tell him I'll call the guy and arrange to meet him for lunch. Then I hang up and forget all about it.

But Marbout wouldn't leave me alone. Over the next few days, he kept calling and leaving me messages about how the guy was still waiting. Once he even called me at the Cantina.

The following evening, just as I am about to go out, the phone rings. It's Marbout again. He tells me the man is leaving tomorrow.

"He's really a great guy," he says.

"I'm sure he is," I respond wearily.

"He wants to meet you before he leaves town," he insists. "You would love him. He's a true Palestinian patriot."

"Okay, okay, what do you want me to do, date him?"

"No, just meet him."

I tell him I will.

I get to the Hilton the following day and meet a man in his late fifties who, like most other Palestinians his age, has a gut sticking out. What makes it worse is that these guys always wear their pants over their gut, which makes them look obscene. And regardless of how expensive or well-tailored their suits are, they still look awful. Mashoub, which in Arabic means "taken away," also sported a super-long necktie that he had tucked into his pants.

"Let me shake the hand, the very hand—and may the Lord bless it with eternal eloquence—that wrote *The Disinherited*," he gushes.

I'd forgotten all about the flowery, ornate, syrupy-sweet formalities Arabs exchange when they meet.

So we ordered lunch, and he asked me if I drank.

"Oh, I guess I drink sometimes."

He ordered us a bottle of good wine. He was polite and anxious to please; I really liked him. We talked about this and that during lunch, and I finished off the bottle. He didn't drink, he said, not because he abstains from alcohol, but because he has an ulcer.

He asked me what I was doing lately, and I said I was writing a new book. That's the mythical book that my editor thinks I'm working on night and day. He wanted to know if, when I wrote a book, I needed "isolation from the world."

"Don't you go to the country somewhere and isolate yourself in the woods?"

"As a matter of fact I don't," I said.

I told Mashoub that I was not a best-seller writer who made a lot of money and could afford country retreats.

"Well then, I have got the answer for you," he said. He explained that he had a $4 million home in Palm Beach, right by the water, and no one lived there at the moment. Would I be interested in flying down there to finish my book?

I sure would.

The house was indeed right by the water, had about ten rooms (each the size of my entire apartment), a guest house, a swimming pool with a waterslide, and a huge backyard overlooking Lake

Worth. Inside the house was lifeless and tacky. Mashoub had expensive antiques, but next to them he had placed cheap packed-wood chairs and side tables. He had an elegant chandelier in the living room, and a plastic bunch of roses in a glass bowl on the piano that he'd picked up at Kmart for $2.95. Also in the living room was a $50,000 silk, Persian rug (so exquisite I thought it should've been in a museum) yet his coffee table was a glass top resting on an imitation rock—another Kmart special.

In spite of that, I thought I liked the place the moment I saw it. But I didn't do much work there. In fact, I didn't work at all. By the second or third day I started hanging out with a bunch of crazy people I'd hooked up with at Bradley's and Alligator Joe's.

Palm Beach was my kind of town, I can tell you—there was nothing else to do but party. Every night, after last call, we would party all night, passing joints, lines, and drinks around until we passed out by the pool or in the living room, with the Doors, the Stones, Bad Company, or the Clash blaring away.

After a couple of weeks, I started to miss my friends in Washington and called up Mark, inviting him to come down with Trudy. I told him to feel free to invite any number of our friends to come too. As it happened, Trudy was too busy at the *Washington Post* to leave. Sandy couldn't make it either because it was her busy season. (As I discovered later, she was also busy seeing another florist.) Mark, who free-lanced as a consultant of some sort, was able to get five days off. Clay had no gigs coming up for two weeks and came down with Lulu, his girlfriend, who decided there and then to give up her waitressing job. Janice, who set her own schedule at the office, also came down along with Rich, who knew that he could deal in Palm Beach as well as Washington.

After they arrived, I decided to have a party to which I invited around twenty of my Palm Beach friends. The drugs that were snorted, smoked, dropped, eaten, and chewed at the party were awesome. In addition to coke, there was hash, pot, mescaline, acid, quaaludes, mushrooms, opium, and speed.

At eight in the morning, who should turn up but Mashoub himself! Some of us were still partying, and there were bodies sprawled all over the place and seminude couples passed out in the various bedrooms. Hundreds of empty beer cans were scattered around, twisted, bent, some half full with cigarette butts floating in them.

The cans were lying on the coffee table, on the piano, on the TV set, on the floor, on the mantlepiece, on the couch, on top of the *Encyclopedia Britannica*. Dirty glasses and cups and half-eaten plates of food with cigarette butts stuck in them were everywhere, along with numerous empty bottles of scotch and vodka. And less than ten minutes before Mr. Rich Man from Palestine had opted to drop by and bust us, Mark and a couple of waitresses had gone skinny dipping in the pool.

At first Mashoub was just too stunned by the spectacle to say anything. I thought he was hyperventilating as he surveyed the scene with silent fury. He just stood there, transfixed. Then he let out a scream that my mother must have heard in Beirut—a scream directed at no one in particular, but since he was looking up at heaven, it must have been meant for God.

"Get out!" he hollered, his hands spread out before him, as if to beseech the walls, the city, the Keys, Cuba, Peru, and the South Pole. "Get out of my house! All of you!" As he hollered, he moved his body full circle to ensure that everyone could hear him. "Get out! I said get out!"

There was a plastic duck in the pool whose head had been twisted off by some destructive drunk last night. When Mashoub saw that, he started hollering: "What have you done to my goose? What have you done to my goose?"

As Mark and the women got out of the pool, the headless duck bobbed up and down.

"Get out, all of you, get out!"

I was beginning to feel guilty. I guess it was my fault. But he wouldn't let up. When he noticed that these people were taking their time getting out (cokeheads and drunks move slowly at the best of times), he began to howl like a hyena, this time in his ornate Arabicized English: "Get out of my humble abode, all of you, who have been cursed by both parents, by the Prophet and his Companions and by the Angel Gabriel. May the Lord pour acid on your souls and destroy the house that your ancestors built."

On the flight back to Washington, Mark and Rich and Clay and Lulu and Janice and I were drinking ourselves silly and laughing so hard about what had happened that the flight attendant told us to be quiet. We were quiet for a couple of minutes, but then Clay, who had the seat behind Lulu, leaned over and said: "May the Lord pour acid on your soul, bitch!" and Lulu responded: "Shut the fuck up you, who is cursed by both parents." We all doubled up with laughter. When Rich accidentally spilled his drink on Janice's pants, Janice grabbed *her* drink and poured it playfully over his crotch. The flight attendant came back and told us that she wasn't serving us any more drinks, and if we continued to be a public nuisance, she would have to tell the captain, who would radio the airport police and have them waiting for us in Washington.

Most of us were holding, so we shut up.

...

One day Janice scores a half-ounce of pot that's so powerful that you do a couple of hits and you start seeing the world in technicolor and hearing its sounds in stereophonic waves. It makes you imagine that the sounds are coming from opposite directions. I give Janice her hundred bucks, my share of the stash, and we roach out a joint before she leaves. I lie down on the floor in the living room, tripping and listening to Jimi Hendrix.

The phone rings. It's my kid brother, Samir, in Paris.

"Hey, I've got bad news," he says.

"What's going on?"

Sam and I communicate in French or in English. Hardly ever in Arabic. Living in Paris, buying and selling (what else?) wine, and having pretty much grown up, gone to school, and gotten married (and divorced) in England, he feels more comfortable in those two foreign languages.

"I just heard," Sam intones. "Mom is dead."

"Gee, that's too bad."

"Yes it is," he says, sounding genuinely bereaved.

"How old was she?"

"Mom was seventy-one."

"Oh really, *that* old? Wow, I didn't know."

He makes no comment.

"Say, are you still coming to my next birthday party?" I ask him.

He still makes no comment. But I could swear Jimi Hendrix was now singing in French about someone being an *espèce de cochon, fou,* and *affreusement affligéante.* "What'd Mom die of?" I ask Sam.

"Old age, asshole."

"Old age, wow, cool."

"What are you talking about?"

"I mean, like, you know, Mom dying of old age and all."

"What's so cool about that?"

"I mean, like, you know, cool."

"Are you stoned?"

"Yeah, right, like I took a couple of hits on a joint a short while ago. Why do you ask?"

"Because you're not making any fucking sense."

"I ain't?"

"No, you ain't," he mimics.

"Yeah, right, wow."

"You're an idiot. You're flushing your talent down the toilet with all these drugs you're doing."

Not that again. If I hear that you-are-wasting-your-talent crap once more, I'll scream. Even my own kid brother is on to me now.

"You're an idiot," he presses.

"Hey, what is it with you kid? Come on, cheer up. And say, Sam, are you still flying to Washington for my birthday party? Everybody is gonna be there, man."

"And I'm more of an idiot carrying on a conversation with you," he says and hangs up.

I play back that track by Hendrix and the guy is singing in English again. What's going on here?

A short while later, the phone rings again. It's my editor calling from New York.

"How's the book coming along?" she asks evenly.

"What book?"

"The book you're working on, dummy."

I think for a minute. "Oh, that. Yeah, I'm working on it."

She says it's been awhile and asked when I was going to show her something. My contract, after all, stipulated a deadline.

So I say, just off the top of my head: "June 10. I'll show you something June 10."

It's my birthday.

"You're going kind of slowly, aren't you?"

I really have to speak to Barbara about this. Otherwise I'll get a faster typist.

Later in the evening, after I'd come down considerably, Sandy came over to tell me she wanted to break up. Only she wanted to do it like Doris Day and Rock Hudson, with Doris looking lovingly into Rock's eyes and telling him she still loved him but there was another man.

Spare me. It's no big deal. She collected her things, and we kissed good-bye at the door.

"I have to run, babe, it's my busy season," she said. And she was gone.

Everybody else is off and gone, so why not Sandy? I thought about my mother, having gone off too. She, like my father and their whole generation of Palestinian exiles, just never knew why it all came crashing down on them like that. Inhabiting the land of others, you never know anything. Even the seasons there are vague, and one finds more than a single answer to every question. My mom and dad's generation, coming from their simple world, could not cope with that, so they willed themselves to death. And here I am doing the same thing. But death is like being born. It is important. Oh, I'm such a good goddamn *Americani* now. I'm a cokehead. I live in a place where death is writ large. My people are a community imbued with its own primordial tribalism, its own contrived hipness and blind obedience to a rush. In such a community, people do not bother their heads with identity, responsibility, and values. The only social contract there is between the citizen and his connection, between the drug and approaching death. But this is still the land of others for me. Deep in my heart, I know it is. I still wake in the middle of the night, or when the night is fading into day, the moment one is neither here nor there—a safe time to think—and I think about Palestine and olive trees, about my childhood in Beirut and my sister in her grave, about how death is an art and solitude a promised land.

I will die, the way I'm going, from coke; or I will die, the way my father did, from not knowing; but I'm not letting anyone greet me hello or wish me farewell. I'm not letting anyone offer me a rose because I don't want to show anyone my strange sorrows. I don't want anyone to profit from my tragedy. I don't want anyone to see me cursing, praising, the time the chain was undone, the hinge came loose.

•••

A few weeks later, Raja, an old friend from my PCNA days, called to invite me to a lecture in Knoxville, Tennessee, where he now lives.

I told him I wasn't giving lectures anymore. He said this was a case of "equal time," and he didn't want anyone else to represent the Palestinians. The university had invited the former Israeli foreign minister Abba Eban to speak and wanted to give a Palestinian equal time. Besides, my name and Eban's had been linked since November 6, 1974, when the *New York Times* had published an op-ed piece of mine, "On Roots and Exile," illustrated with barbed wire and a pen, and the following day they had a piece by Eban on the same subject with a similar illustration.

"Besides, the Palestinian community, the students, they love you, they want you down here to speak," Raja insists.

"I'm sorry, I can't do it, buddy."

"The university is paying $3,000, the same honorarium they paid Eban."

"Is that right?" I ask. Then I add, "Okay. I'll come then."

"You will?"

"For the buckeroos I will."

"I don't believe you mean that."

Well, let him believe what he wants. Why disabuse him of his romantic notions? Raja still thinks I'm a big-time activist who goes around speaking to audiences throughout the country solely for the cause. He doesn't know how expensive coke is and how much money it takes to support my life-style. He'd be shocked to know that I've drawn on every penny of my savings, sold my beloved Jacques Le Nanteque sculptures and my Persian rugs, run up my credit cards to the limit, cashed my puny royalty checks, and scammed an advance from my publisher for a book whose subject matter I now only vaguely recollect. Heck, I'll go to Knoxville. It will be easy and painless because I'll merely go through the motions—the emotions I have long since left behind.

So I lounge around the apartment, play James Brown, drink a beer, and compose my notes for the lecture. When I look in the fridge to see what I can cook for myself I find precious little. So what the hell, I'll walk down to the Childe, order a hot meal with a cold beer, and then head home. I have a flight to catch tomorrow at 8:00 A.M.

The bar is not only packed but in a frenzy. At first I don't know what is going on, but when I see everybody dressed in green and drinking that dreadful green Irish beer that looks like Windex, it suddenly hits me that it's St. Patrick's Day. I'm there until closing time and bring a bunch of drunks over to my place who stay until 5:00 A.M. I set the alarm for 6:30 and thus get one and a half hours of sleep, lying on the bed with my clothes on. When I get up, my one comforting thought was that I could do a line and that would see me through the morning. But I can't find my stash. Where the fuck is my coke, man? You can't trust your best friends anymore. Your own guests from last night. Bunch of scumbags. Coke whores. Leave a half-gram on your coffee table, and your wallet with a thousand dollars in it, and they would take the coke.

On the plane I have a couple of bloody marys and begin to feel better, but my eyes are like slits and I look like death warmed over. This is not worth three thousand dollars.

At the airport there was not only Raja waiting for me, but the dean and the chancellor and the president of the Asia Club and the head of the local chapter of the General Union of Palestinian Students and prominent members of the Palestinian community. I'm introduced to them all, but I remember nothing. We eat lunch at the faculty club, and I gulp down a gallon of coffee and five gallons of water to combat my dehydration. I don't feel any better until I get to the lecture hall and climb on to the stage, stand in front of the microphone, and watch the audience give me a standing ovation. That's when the adrenalin starts working. I don't feel the hangover, the fatigue. I feel instead the exquisite nexus between me and the audience. I'm enfolded by their evident adoration. When it's all over, Raja drives me to my hotel, and I sleep for six hours.

"I'll be back for you around eight this evening," he offers, "and we'll go out and party."

By eight I'm roaring to go. We spend the first part of the evening at Raja's mom's place. Raja is twenty-nine and still lives at home. Mrs. Suleiman had been cooking all day and had set up an elaborate sit-down dinner for ten. One of the guests is Clovis Maksoud, the new ambassador of the Arab League in Washington. He is short, fat, and balding, and so nearsighted he would have to stand five inches away from you to recognize your face. He is full of himself and the fluffy values of established Arab society. He truly comes into his own, though, when he gives speeches. He thinks in Formal Arabic, which he stylizes to mimic Classical Arabic, and then translates his comments into English. The result is hilarious. Sentences go on and on, interspersed with flowery parenthetical phrases, but he forgets, or never bothers, to bring them to an end: "The sublime glories of the nobility of the deeply profound essence, nay quintessence, of the edifying qualities of the literature of the Arabs whose contribution to the West, nay the world, a world that owes a debt, a great debt, without which the renaissance of the Western spirit would not have survived the challenges of a historical experience that the Arabs, by their glory, enacted."

Maksoud is telling me how much he admires my work. Would I be interested in getting my "American writer friends" together at a gathering at the Washington Hilton that would be sponsored, nay paid for, by the Arab League, where he might address them on Arab literature? But I don't know any writers in Washington. Just bums and cokeheads.

"Sure Clovis, I'll think about it," I say.

A week later there is a message on my machine. "This is the secretary of His Excellency, Dr. Clovis Maksoud, the ambassador of the Arab League of States in Washington." She wants to know if I have considered "His Excellency's proposal" to address "your American writer friends" at the Washington Hilton. I ignore the call and go about my business. But Maksoud's secretary will not leave me alone. She keeps leaving messages and once even caught me at home, addressing me as "the brother struggler." I told her I was still working on it and hung up. But I was in a funky mood that afternoon, and I figured, why the hell not? This is a great opportunity to get my revenge on the Arab establishment. Why not go to Dupont Circle Park and invite all the bums, homeless people, street musicians, chess players, and other shady characters to come for a free dinner at the Washington Hilton?

The more I think about it, the more I love it. So one day I'm at Hell and meet Clay and Lulu and I tell them, over beers, about my plan. They say, no, man, invite your friends. Invite us, Lulu says, the whole bunch of us, and we can party together.

I get in touch with Maksoud's secretary and arrange for the event to take place on a Friday night three weeks hence. Clovis calls me back himself, and he's all over me with gratitude. So I invite all my friends—thirty in all—along with a bunch of their friends. I tell them what it's all about. They love it.

On the night of the party—for that's what it was, compliments of the Arab League—everybody is getting progressively drunker as the evening moves along. We listen to Maksoud tell us all about how everything Western—from math to chess, from democracy to law, from medicine to art, from literature to respect for human rights— originally came from the Arab world. The drunker the audience got, the more they applauded. Poor Clovis thought they were applauding his ideas. The more applause he got, the longer his endless sentences became. And the longer his sentences became, the more we loved it. At one point he actually talked about women's liberation in the Arab world, and all he could say was that Arab women have liberated men to the point where men now do everything in the house.

"Men work in the kitchen alongside their wives," he thundered. "They help rear children. They cook. They mop floors."

The highlight of the evening came when Clovis tried to say that the Arab League had budgeted enough money to make this a breakthrough year for public relations and the dissemination of information in America about the Arab world. Since he was translating the word *ikhtirak* literally from Arabic into English, a word that means "to enter or to penetrate," this is what he came up with: "And we at the Arab League have determined that this year shall be the year of penetration. We shall penetrate as hard as we can and as forcefully as we can. We shall penetrate with all our might."

He got a standing ovation! Everyone was on their feet applauding, whistling, demanding "more, more," and egging him on with shouts of "penetration, penetration, penetration."

After the speech, Clovis came down from the podium and circulated for a while.

"I am John Updike," Clay says, introducing himself. "And this is Norman Mailer," he adds, introducing Rich. Liz was Gloria Steinem and Edward was Walker Percy. Andrew apologizes because, he says, he shouldn't really be here since he is, strictly speaking, a journalist and not a writer.

Clovis pulls himself up to his full height of five feet, five inches. "But welcome, welcome, I say to you, dear sir, welcome, welcome. You, journalists, are the yeast from which the febrile elements of the news, nay, the information which is firmly localized in our consciousness, rationally spent, elucidated in the utilitarian and pragmatic vocabulary of the mind, artfully recorded in newspapers, benevolent to the heart, yet transposed equally to the brain. That is the yeast of your profession as a journalist. Welcome, welcome. I say, dear sir, welcome, welcome."

I'm thinking any minute now, the gig is gonna be up. Any minute I feared he would recognize the names of these famous writers my friends were giving him. But he didn't catch on. After circulating for half an hour or so, he left, innocent of anything untoward.

Clovis had been kind enough to supply us with our own open bar in the Hemisphere Room. We finished off everything in it long before closing time.

"Annie, baby, you having a good time?" I ask Annie at the bar.

"Don't you dare call me Annie," she responds with mock indignation. "My name is not Annie. I'm Pearl. Pearl Buck. And yes I am having a great time." I get a hug.

So welcome, welcome, dear friends, I say welcome, welcome.

...

One afternoon I'm in Georgetown going from bar to bar frantically looking for a connection of mine, and who do I bump into on Wisconsin Avenue but Georgina, a Palestinian from the West Bank who has hustled her way to a position of real power and prestige in the PLO. It wasn't hard for her to do that. To begin with, she came from a prominent family with land and wealth (or whatever land and wealth the Israelis have let them keep). I first met Georgina years back in New York. She was then married to an older man—a banker or landlord or money changer or tax collector or some other exploiter of the poor. We were all in a car (about six of us) heading to some restaurant uptown. Miss G had been flirting with the guys all night, and hubby copped an attitude. So he and Georgina get into an argument that degenerates into a fistfight—mostly Georgina's fist slamming with a thud across his earhole.

That was then. Today Georgina is "connected" and runs a lot of "PLO shops" from Nablus to Washington. The shopkeepers she has appointed to run the business (mostly publishing smudgy magazines with typos in every paragraph, semiliterate tracts on the Palestinian struggle, "news and views from the Occupied Homeland," and the like) are fiercely loyal. She controls millions of dollars, a fraction of which is spent on PLO work and the rest pocketed by her and "the brother strugglers." She and her supporters live in fancy homes (Georgina owns about five in North America and Western Europe), drive luxury cars, and take expensive vacations. They make money the old-fashioned way: ripping off their own people.

Georgina insists that we meet later for dinner.

"You must come. My treat," she gushes. "Besides, I want to discuss a project with you. Give me your address, and I'll come and pick you up," she continues, as she struggles to put down her shopping bags, printed with the names of Georgetown boutiques. "I've hired a limo and a driver to take me around for the week I'm here."

It's people like you who've driven me to this, I think. But I don't care anymore. I don't believe anymore. I live in my own world and they live in theirs. And never the twain shall meet.

We go for dinner at Mr. K's. I have a couple of cocktails before dinner, go through one and a half bottles of wine with the meal, and drink three Courvoisiers afterward. That gives me a bit of a buzz.

"Let's go for a drive by the Potomac," she says.

We hop in the limo, and she sits very close. "I gotta write me a book, honeybunch, a book as cute as your *Disinherited*," she says in her heavy Palestinian accent.

"So what's this project you've got in mind?" I ask.

"Well, very simply," she says, "I want you to come work for me."

"I don't work for anyone," I say.

"I mean you will work with me. You'll run things."

"I'm not looking for a job."

She giggles. The girl is drunk. "I like you. You're a sweet guy." She moves closer. "Well, if you won't work for me and you won't work with me, how about if you work on me?" And suddenly she's got her tongue down my throat. I'm loaded enough not to care. I put my hand between her legs, but she brushes it away. She just wants to neck like kids in high school in the Fifties. What am I doing here?

"You do coke?" I ask Georgina.

She thinks I mean Coke the drink.

"I mean coke the drug," I explain.

"No, no, no," she says, sitting upright and looking as if I'd smacked her. "I say no to all drugs."

I ask the driver to take me home. Before I get out of the limo, she grabs me and sticks her tongue down my throat again.

When I get home I look at the time. It's only 11:00 P.M. Time to get out of my straight clothes and into my regular ones, and go out looking for some toot. It's Friday night, for crying out loud.

...

Tonight at the Childe, everything is cool. Everybody is high, and we're flirting with Lynn, the bartender, and playfully hitting on the women in the bar and from time to time circulating around the place to exchange gossip about who is screwing who, who broke up with who, and so on.

Mark, Clay, Rich, and I were still there for last call. Lynn wouldn't let us leave without doing four blow jobs—these are shooters, served in pony glasses and made of half Kahlua and half Bailey's, topped with whipped cream. You're meant to clutch the drink between your lips and after downing it, put the pony glass back on the bar without using your hands. We shoot these quickly and leave. The four of us hop in Mark's car and head to Mark and Trudy's houseboat.

No sooner do we get there than Trudy wakes up and starts screaming. We're being inconsiderate, she says, and we should be quiet or get the hell out because she has to work in a couple of hours. So we hop back in Mark's car and head to Clay's place. Clay assures us he's got some killer weed at home that will blow our heads off. Soon after we walk into his apartment, Lulu wakes up, wanders into the living room with her panties on and nothing else, and starts screaming at us. She calls us "a bunch of drunken dickheads" who had no consideration for other people who had to work in the morning.

Hell, it was morning already. So Clay grabs his stash box and we drive to my place. At least *I* have no chick there to give us a hard time.

We get to my apartment, pass a bowl around, and sit back to listen to Iggy Pop and the Clash. That's what did it. Some irate neighbor called the cops. The men in blue turn up, but they are nice and just tell us to cool it. The guys get paranoid and decide to call it a day.

"Come on, you guys, let's go get a couple of six-packs at Seven-Eleven and hang out at Dupont Circle," I say.

They're not keen on the idea. I call Roger. Sally answers. It's six in the morning.

I say, "Hi Sally," and she tells me, "This had better be good."

"Give me Roger."

Roger comes on the line.

"Hi Rog, how you doing?"

He knows what I want.

"You want a six-pack?" he asks, using our code word for a half a gram.

"I want a whole case," I tell him.

"Well, it's your funeral."

I guess the son of a bitch meant that literally.

"You'll cover me on that?" I ask him.

"You owe me already."

"I know. My royalty check is on its way."

"Okay. Come and get it."

What are buddies for?

I could hardly wait when I got back with my treasure. I pulled down the blinds, took the phone off the hook, then sat back on the floor in the living room, leaning against the couch, with my stash on a mirror. This is heaven. I owned the world. This is it. This is paradise. Me and my Lady. This is heaven, I tell you.

And hell.

I woke up sometime later. I didn't know whether I had slept for five days or five hours. I looked out the window and tried to figure out whether it was dawn or dusk. I didn't know. I tried to figure out what day it was. I didn't know. I wondered when I had gone to sleep. I didn't know.

I was on the brass bed in my bedroom. I raised myself up but it took such an effort that I felt as if my bones were going to break. I dragged myself to the edge of the bed and tried to get to the bathroom. I fell face down on the floor. I had absolutely no motor control over my body. I had been drained of energy. I had not an ounce left, even to lift myself up off the floor. My nose was bleeding badly. I don't know how long it took me to get to the bathroom, but when I saw myself in the mirror, I was convinced that I was dying.

Jesus fucking Christ, I'm dying. This is it. But how crude and banal it will be.

Jasmine, I am dying. They have given me my poison. I am going to die like you did. Jasmine! I am lurching forward, like you did, like a bull gored by too many picks. I don't want to die I don't want to die I don't want to die. *Jasmine Jasmine Jasmine. I am dying too.* Like you. You can't defy Tradition. *Baby. Baby. What was behind the mountains? You died too young to find out. I'm dying too old to bother.* And the pigeons kept coming back and coming back and coming back to search for their coop that wasn't there anymore. They kept coming back to search for what wasn't there.

Jasmine. I am tangled in your memory. All these years I've tried to set fire, like you did, to God's universe. I ended up dwelling on the hill of our crazy sorrow, begging for bread from the angels. And all they gave me was what they gave you. The fuckers. They write books about our pain and send us prophets dressed in uniform, to pass their hands over our wounds. And then give us new names. We are just images on their screen. I want to come back. I ache to see the olive tree the brown house the *dabki* tune the dirt track the animate stone the metaphor riding atop the waves of our ancient sea. I'm tired of wrapping my legs around the neck of so many winters screaming helpless American jokes.

...

I regain consciousness. I open my eyes, sprawled on the bathroom floor with blood still trickling out of my nose.

I'm not dead.

I crawl to the living room and reach for the phone.

"Hey, guess what?" I tell my good friend Hassan. "I think I'm dying."

"What's the matter, brother?"

"I'm dying."

"I'll be right over."

And he was.

11

Last Glimpses in Palestine

I'm escaping this place in three days—after I meet with a Hamas official tomorrow morning in Gaza and with three representatives of the underground in Haifa the day after. *Intifada* activists deem it eminently more sensible to conduct their business in Israel than in the West Bank.

It is January 11, 1991. Allied forces in the Gulf are poised to attack unless Iraq meets the deadline, four days hence, and evacuates its occupation army from Kuwait. War seems inevitable given Saddam's adamant position and the allies' proclaimed intention to follow through on their threat. Most airlines are canceling flights to and from Tel Aviv. Those still operating have put advertisements in Israeli newspapers advising the public that the last flights out will be on January 14, one day before the deadline, with an additional $130 on fares to Europe "because of the increase in insurance premiums." Visitors in Israel are scrambling to get out. Americans who called their consulate in Jerusalem were advised to leave. If they didn't, they were told, they would be "on their own."

I leave Jerusalem the day before my meeting and arrive in Gaza late in the afternoon, driven there by one of Leila's contacts, a youngster in his early twenties with short, curly hair, and a china-white face. His name is Jawad.

The dour desperation of Gaza hits you like a gust of wind and crushes you like a stone the moment you enter it.

Gaza is a nowhere strip of land. There is the Sinai Desert to the south, the Negev Desert to the east, the Mediterranean to the west, and Israel to the north. Like any other community, it is attached to a distinct geographical area, and this in itself is one of the crucial elements of its social composition. So when the bitter desert wind from the south and east, the cold sea air from the west, and the rule of the gun from the north combine, Gazans have no way out, around, or through their condition.

I walk the overcrowded streets of Gaza City with Jawad for an hour or so (the day comes to an end around 7:00 P.M. here, as it does in the West Bank) before going to his parents' place to spend the night. I feel about to suffocate from the fetid smell of open sewers and the stench from uncollected garbage dumped at street corners. A blizzard of flies swarms everywhere in the marketplace, buzzing around vegetable stalls, butchers' shops, falafel stands, grocery stores with rickety awnings, and tailors' shops with naked dummies in their windows.

I am in a vortex of faces and sounds and smells and sights that come at me from every direction. The incongruent symmetry of the streets and the alleyways overwhelms me with vertigo. There are no colors that unfold and move before one's eyes, only a cruel, gloomy gray. Everything breathes fatigue, resignation, stoicism, a kind of aridness in the soul.

Such is the harsh sense of despair Gazans feel that, I notice, not one person out of the thousands I see walking the streets of this city—not one man, woman, or child—seems to smile. They hardly look human anymore.

Two blocks up, the streets resound with the laments of mourners. Gazans are burying yet another "martyr" who had fallen "in the arena of struggle." The women wail and wail, but the sounds that come out of their throats are strangely like laughter. They hang in the air for a long time, as if by a law of their own making, sounds that haunt me to this day.

Everything about this place is sad in the extreme. Its sadness plays on my nerves with a vehemence all too real. For a moment, yielding to some private obsession from my past, some dark need for expiation, I want to be one with these people. I want to be home with these people. But I finally turn away from their unendurable anguish as if at the nakedness of a stranger, for I know my home is not, as it is meant to be, where my heart is. I cannot claim as mine this pulverizing pain that Palestinians endure. Palestinians in the homeground are knit by blood, anguish, and death. A different shadow of damnation stalks my life in exile.

On the way home to my host's place, Jawad asks if I want to go to the local mosque for evening prayers. The mosque is already filling with worshippers, including many of the mourners from the funeral. I say no. Who are these people worshipping anyway? There are no believers here anymore. God's last worshipper died on the cross in this tormented land two thousand years ago.

Jawad's parents, by Palestinian standards an affluent middle-class couple, are waiting for us with an elaborate dinner. They are an elderly, pious Moslem couple who practice and take Islam very seriously. "Oh, my son," Um Jawad says to me warmly, "you are from the Outside!" She is a strikingly dignified woman in her early sixties. Palestinians in the West Bank and Gaza often speak of Palestinians living elsewhere as the Outside.

"You live in America!" Abu Jawad says. He is dressed all in white—white *Jalabiya*, white knit cap, and white slippers—and stringing prayer beads.

I tell him I do.

"May the Lord bring plague to their lands and pestilence to their homes."

We sit down to eat dinner—a giant platter of glistening rice topped with almonds and sesame seeds, its sides lined with lamb chops cooked in yogurt sauce.

"Tell us about the Outside," Um Jawad demands.

What can I tell these people? I'm a reformed alcoholic and addict who now lives with a woman to whom the most exciting event in existence is to come home with a new CD and sit there dreamily listening to it over and over again. My lips involuntarily part to tell them about that, but I decide to tell them instead about my childhood years in Beirut and my trip back there in 1979. I talk about my cousin Abla who died in an Israeli air raid that year and how I saw, among the fleeing refugees, a woman with two children push them to the ground and fling herself on top of them, her arms stretched out in both directions.

"You have suffered a lot in the Outside," Um Jawad says, patting me on the wrist. Then she tells me angrily about their two sons who are now in the Gulf and have not been able to return home for the last six years because they have "overstayed"—lived abroad longer than their exit visas allowed—and the Israelis won't let them in again.

"May the Lord pour acid on the soul of the Israelis. The Israelis are sons of whores. They are sons of whores, all of them!" she says vehemently. Then she puts her fist to her mouth, as if stunned at her shamelessness.

Over tea Abu Jawad says, showing me his Israeli-issued ID, tattered and worn, as though it had been thumbed by countless soldiers, "The Israelis are brutal with us, but I'd forgive them everything if they would only let my two sons come back home. I tell you, we are not even accorded animal rights here."

I go to my room later, feeling a little envious that I did not suffer as much as people did here.

As I undress, I fumble absentmindedly in my coat pocket. Inside, I find a book of matches from the Tucson Cantina, the stub of a ticket to a Bad Company concert at Merriweather, a gum wrapper, and a Visa receipt for the purchase of two books and one tape at Olsson's in Washington. So much for suffering.

Outside, the night exudes a kind of dread. Gaza, exhausted by the dreariness of its own existence, sleeps in darkness and in silence. Gazans will wake up tomorrow, with the *muazzen*'s call to prayer, and repeat themselves one more time, just as they have done every day since the occupation began almost a quarter-century ago.

That night I dreamed I was in the town square, shouting at Gazans to watch out for an imminent danger, but I was unable to make sounds come out of my throat. I was unable to move my arms, and my feet were soldered to the ground. I thrashed around and cried and cried, but no sounds came.

In the morning, Jawad walks me seven blocks to a residential area in Gaza City and points to a squalid three-story building where I was to meet Izhak Bakri, a top leader of Hamas, the influential Islamic movement. The meeting had been arranged by Leila, and Bakri had agreed to it only after discovering that I was a *hajji*, a Moslem who had made the pilgrimage to Mecca. My intention was to determine how Hamas leaders have grasped Islam and come to define it in the modern age.

The influence of Hamas has been increasing all over the territories, but in Gaza it reigns supreme, pervading every aspect of life.
Its charismatic leader, Ahmad Yassein, a disabled man who moves
around in a wheelchair, has been arrested by Israeli authorities and
is now under preventive detention.

We climb to the top floor and knock at one of the two apartments
there. Bakri opens the door and greets me quietly, kissing me, Palestinian fashion, on both cheeks. He directs me to a bare room where
we sit on the floor and exchange a few polite words. Two companions serve us tea and then sit on either side of him. Jawad sits unob-
trusively to my left.

Leila had warned me not to toy with this man. His faith in Islam
is so desperate and so absolute that a perceived levity on my part,
real or imagined, could cause trouble. Though in his house I'm pro-
tected by my status as a guest—an exalted status indeed in Arab
culture—heaven knows what could happen to me once I leave it.

"Welcome, welcome, *hajji*," he says.

Bakri is a gaunt, almost skeletal man in his middle thirties with a
thick, bushy beard. He sits sprawled on a straw mat across from me,
his chin resting on one hand. His hair is thick and curly, but coarse,
like lichen.

The man has not smiled once since I walked in, and now as he
exchanges pleasantries with me, his face already is contorted with
furious concentration. I ask if he would object to my tape recorder.

"Not at all, brother, not at all," he says with effusive sweetness.

I'm beginning to feel uneasy. Does Bakri think I'm a real *hajji*, and
thus a devout Moslem? Knowing I don't approve of the PLO, does
he assume I support Hamas? I feel a tug of nausea at my throat, but
that is probably because the apartment smells of kerosene and stale
food.

Bakri, Leila had explained, was a highly educated individual with
degrees in anthropology and philosophy from Cairo University. Until
four years ago, he had been one of Fatah's most ardent supporters
and activists, an Arafat man from his teens.

"Before I found the path," Bakri tells me bitterly, "I thought
Fatah was the only way to go to find what we used to call in those
days national liberation." He sniffs at the term. "I thought Yasser
Arafat was our only leader. I was so proud to be a member of Fatah.
So proud of the chairman. I remember traveling to Amman once,

with three other students, where Arafat received us. He had a cold then. A bad one. He kept sneezing the whole time. I couldn't believe that I was sitting across from the chairman of the PLO. I was so proud to be with him. I was so proud the next day when I discovered I had caught his cold." He doesn't smile even at that.

"Why did you defect from Fatah?"

"I did not defect. I simply realized that the secular nationalists were divorced from reality as God defined it. I had departed from the path, and today I'm back on it."

"Brother Izhak," I say, "we in the Outside are told that you have waged a campaign of killing against fellow Palestinians."

"No, that is false. The enemies of Islam fabricate these tales to alienate our followers from the true path of God."

"Is it true that you demand total obedience from your followers?"

"We are not different from any other organization in that regard."

I remembered the story that Leila had told me about the blind, neurotic loyalty the followers of Hamas show toward their *masouleen*. In late 1989, a panel discussion took place at Najah University in Nablus in which a Hamas discussant participated. Hamas supporters attended in force, and so many of them were standing on the stairway leading to the second floor of the lecture hall that the university authorities feared it would collapse. Pleas to clear the stairwell were to no avail. Even the dean, called in to deal with them, was ignored. Finally the dean appealed to Bakri, who was sitting in a front row of the lecture hall. Bakri simply went over to his followers, and, without saying a word, gestured distractedly with his hand, indicating that he wanted them all off the stairway, and walked back to his seat. Immediately the stairway was cleared. With Hamas followers, Leila had elaborated, spontaneous thought is paralyzed, and action is turned into mechanical response. The ritual weight of doctrine pervades every aspect of their lives.

"Why have you refused to cooperate with Fatah and the other groups in the uprising against the occupation?" I ask.

"The other groups, such as the Marxists, are servants of the West," he answers quietly. "The Fatah people are misguided because they fight for half a cause. Man's soul was given to him in trust, by Allah, and when you fight for half a cause, you betray that trust."

"By half a cause you mean . . ."

"By that I mean they call for a little state on less than one-third of our land."

"You seek the total liberation of Palestine?"

"No question, no question. If the cadres of Fatah had followed the true path of God, they would have known they were wrong."

"Does that mean the dismantlement of Israel and the expulsion of the Jews from the area?"

"Dismantlement yes, expulsion no," he responds as he stares at his hands, head bowed. "The Jews can live here if they so desire. We intend them no harm. The Jews are people of the Book. And the Prophet told us that he who harms a believer harms Him. The Jews can live in Palestine as they lived in the Islamic empire. They can play as constructive a role here as they have done in the States, in Norway, in France, and elsewhere."

"What are the means at your disposal to fight Israel and finally dismantle it?"

"Once we are ready to be martyred for our cause, the state of Israel will crumble. We are not planning for today or tomorrow. We are planning for the next fifty years. Once you fight for your rights, you fight for God. We in Hamas say that if force is what maintains a hated ruler in power, then only force will overthrow him."

Bakri would doubtless have been surprised to know that this was not an original thought.

"What about the role of women in a nation governed by Islamic fundamentalists? Do women, for example, have to wear scarves to cover their heads?"

"First of all, we are not Islamic fundamentalists. The term derives from the West. Fundamentalism is a function of the historical development of Christianity, not Islam. We are Moslems, period. And as far as scarves are concerned, you'll find that once the majority of women wear them, the minority will too."

"I'm asking this: If a woman doesn't want to wear a scarf, what will you do?"

"How did she acquire this taste?"

"I don't know. I just want you to tell me whether she'll be allowed to do it or not. And if not, what happens to her?"

"In schools in the West, girls have to wear uniforms, don't they? So why are scarves a problem?"

"The problem lies in regimenting the norms of social life."

"What's wrong with regimenting society? Aren't people regimented when they work from nine to five, as they do where you live in the United States; when they have to observe a dress code; when they have to wear their hair short; when they have to conceal certain parts of their bodies, and so on?" Then he plunges into a long analysis of what it says in the Koran and the Hadith, the book comprising the Prophet's sayings, about social ethics, public morality, and individual initiative in Islamic society. Halfway through his narrative, he starts whispering and uttering his words in monotone. I can hardly hear him. And every time I ask him to repeat something, he looks annoyed and goes on talking as if I weren't there.

Finally he looks blankly at me. I hadn't understood a single word. All I could say was: "So you insist on women wearing scarves at all times?"

"Yes, that would be better."

"And men decide that for them?"

"Yes. In the Koran it says men are superior to women. They contribute more to society. That has always been the case in history. God has chosen all his prophets as men. Men are tough, and those who are not can easily be made so."

Leila told me that when Bakri was a child, his father emigrated to Nicaragua to open a business. Soon after his arrival there, he wrote a letter to his wife asking her to tell young Izhak that if he wanted to join his dad in Nicaragua one day, he had to realize that it takes tough guys to put up with the tough life there—so tough, in fact, Bakri Senior wrote, that "a man must be able to hold burning coal in the palm of his hand, close his fist on it and not wince at the pain." Mr. Bakri had not meant that literally, of course, but was simply using an old-fashioned saying in Oral Arabic that defined tough. Well, young Izhak did take it literally. Wanting to prove that he was qualified to join his dad in Nicaragua, he went over to his mom's *mokadeh* ("cooking stove"), took out a burning coal, held it in his hand, and closed his fist on it. Within seconds he dropped it and went screaming to his mother: "I can't make it. I can't make it. I can't go to Nicaragua."

So now I ask Bakri: "I understand you to mean that women will play a subordinate role in society."

"Why do you call it subordinate? Is raising children subordinate?"

"Look at women in Saudi Arabia."

"Why Saudi Arabia? Look at Iran."

"You consider Iran a progressive model?"

"Good model, yes. Not progressive. There is no progressive and nonprogressive in Islam. Palestinians, like their brothers in Iran, have rejected all political conviction and ideological dogma. With us, the worth of an idea is defined by its point of origin. It is worthy if it derives from Islam and worthless if otherwise."

"And you think Palestinians here, considering the nature of their social development, will go along with the type of society you're calling for."

"Look," he says placidly, "we Moslems from Hamas did not come on the Palestinian stage without being summoned. The people want to return to the path of Islam, and we came to lead them." His words, delivered with stony calm and strange cunning, hit me with their simple truthfulness. Different Islamic cultures, in different ages, have worked differently with Islam. Reared on violence—the violence in the soul, the violence in tradition—a whole generation now finally has resorted to violence to confer meaning even on the Word. What Jacques Necker said of religion in fifteenth-century Europe, that it was "a heavy chain and a daily consolation," might equally be said of Palestinians under occupation today.

"I hear you want to ban music."

"What kind of music? Disco music? This type of Western music has a corrupting influence on public morality."

"Don't you think human beings should listen to whatever kind of music they want?"

"No."

"You deny me that right?" I ask incredulously.

"In equal measure as you are denied it in America. In the United States you have the Federal Communications Commission that monitors what kind of music you listen to," he persists.

"That monitoring is directed at obscene lyrics and the like."

"What constitutes obscenity here may not constitute obscenity there."

"But in the United States I am able to decide what kind of music I listen to."

"Yes, but in the United States the Federal Communications Commission decides, before you decide, what music you listen to, just as the *New York Times* decides for you what news is fit for you to read. Here we have neither. We have instead the Word of God that guides us to the right path."

I pursue that discussion further, but every time I argue against the logic of a certain notion, Bakri simply replies that God said this or the Prophet advocated that. My objections come up against a solid barrier, like a growing plant meeting a wall.

"Brother Izhak, I want to tell you the truth. I'm afraid of what will happen if you take over power here."

"What are you afraid of?"

"Of not being able to do whatever I want."

"There is no place on earth where you can do whatever you want."

"You've killed Palestinians who didn't agree with you?"

"You have asked me that question already. It is an outrageous lie."

"You deny your group sanctioned the killing of any Palestinians?"

"No. We have killed collaborators. We don't kill people who disagree with us. There are a lot of people who don't agree with us, and they are not dead. There are times when some of our followers have acted rashly, in order to prevent and deter, but we don't sanction killing."

"You have called the Palestinian flag 'dirty cloth.'"

"It is that. We already have a flag, the flag of Islam."

"You have called the cadres of Fatah groups of decadent homosexuals."

"No, that is not true."

"Do I take it you consider homosexuals to be deviates?"

"Yes, I do."

"What would you do to them in an Islamic state?"

"That depends on what they do. If they corrupt public morality by preaching homosexuality, they will be dealt with by the edge of the sword."

"Will you cut off the hands of thieves?"

"In Islam it is dictated that we cut off the hands of thieves after it's proved, as you say in the West, beyond the shadow of a doubt that the accused was in command of his faculties, that there was no compelling need to steal the property of others."

"But . . ." I falter.

"Islam provides for people to live in dignity, where there is no reason to resort to theft."

" . . . isn't it too much to cut off someone's hand for stealing? Isn't the punishment excessive?"

"Not at all," he offers simply.

"What about people who do not believe in Islam?"

"Moslems?"

"Yes."

"Islam is not a game. There is no mercy shown you here even by your own mother. The punishment for apostasy and atheism is death."

I say nothing to that.

Bakri extends both arms in my direction. "In the United States, what would happen if, say, the secretary of the treasury were to confess that he was a communist?"

"I don't know, but we wouldn't chop his head off."

"It would be better if the man were to have his head chopped off, because surely after his confession, he would be excommunicated by society and find it difficult to make a living."

Or he could write a best-seller, go on the lecture circuit, and finally get his own talk show.

"Are you a believer, or have you retrenched?" Bakri wants to know, giving me a cold stare.

What is that I'm feeling in my veins? Has my blood frozen?

"Who, me?"

"Yes, brother," Bakri says, head now bowed, eyes closed.

The room is cold and the air in it stifling. Suddenly it has grown smaller. The door leading to it looks menacing, as if it were the door to a dungeon. I feel this urge to slip away quickly, before I say anything out of control.

"Oh, you must understand," I find myself reasoning with him as I would with a mugger. "I have lost my path here and there, but I still believe. Thank God for the blessing of Islam. I am a believer. Oh, yes, I'm a believer."

"We shall save the earth from the evil of those who think apostasy is a game."

There is a gap of light-years between the free spirit of classical Arabs who spoke coherently to and from Islam and the spiritual deadness of spirit of today's Moslem Arabs. Theirs is a mere parody of Islam. They go around terrorizing unbelievers and enforcing their submissive norms. These Moslems are far from being an active echo of the poetry of Islam and the beauty of its Koranic traditions. They echo the temper of their age and their botched social consciousness.

Yet other Moslems have found in Islam a force for genuine human liberation, like my friend Hassan who went with me to Mecca. After he had returned to Washington, I discovered that he had found something in Islam that an Arab Moslem would not have. He, an African American, had found an answer to the riddle of racism in his own society. This was essentially the same double-take that Malcolm X described in his *Autobiography*. Here was Hassan, interacting for days with Suleiman, a blond, blue-eyed man, who did not exude a hint of racial consciousness in his encounter with a black person. For the first time in his life, Hassan told me, he felt unconscious of the color of his skin when he spoke with a white man. Not all white men, he discovered, as Malcolm had done earlier, are devils.

Islam, in many places and across many centuries, has transformed men and women who have used its teachings as a vehicle for liberation; but Islam has also, like other religions before and since, been used as a vehicle for oppression. The latter case seems to apply in Palestine and the rest of the Arab world today.

Back in Washington, Hassan and I saw less and less of each other as time went on. He was naturally scandalized by my drunkenness, drug use, and womanizing. But he was there when I needed him. It was he whom I called when I OD'd. And he was the man to arrange for my detox program and, afterward, for my integration back into the mainstream of humanity by sending me to stay at a friend's house in San Diego for several months. And it was there, walking on the beach every day, now clean and sober, that I realized that I had cheated myself of the right to a productive life. What is broken, I realized, can be mended. A dreamer must learn to take affront because his dream will be assaulted by the enemies of change. I had accommodated these enemies when I had nonchalantly taken poison, as my sister had, by helping to kill the dream by killing the dreamer.

After I came back from California, I attended daily meetings at AA and NA. The white stuff—even the mere mention of it—continued to tease me, to tantalize me, to torture me, for a long time, even to this day.

I also realized something else. Exile and the homeground are an indivisible part of each other. I cannot sever myself from my archetypal roots. I may have lived a different life from other Palestinians, but I have nevertheless lived a quintessentially Palestinian life, its rhythm mysteriously paralleling the ebb and flow of the national struggle. As the Palestinians rebelled in the late 1960s, seeking to transform their lives, so did I. As they withdrew into the anarchic confusion and the self-destructive compulsions of the 1980s, so did I. As the *Intifada* began to heal the choked psyche of Palestinian society, so did mine begin to heal. I have thus not strayed too far from Palestine and the search for meaning over this last quarter-century, though I have escaped the shackles of tradition and scaled the wall, as rigid as an iron curtain, that it has made between us and the modern world.

Tonight in Haifa, when I meet the three representatives of the *Intifada*, I will find out if our revolutionary underground are planning that escape for Palestinian society and preparing it for a charge against the ramparts of tradition.

...

We arrive in Haifa early in the evening, and Jawad drives us to a small house in the Port District, close to the sea. There we are received by a sweet old Palestinian man—an Israeli-Arab, as Palestinians who stayed behind after 1948 came to be known—who directs us down a dim hallway to a living room jammed with oriental rugs and Middle Eastern artifacts. He is the grandfather of one of the three men I am meeting tonight. After he makes tea and serves it to us in little glasses, he retires to another room where he begins to recite loudly verses from the Koran dealing with the dead. Both his wife and daughter had died within four days of each other less than a month before. He lives alone except for occasional visits by various relatives who also live in the city.

The three men, I discover, will be arriving, separately, in two hours. I will, of course, be more familiar, not to mention more comfortable, with these fellows than I had been with Bakri. They are, after all, PLO boys, though as underground activists, they are honed at the whetstone of the *Intifada*'s rebellious élan.

With two hours at hand, I go for a walk on the beach, two hundred yards away from the house.

It's good to be back in Haifa again, away from the torment of Gaza and the muted hysteria of the West Bank. It's good to be sitting here by the sea, our ancient sea, contemplating its mastery over man and land, plant and soil, heaven and earth, indifferent to who rules and who is ruled. To those of us who have grown up by its shores, there is animate logic in the sound of its waves, a mystery of meaning in the blueness of its blue. The spirits of our dead lie tangled in its eternity.

Soon after I return, the first fellow arrives. He is a youngster in his early twenties who looks bored and sulky. He gives his name as Mohammed. You can't go wrong with a name like that in this part of the world.

"I can only stay for an hour," he says, in a distracted manner, without further elaboration.

After the old man brings more tea, Mohammed engages me in an after-you-doctor routine. Palestinians call you "doctor" even if you don't have a degree in medicine or philosophy.

The second fellow arrives ten minutes later. He is tall and athletic, in his late twenties, and decidedly more pleasant than Mohammed.

"I am Zakharieh," he introduces himself. I have a feeling it is his real name. "It's an honor to meet you at last. You see, I feel I know you already, because when I was a student, we had to do your first book as required reading at Beir Zeit University, along with your poetry collection."

Zakharieh also cannot stay long—something to do with "not safe today."

The third man doesn't show up at all.

"Brother, you have written a lot of anti-PLO stuff. Does that mean you're against the organization?" Mohammed asks. Then he pauses and tilts his head forward, his eyes saying, "Well?"

Hey, who is interviewing whom?

"I am all for the idea of a PLO," I respond evenly. "I am all for the idea of an organization that would embody within its institutional structures—provided, of course, they are democratic—the aspirations of the Palestinian people." I find myself adopting a pedagogic manner as I tell them how I am adamantly opposed to the excesses of PLO officials, some of which I have observed firsthand.

"Let me tell you the truth," Zakharieh puts in. "We feel the same way you do. We have been debating this for the longest time. The issue of reform is pressing and necessary. PLO officials have gotten too fat, both literally and figuratively."

"So what's the problem?"

"The problem is we feel this is not the time to bring this up. There is a lot of friction going on—a lot more than you can imagine. There is currently friction here between the leadership aboveground and the masses; friction between the leadership aboveground and the leadership underground; and friction generally between the Outside and the Inside."

Good as his word, Zakharieh tells me the truth. The PLO Outside, he explains, does not want the leadership Inside to become too popular because that would ultimately supplant it and render it irrelevant, perhaps even reduce it to taking orders from the leaders of the West Bank/Gaza. The PLO does not want that to happen under any circumstances.

"Nor does Israel want to see that happen," Mohammed interjects. "Because if it does, then we become an authentic leadership that Israel will have to speak to and negotiate with."

When I ask about the underground leadership and its relationship with the leadership aboveground, such as with Faisal Husseini, in terms of who has the upper hand, they both say, "We cooperate."

"You have to realize, Doctor," Zakharieh offers, "our concern is not just to confront Israel as an occupying power but to confront, as well, the many, many social problems that face our people here in their daily lives." He explains that there has been a qualitative shift in the social needs of Palestinians in the territories. "Take the health services here. These have deteriorated dramatically during the past decade. According to the Geneva Conventions, Israel, as an occupying power, should provide us with adequate health services, but it has not. What Israel spends annually on that in the territories is less than what it spends on one hospital in Israel. So this is where we come in. We can't leave our people at the mercy of Israel or UN resolutions and so on. We have to take matters into our own hands."

They both explain that with help from the European Community, the World Health Organization, and the Islamic Bank, Palestinians in the territories have already established "at least eighty-three centers of preventive dentistry and 560 societies and organizations" that help peasants, artists, teachers, builders, farmers, researchers, and others.

"We deal not with a government but with our own grass-roots organizations," Zakharieh says proudly. "We have created a lot of institutions here, despite the difficulties that the occupiers put in our way. We have created cultural councils, artists' leagues, folklore groups, and so on. We put on plays, musical festivals, embroidery exhibitions, seminars, workshops, and poetry recitals. All of this goes on, I say, despite the difficulties Israel puts in our way. We in the *Intifada* must do our work from the standpoint of the fact that we are a living nation. Our culture should be nourished in equal measure as should our political consciousness."

I ask them about the Strike Forces and their excesses.

"Don't forget we're under occupation," Mohammed says defensively. "Tensions emerge."

"Is there a chance that one day the leadership of the *Intifada* will come forward and declare itself the legitimate representative of the Palestinians, or at least of those who live in the West Bank/Gaza?"

"None! The Outside and the Inside complement each other," he answers with finality.

"None whatsoever," Mohammed adds. "Actually, even if we were desirous of that, which we are not, we know from experience that the moment we create an aboveground, centralized body to represent us here, we'll be destroyed. We will, you see, become a target of daily pressure by Israel to follow its rules—or else."

He reminds me of the National Guidance Committee that operated aboveground in the late 1970s and how its leaders, mostly mayors, teachers, union officials, and notables, were all finally deported, imprisoned, had their legs blown off by members of Gush Emuniam, or were killed.

"We have two options here. We surrender and be liquidated," Zakharieh says simply, "or we resist and rise to the challenge. I give you as an example the issue of schools. The Israelis, as you know, have closed all our educational institutions, so we took our schools underground. We teach our kids in private homes now. We have to exercise authority over our lives. You may not believe this, but we already possess an infrastructure, a network of institutions, to deal with everything. We are ready. When the state is established, we'll be ready for statehood, believe me."

"Has the PLO played a constructive role in any of this? And will it, considering its track record, play such a role in the future?"

"The PLO is all we've got," Mohammed answers with ponderous dignity. "It will remain so."

"Palestinians here will never become alienated from it?"

Mohammed responds, without looking up: "With Palestinians the PLO will remain popular, though it has, over the years, lost much of its prestige in Arab capitals and, recently, much of its influence there because of the position it has taken on the Gulf crisis."

And after the crisis is over, I say to myself, the organization's officials will retain about as much prestige and influence as actors in a play that closes on opening night.

When I ask what they think of Saddam Hussein, both, surprisingly, express dislike of the man, distrust of his motives in invading Kuwait, and suspicion of his pro-Palestinian professions.

"Saddam is as ruthless as Hafez Assad," Mohammed tells me, and Zakharieh nods in agreement. "He has massacred his own people just as Assad has in Hama. He is also a hypocrite. His war with Iran was simply his way of going about gratifying his ambitions for leadership of the Arab world. His hypocrisy was evident in his dealings with Egypt. You may recall that he was the first Arab leader to call for the isolation of that state from the Arab fold following its Camp David treaty with Israel and the first to rehabilitate it during the Iran-Iraq war because of his need for Egyptian weapons."

"Saddam lost the war with Iran," he adds, "because he miscalculated the deep feelings Iranians harbor for their revolution, and the personal stake they have in its survival."

"More than that," Zakharieh elaborates, "Islam for Iranians was something they genuinely believed in as a binding social ideology. Baathism is hardly that for Iraqis."

"What's the most important contribution the *Intifada* hopes to make, or will have made before independence, to Palestinian society?" I ask.

"I have to tell you this," Zakharieh explains reflectively. "Our contribution has to be more in the arena of culture than in that of politics. You see, our people, like other Arabs in this Arab world . . ."

"In this whorehouse called the Arab world," Mohammed corrects his friend with a mock-serious expression.

". . . have been reared on defeat. They have known nothing but defeat. Ours is a culture of defeat. In 1948, Palestine was dismembered in six months. In 1967, the Arab armies were defeated in six days. In 1982, PLO forces in Lebanon were overrun in six hours. And the wars of 1956 and 1973 were no victories either. Each war instilled in Arabs a sense of impotence about their role in history. So our role here is to reverse this process. Our politics will remain archaic so long as our culture is archaic, for surely, the politics of a society reflect the design of its culture."

These two children seem to be addressing no less than the root cause of all that is helpless in the Palestinian condition. Maybe when they are done, the dreamer will no longer be seen in Palestinian society as the anti-Christ and the idealist as a heretic. Maybe with a shift in social perception, there will be a shift across the board in social expression, especially in formal Arabic, a language that is not suited for logical thinking, a language that considers the tree not to be wood and the mountain not to be stone. Just maybe, like a blossom breaking from the bud, or like a poem coming into form, a new consciousness will emerge here. Maybe—and this is not altogether inconceivable—one day someone will put a stop to the debauchery of Arab leaders and Arabs will again be masters of their destiny, no longer, as they have been for the last five hundred years, mere ephemera in history, passing across its stage like so many fireflies, flitting around chaotically before they settle into darkness.

I walk Mohammed and Zakharieh to the door.

I like these kids. Our traditional leadership, by its cynical follies and blatant corruption, has destroyed much of the meaning in the Palestinian people's call for justice. But in the life of a nation, as in the life of the physical world, nothing is created or destroyed. All decline is compensated for by some simultaneous advance elsewhere. Cynicism and corruption in one sector of society yield their antithesis in another. And the leaders of the Children's Crusade, children all, imbued with the ardor and optimism of children, may just be agents of that change.

We hug good-bye.

"You take care as you listen to your soul," they say to me at the door, in a typically Palestinian farewell.

Sure, and you take care as you listen to yours, especially at the gap between the sounds.

It is enough for me to discover, as I have done by talking to these kids from the underground, that Palestinian society has a future. The *Intifada* has proved that the will to meaning which lies beneath the ice crust of tradition is alive in Palestinian life. The dream of freedom will remain magnetic here—there is no going back, for the idea is already ingrained in the national consciousness—but the challenge of the Palestinian struggle will remain an internal one: whether its leaders recognize that what Palestinians should pursue is not just the right to establish a state but the right of their society to liberate itself from neobackwardness. For it is doubtful that national independence alone can lead to modernity and cultural emancipation. Arabs elsewhere have long since had their independence, but the repressive societies they built succeeded only in producing generations of automatons responsive to the notion that repression is a given. The notion is now so ingrained in the sensibility of Arabs that it is like a second skin. The only cure for this morbid outlook is a genuine engagement in the global dialogue of cultures and a willingness to open one's self to the solicitations of another way of life.

It happened to me in Australia.

When I was twenty-two and a student in Sydney, I toyed seriously with the idea of joining the Communist Party. I finally did not because I discovered I had major problems with the Marxist model, which denigrates the status of the subjective world; and because Australian communists, true to the Puritan tradition of their ancestors—who banned bear-baiting not because it gave bears pain but because it gave men pleasure—were motivated more by their hatred of the ruling classes than by their love for the workers. It happened that one of my communist friends that day had lent me a book. As I walked down the street with it under my arm, I felt a formidable sense of fear. My God, I was saying to myself, what if I get stopped by a cop and I am caught with a proscribed book like this on me? I came from a world that banned and censored and burned books, a world that imprisoned and tortured and killed men and women who wrote books, a world whose regimes are engaged primarily in defending themselves against the ideas contained in books. The terror had stayed with me. I knew that my fear was irrational—I was in Australia after all but that fear continued to haunt me for a long time. If I had stayed in the Arab world and acquired a past and a consciousness there, I would not have seen anything unusual about such a state of affairs. It was only after I went away and lived in another world that I came to know my own.

That is why it is not enough for the Palestinians to just call for the establishment of an independent state. It is, as the boys from the underground seemed to imply, necessary but not sufficient. An independent Palestine without a liberated Palestinian culture is just another Arab state. Who needs that? There are twenty-one of them already, all remarkably unfree and inhospitable.

It was not the mere existence of oppression that made Palestinians rise in revolt but their unbearable consciousness of it. In like manner, the liberation of Palestinian society will only come about when the Palestinians themselves recognize their neobackwardness and begin an *Intifada* against it.

...

I go to sleep thinking, this is it, my last night in this land. The land where my birth certificate was issued. The land, as they say in certain quarters, of my ancestors. The land that haunts us still with its terrible message that human beings are responsible for the gift of their humanity.

I wake up two hours later to the sound of loud chanting. The old man is going around the various rooms, including mine, holding a copy of the Koran, praying, bowing, and mumbling to the corners and the walls, and calling for a union between God and his dead wife and daughter.

This man looks like my father, I say to myself.

"*Allah homma rahmalika,*" he intones, seeking to unite *el rahman*, the Merciful, with the object of His creation. Then he appeals to *el jinn*, the creatures of the underworld, not to hurt his dear departed.

"I do not understand," the old man continues, "why you have taken my wife and daughter away from me. I do not, oh Lord, seek to understand. For he who understands Thee shall forever miss the fabric of Thine essence. Show mercy, oh God in heaven, on my wife and daughter. Let them rest with Thee and Thine angels in eternal grace."

He even sounds like my father—the way he used to mumble about how soon, for surely it must be soon, he would return to Haifa.

An hour later the old man retired, sufficiently exhausted, to his room. And I responded to the stillness that engulfed the house. A residue of meditative ardor hung in the air, as did the old man's words, as if they were now creatures with a right to live that went beyond the being that had given them utterance.

It is dark out. I am wide awake, and now I feel a formidable urge to see the Mediterranean one last time.

I get dressed and walk in the dark the two hundred yards to the water. I sit there alone, thinking now of my father. I can't get him out of my mind. I think of the day we left Palestine. I think of our first year or two in exile. I think of his dream that one day soon he would return to the city of his birth. I think of that city, the city of my childhood, as it was before we fled, with its forlorn bleeding eyes, uttering dying cries in the solitude of a promised land, and of how the sea sits here and contemplates its wounds. I take in its smell of a hundred centuries of prickly pears.

Time slides past as if I am not of it, the way it does at moments when we feel the tug of memory at our center. I'm sitting on a flat rock, engulfed by a quiet, almost sensual solitude, thinking about my father. Then, in the quiet darkness of night, I hear myself whispering his name: "Dad, Dad."

"Dad," I say again, louder.

In the middle of the night, or where the night is just about to fade into day, a gust of wind, accompanied by a faint moan, moves across the water. As it gets closer, it becomes a kind of gradually deepening drumbeat. Every part of me shakes with fear, like a tree in a storm. Then I see a figure standing still before me. It stands where I stand, in the same space I am occupying. It is darker than the dark. I know, I sense, that it is my father. Our beings touch in a kind of fulfilling embrace. I feel his lips brush my forehead.

"Dad, Dad," I repeat, tears falling down my cheeks. And I hear his words echoing back at me, exactly the way he used to say them in life: "He has infused a logic and a reason to every act in His creation, and it is all in the heart of the poet."

Dad, you are here. You have made it. You have returned to Haifa. Your spirit has journeyed back home.

From somewhere behind Mount Karmel, preceded by a soft dawn, the sun begins to creep into the city, and with it human beings and human voices and human stirrings.

I walk back to the house and stop by the road. People pass me silently, and I watch them as if I were master of some ceremonial review. These people live here now. This is their city, their dawn.

Hey, you, you love and guard this land that sustains you, do you hear?

Dad is home. I know that now. His wish to die, which he had

uttered just before passing away, had had the logic and reason that are found in the heart of the poet.

Even Jasmine, in a way, is home. She had looked for a world beyond the dictates of tradition, and when she couldn't find it here, she went looking in the Otherworld, behind whatever mountains may exist there. Every dreamer is accountable for his dream. Between dreamer and dream the accounts always balance one day.

I too have found a home.

My last glimpse of this land as I was being driven to the airport the following day was of a Palestinian kid in an Arab village, standing silently at a street corner, leaning against a wall, contemplating life with eyes that stared from the slit of his checkered *hatta*. His eyes seemed to mask a hot rage, a readiness to combat all of life with brute ferocity. He looked so native to his world, so rooted in its harsh realities. So confident about its codes of meaning.

I am a madman to have attempted a journey to the desolate frontiers of Palestine's soul. I am so little worthy of taking on this task, for I come from a hollow place where I have silenced all the voices from my past. Oh, yes, I am used to dread and to its language of divine resurrection. I have run into the Palestinian storm and become woven in its dance. But no one, not even the god before God, can make an echo without a voice.

Now I am ready to go home. I love this land. Everything about it, like a beautiful tree visible from all directions, bristles with conjecture about life. I love it the way it wants to be loved, in a holy way. But I am also weary of it. I am tired of its people's shadows, its people's plaints, its people's darkness. I am tired of the way they have debased it by their fighting. I have better things to do than concern myself with the trivia of nationalism. I have to look, before I die, for one last land behind the mountains, even if the search should lead, as perhaps it may, to Desolation Row. My people are everywhere because they come from everywhere. I don't want to kill anybody's soul. I am, in the end, who everyone else is.

Epilogue
The Land Behind
the Mountains

When I left Palestine on January 14, a day before the Gulf War started, I believed that peace between Israelis and Palestinians would remain an elusive dream. Like most other observers, I was unaware of the shifts of political sensibility, already dimly at work, that would soon declare themselves with sudden force. The notion that representatives of the Israeli government and the PLO would, within less than three years, recognize each other and sign a peace agreement on the White House lawn did not seem to belong to our time. Even more remote was the possibility that, at long last, the Palestinians would soon be statehood-bound, or at least become a people *enracinés* in one form or another.

Palestinians and Israelis had demonized, fought, and killed each other for eighty years. Being an outright pessimist, I was convinced that they were destined to chew their nationalist slogans to the marrow and live out their flat and shoddy political lives in constant conflict for eighty more.

No one, at any rate, was much concerned then with the fate of the Holy Land and its two peoples.

In the middle of January 1991, the world's attention was focused on the Gulf War and Iraq, getting decidedly trounced. The allies were able, in a comparatively short time and with little cost to

267

themselves, to crush Saddam's forces, expel his army from Kuwait, effectively disarm him, divide his country into three parts—two of which would remain outside his control—and bring him to total submission.

The mother of all battles was over for the Iraqi dictator, but not for his suffering people who would shoulder its disruptive and painful consequences for years to come.

Not only did Saddam fail to resign in disgrace for the catastrophes that he had brought upon his people, he had them out in the streets that year to celebrate his birthday and later opened something called the Museum of Steadfastness and Defiance so that they would "remember the heroism of the Iraqi army."

Saddam was not a rhetorical bully like Adolf Hitler—Saddam could not even speak well publicly—but he was, like the other "brother strugglers," a polluter of language who delighted in creating a make-believe world for his people to inhabit. It is doubtful that after their debasement at his hands words like *mother*, *celebrate*, and *heroism* would ever recover a sane meaning in the Arabic language.

On the last day of war, for example, his supporters, especially the Palestinians among them, refused to believe his speech of surrender to the demands of the allies. Nora Boustani, *the Washington Post* correspondent, reported from Amman that several people she had interviewed were convinced that it "was not read by Saddam but by someone else impersonating him."

The Gulf War, like no other event in modern Arab history, shook long-held assumptions about pan-Arab solidarity—wobbly notions to begin with. In its wake, the Arab world stood divided and helpless.

In the Arabian Peninsula, the oil states were no longer rich. Their stability had been undermined by unrestrained spending, huge military purchases, bizarre banking practices, and enormous expenditures on the war itself. Saudi Arabia, the richest among them, which had had $121 billion in financial reserves a decade before, was now in deficit. In the Fertile Crescent, the confrontation states bordering Israel, hit equally hard by their loss of military, economic, and political support from a collapsed Soviet Union, were in no position to confront anyone. The Maghreb countries in North Africa were experiencing unprecedented turmoil resulting from Islamic fundamentalism and economic dislocation. Egypt, which had ceased to be a player in inter-Arab politics after the signing of the Camp David Accords in 1979, was helpless in the face of its own Islamic terrorists. And the PLO, ostracized by the Gulf Arabs and denied financial aid, was broke and teetered on collapse.

The stillness that followed the Gulf War spoke directly to the ruin of the Arab spirit and destroyed the Arab people's hold on long-cherished ideals about both individual and national identity.

The Arabs, in effect, were being summoned to join the new world order and to rethink their assumptions about confrontation with Israel.

Israelis too had no workable alternatives either. They also had to rethink their assumptions about the enemy and try to reach an accommodation. Otherwise, they were left with the nightmare choice of dominating a people who would only be ruled by repression, followed by revolt, followed by more repression and again by revolt. This was a situation that, especially since the start of the *Intifada*, had taken its psychological toll on Israelis.

Peace talks seemed an inevitable outcome of the new order in the Middle East. Yet when these talks were finally convened, initially in Madrid, between Israel on the one hand and Syrians, Lebanese, Jordanians, and ostensibly non-PLO Palestinians from the territories on the other, they went nowhere. Even after the talks were moved to Washington, they dragged on interminably, with neither the participants nor the Americans able to breathe life into them. One dreary session followed another over almost two years.

Concurrently, and with everyone kept in the dark, representatives of the PLO and a new Labor government in Israel responsive to the idea of territorial compromise convened talks in Oslo that finally resulted in a breakthrough on August 20, 1993—an agreement nicknamed "Gaza and Jericho first," which led to an exchange of letters of mutual recognition between Israel and the PLO, followed by the ceremony on the White House lawn on September 13.

The world stood transfixed by the event and not only because the leader of the hitherto untouchable PLO shook hands with the Israeli prime minister but also because the agreement bore the mark of historical magnitude. This was not an agreement between Israel and an Arab state over a territorial and diplomatic dispute, but an agreement between two peoples, two rival nationalisms, that for eight decades had vied for self-definition on the same piece of land.

A quarter-century after Golda Meir denied that a Palestinian people existed, while the Palestinian National Charter denied Israelis their right to statehood, both peoples realized the biblical truth that you have to know thine enemy to deal with him. How your enemy defines himself is important; how you define him is not.

It would be a long time before this agreement yielded its full political and economic fruits. But clearly, this was a reconciliation more than an agreement, the feast that comes after a long fast.

We remain too close to the fact to predict whether the Palestinians, as they begin to rule themselves, will go from "Gaza and Jericho first" to full-blown independence, or whether they will fail, as so often in the past, to embrace the turning points in their history.

Will the PLO, given its record of corruption, ineptitude, and cynicism, be equal to the challenge? Will it yield to the forces of modernity growing in Palestinian society, to the representatives of the Children's Crusade whose uprising was largely responsible for the groundswell that led to the ceremony on the White House lawn? If this Palestinian entity is to be democratic, as I understand young Palestinians like Zakharieh and Mohammed (the boys from the underground) would want, can it deny Islamic activists self-expression and assembly and, potentially, political power? And what of other dissenters (not all of them rejectionists or fundamentalists) who will form an adversarial current in society? Will the PLO send its police after them, as any other Arab regime would do, to silence their voices and break their heads? Will we in other words, see yet another dreary Arab state where the night knock on the door, and dragging off dissenters to the gallows, would be all too common?

To go from Gaza, a grim, turbulent strip of land inhabited by 800,000 souls, and from Jericho, a mere dot on the map, a dusty outpost by the Dead Sea whose sedentary population was the last to join the *Intifada*, to a promised land of independence and stability is a trip that shakes our grasp on the "reality principle."

The whole experiment may go haywire. After all, it is the PLO that will be custodian and overseer of the Palestinian future in the West Bank and Gaza. And lest we forget, the Palestinians are a little people, unprepared for the challenges of modernity, a community that still moves around the treadmill of immemorial traditions and beliefs, which is one reason that no other people in the world has repeated its history as Palestinians have.

Yet we should not be given warrant to see nothing but a bleak future for Palestine. Young Palestinians in the West Bank and Gaza, who comprise the overwhelming majority, possess large reserves of political consciousness and new social habits honed by years in the underground. These will finally take root. I am convinced that in a future Palestine we will hear the *Intifada*'s shaping echo, not the strident voice of a tyrant "brother struggler."

...

Meanwhile, what is to become of the four million Palestinian exiles descended from the refugee exodus of 1948? The fact that they were not mentioned in the peace agreement, the shock of realizing that they will never go home, will profoundly alter the way they see themselves and the world around them.

While Palestinians in the West Bank and Gaza will be engaged in nation building, Palestinians in the diaspora will lose much of their accustomed bearing. For years they will feel a loss too grievous to contemplate—and not only because, for the first time, they will no longer share a vision of the future with Palestinians who live on the Inside.

For almost half a century, the concept of the *awda*, the return to home and homeland, formed the pivot of an exile's inward life. The idea shaped the sensibility of Palestinians in whatever host state they happened to live. As the possibility of returning to Palestine faded over the years, the image of the *awda* still glowed vivid and real in their lives. If pressed, no sane exile would say that his expectation of returning to Haifa, Jaffa, or Lod was realistic. But Palestinians in the diaspora needed to believe that one day they would return. Not to believe would have torn up the roots of their identity. Like the square root of minus one, the *awda* was a big lie, an imaginary notion, a state of fancy. But just as this imaginary value is integral to the order of mathematics, so was belief in the *awda* necessary to the lives of Palestinians in exile.

Yet it is not inconceivable that diaspora Palestinians will learn to adjust, especially if the West Bank and Gaza are transformed from a mere homeground into an independent homeland. For then they will know that there is a tiny strip of land, a little corner of the earth tucked between the Mediterranean and the River Jordan, where they can go when the Kuwaitis kick them out, when the frenzied packs come to their refugee camps, when the bullies in their host states begin to snarl at their heels.

We in the diaspora will learn to live with the new realities. We will even learn to live with our memories—memories of a cloudless day on Mount Karmel and of God's rage on the coastal road to Lebanon; memories of exile and of mass graves at Sabra and Shatila. In our minds, these images are not frozen like statues. Every generation judges the past anew. It was the world of our being that created the world of our memories. And once that world is changed, so will our selective use of memory.

I have no doubt that the majority of diaspora Palestinians have felt a dizzying sense of joy that their cousins in the homeground have taken a step that may lead them to statehood, independence, and freedom. We are, after all, the same people, maimed by the same catastrophe in 1948. Yet I see one of the cruelest ironies in our history looming ahead. For once Palestinians in the homeground build their state, there will be nothing "Palestinian" about them. They will be just another people with a state, now cut off from all that the name *Palestinian* has historically conferred on Palestinians everywhere.

For the last half-century or so, to be Palestinian was, in part by upbringing, in part by sensibility, to be a wanderer, an exile, a touch moon-mad, always a little different from others. Our name, which we acquired after 1948, was not so much a national title—we had had no nation—as an existential term. Palestinians enjoyed the freedom to go beyond the confining thresholds of national torpor. We had the freedom to remember, to dream of a different reality, to deliver ourselves into history's keeping.

Now two million Palestinians in the West Bank and Gaza—perhaps more as the figure swells with the influx of exiles—will build their own homeland on their own bit of earth. Many more of us will stay in our adopted ones.

To me, the idea of a nation remains absurdly wrong. I find the idea of unrestrained, militant nationalism to be obscene. In the name of territorial integrity and ethnic purity, men have slaughtered one another for centuries.

Jewish nationalists who believe that the Jewish nation's boundaries include the territories stretching from the Mediterranean to the River Jordan and beyond, have their counterparts among the

Palestinians. I met one of them in Washington soon after the White House ceremony. He was introduced to me as a former PLO fighter on his way to Jordan to be trained as a police officer. From there he would be Jericho bound. A man in his fifties, who wore his hair slicked back on both sides and curled on top like Cleopatra's diadem, he assured me that "in less than thirty years from now the whole of Palestine will be liberated and all the Jews will be gone from our country."

I have always sought to disassociate myself from that kind of venom. And that is why, though I am happy that Palestinians in the West Bank and Gaza will soon be free to determine their own destiny, I will not pick up and go to live in a Palestinian homeland.

Forty-five years of exile are homeland enough. Anywhere where one is free to watch one's favorite movies, reread one's favorite classics, listen to one's favorite music, support one's favorite unpopular causes, and, above all, do one's work without fear of retribution, is homeland enough.

I need not live in Nablus or Jericho or Gaza. I could live anywhere I am with my people—those from any part of the world with whom I share a commonality of values and a certain way of life. Paris, Sydney, or New York will do—especially New York, because New Yorkers are like Palestinians in many ways. They too are born of tragedy. Their ancestors landed at Ellis Island after escaping a czar who claimed to love them, a "brother struggler" who had anointed himself head of the national family, a tyrant who did not like their ethnic roots, a colonial oppressor who robbed them and couldn't care less about their famine. And there are other New Yorkers whose ancestors didn't land on Plymouth Rock; instead—as Malcolm X put it—Plymouth Rock landed on them. Like Palestinians, New Yorkers are a little mad, a little lonely, a little disgruntled. They live with no regard for the concerns of the rest of the planet and stare with murder in their eye if you dare to suggest that there is any place better than where they come from.

And I need not die in Haifa, Safad, or Jaffa. Washington will do. I have lived there longer than in any other part of the world. Nor, when I'm dust and forgotten, should it be of any consequence to anyone where my remains are buried.

Still, even to a hardened exile like myself, the emergence of a Palestinian state touches some covert longings in my soul. It will in

any case compel me to rename myself. Palestinians in the homeground will laugh at those who continue to ascribe to their name
attributes that predate the new Palestine. Henceforth, a Palestinian
becomes what he is because he lives in Palestine. Believe us, they
will say, we built a state because of our need for a safe haven, not for
love of nationalism. Come over here and live with us. We will turn
our soul's concern in your direction. May the Lord pour acid on your
exile and destroy all the houses you've built in it. Come!

This idea of a state is too fantastic. *A Palestinian state*! Surely this
is the stuff of which dreams are made.

I can see myself, ten years from now, succumbing to the fantasy.
In this dream, I fly to Palestine. My plane lands at Jericho airport. I
am traveling light—some clothes, my notebooks, and a toothbrush.
There is no need to bring anything else. This is a modern country,
and I can buy everything I need here. I walk to Immigration and
stand in line. Outside, the sun, as usual, shines brightly. Awaiting
me is a life among the olive trees in a town by the River Jordan. The
official greets me effusively and asks how I feel. I tell him I feel
great, and it is the truth. He stamps my passport and says, "Welcome to Palestine." As I walk out of the airport, I repeat the name
to myself. I want to test the sound of it, to make sure it is real. I
repeat it, once, twice, thrice, then utter it as if in babble, like an
infant who has not yet mastered words. I hop in a cab and am driven
along a paved road hugging the river. The cabbie tells me the road
was completed just four years before, after the PLO lost the vote in
a democratically contested election, and the new president, whom
everyone calls Brother Zakharieh, took on the task of eliminating
corruption and building the economy.

The taxi driver turns on his car radio, and I hear Palestinian folk
music, the lyrics simple and benign and not about struggle or death
or sacrifice or steadfastness in the face of foreign oppressors. I reach
out as if to touch the sounds, to grab them from the air, and rest
them on my chest.

I ask the driver how far it is to my destination and he points
ahead of him. Right there, brother, he tells me, just behind those
mountains in the distance.